Women's Personal Narratives

Essays in Criticism and Pedagogy

EDITED BY

Leonore Hoffmann
and
Margo Culley

The Modern Language Association of America
New York   1985

Library of Congress Cataloging in Publication Data

Main entry under title:

Women's personal narratives.

   Bibliography: p.
   1. American literature—Women authors—Study and teaching—Addresses, essays, lectures.   2. Autobiography—Women authors—Study and teaching—Addresses, essays, lectures.   3. Women in literature—Study and teaching—Addresses, essays, lectures.   4. Women—United States—History—Study and teaching—Addresses, essays, lectures.   5. Narration (Rhetoric)—Study and teaching—Addresses, essays, lectures.   6. Self in literature—Study and teaching—Addresses, essays, lectures.   I. Hoffmann, Leonore, 1929–   .   II. Culley, Margo.

PS42.W65   1985   810'.9'9287   85-329
ISBN 0-87352-342-3
ISBN 0-87352-343-1 (pbk.)

Illustration and type design for the cover of the paperback edition by Marie Mutz. This illustration was inspired by Edmund Charles Tarbell's painting *Josephine and Mercie* in the Corcoran Gallery in Washington, D.C.

Acknowledgments
We wish to thank the National Endowment for the Humanities, Division of Education, for its generous support of the project from which this volume evolved. Special thanks go to Cynthia Wolloch, NEH Program Officer, and to the staff of the Modern Language Association who advised and encouraged us.

The Editors

   Virginia Walcott Beauchamp, "Letters as Literature," is adapted from her essay in *Maryland Historical Magazine* 77 (1982).
   Annette Kolodny, "Captives in Paradise," is adapted from *The Land before Her: Fantasy and Experience of the American Frontiers, 1630–1860*, by Annette Kolodny. Copyright 1984 The University of North Carolina Press.
   Judith Stitzel, "Hearing Voices: Oral History as an Aid to Reading," first appeared in *Frontiers: A Journal of Women Studies* 7.1 (1983).
   "The Diary of Amelia Buss" is printed with the permission of the Special Collections Department, Colorado State University Libraries, Fort Collins.
   "The Letters of Delina Hopper" are printed with the permission of the Western Reserve Historical Society, Cleveland.

Third printing, 1991

Published by The Modern Language Association of America
Astor Place, New York, New York

Contents

Introduction
Leonore Hoffmann　　　　1

Overviews

Women's Vernacular Literature: Teaching the Mother
　Tongue
Margo Culley　　　　9

The Languages of Oral Testimony and Women's Literature
Elizabeth A. Meese　　　　18

Analyses of Specific Texts

Letters as Literature: The Prestons of Baltimore
Virginia Walcott Beauchamp　　　　29

Letters and Diaries: The Persona and the Real Woman—
　A Case Study
Virginia Walcott Beauchamp　　　　40

Writer Anxiety versus the Need for Community in the
　Botts Family Letters
Susan S. Kissel　　　　48

The Pariah and the Author: An Analysis of
　The Maimie Papers
Rose Kamel　　　　57

An Analysis of the Oral Testimony of Edna Anderson
Alice T. Gasque　　　　78

The Oral Testimony of Edna Anderson
Susan Sherman and Alice T. Gasque　　　　86

Captives in Paradise: Women on the Early American
　Frontier
Annette Kolodny　　　　93

Using Personal Narratives in the Classroom

The Usefulness of Women's Nontraditional Literature
in the Traditional Literature-and-Composition Course
John Schilb 115

A Lost Diary Found: The Art of the Everyday
Dure Jo Gillikin 124

Hearing Voices: Oral History as an Aid to Reading
Judith Stitzel 139

Women's Shorter Autobiographical Writings: Expression,
Identity, and Form
Susan Waugh 144

Preparing a Collection of Regional Autobiographical
Materials for Use in the Composition Classroom
Susan S. Kissel 153

Literature in Performance in the Place Where the
Partridge Drums
Susan Ward with Joan Olsen Donovan 162

Telling One's Story: Women's Journals Then and Now
Elouise M. Bell 167

Appendixes

Writing Exercises 179

The Diary of Amelia Buss 182

The Letters of Delina Hopper 214

Editing a Woman's Diary: A Case Study
Elizabeth Hampsten 227

Institute Participants 237

Selected Bibliography and Works Cited 239

Introduction

Leonore Hoffmann

This volume encourages literature faculty to include in their class-rooms the "nontraditional" literature of ordinary women. (These materials are "nontraditional" only in the sense of their exclusion from the literary canon. They are, in fact, women's traditional literature.) The contributors analyze letters, diaries and oral testimonies to suggest the possibilities for approaching these materials as literature and describe the pedagogy for introducing them into the classroom. In recent years, historians, anthropologists, psychologists, sociologists, linguists, and folklorists have demonstrated that in their disciplines such texts can be rich resources. Those interested in the various modes of literary production, broadly defined as the process of giving shape and meaning with language, will also find such materials stimulating and rewarding areas of inquiry.

The texts examined here are primarily autobiographical narratives, though not formal autobiographies. Most were not created for publication, and the voices we hear are not those of professional writers. The focus is not on the achievement of prominent women but on the modes of verbal art practiced by most women who use language to give shape and meaning to their experiences. We do not wish to collapse the distinctions between belles lettres and the forms of "language arts" practiced more widely; rather, we wish to demonstrate that these texts exhibit much of interest to scholars and teachers of literature, no matter what critical framework and vocabulary they choose to employ. Each text constructs a self and tells its story to a real or implied audience. In doing so, they are works of the imagination drawing out themes beyond the limits of their historical specificity.

Schools of literary criticism that place the production of literature within a social context will find these texts of particular interest. Feminist criticism, reader-response theory, and the "new historicism" all view literary creation as a complex interaction between writer or speaker and audience, each embedded in the specifics of culture, in-

1

cluding the specifics of gender, race, and class. As texts become more than objects of aesthetic interest, the forms of discourse appropriate for study become more various. If one is interested in the woman artist, for example, one must look beyond the forms created for public, commercial distribution to the forms most women have used, such as personal narrative. And as the contents of this volume indicate, these narratives can be valued within multiple frameworks—including the aesthetic—and will provide rich resources for classroom use.

The project out of which this collection evolved was supported by two federal grants (the Fund for the Improvement of Postsecondary Education and the National Endowment for the Humanities) and sponsored by the Modern Language Association. It enabled faculty primarily in English to recover, analyze, and then teach the personal narratives of ordinary women. An earlier volume, *Teaching Women's Literature from a Regional Perspective*, edited by Leonore Hoffmann and Deborah Rosenfelt, emphasized pedagogy. Students discovered the documents of women in their region, analyzed them, and then presented them to others through published booklets, oral presentations, dramatic skits, videotaped interviews, poems, and short stories. The present volume continues the pedagogical implications of familiarizing students with noncanonical materials but also strengthens the analytical dimensions of this project. This volume emerges from an NEH Humanities Institute held in the summer of 1979 at the University of Alabama.

The opening two essays provide overviews of issues related to the use of nontraditional literature in the classroom. Margo Culley's "Women's Vernacular Literature: Teaching the Mother Tongue" not only places in historical context the struggle of feminist literary scholars to include literature by women in the canon but also warns these same scholars not to repeat the mistakes of their male predecessors by establishing a canon of accepted works and thus excluding the materials of ordinary women. Elizabeth Meese in "The Languages of Oral Testimony and Women's Literature" constructs some necessary bridges between oral and written materials and suggests some familiar criteria and methods for identifying literary qualities of oral material.

The next group of essays analyzes texts by means of such familiar literary criteria as audience, voice, and narrative structure. Virginia Beauchamp's two essays, "Letters as Literature: The Prestons of Baltimore" and "Letters and Diaries: The Persona and the Real Woman—A Case Study," use a collection of letters by an upper-class white woman living in Baltimore in the mid–nineteenth century. Audience, in this case her young daughter, was crucial in determining both the content and the form of her letters. The first essay concentrates on Preston's artistry or, perhaps, artifice. The second is concerned with the language of silence. A researcher's dream come true, Preston's diary, written concurrently with some of the letters, is extant and reveals emotional upheavals that the letters conceal. With this knowledge Beauchamp analyzes the letters in an effort to decode ambiguous passages.

Another way to approach these materials is through a discussion of voice. Susan Kissel in "Writer Anxiety versus the Need for Community in the Botts Family Letters" analyzes a collection of approximately one hundred letters written by carpenters, farmers, hardworking mothers, and wives to Emily Botts in Boone County, Kentucky, from 1820 to 1880. We hear many different voices and points of view. At first the reader is puzzled, but gradually the "collection's emotional power, like that of a piece of fiction or a dream, builds . . . as the reader becomes more and more immersed in the world that has been created."

Perhaps the most important function of writing, self-discovery through self-revelation, is exemplified by two texts: a collection of letters, published as *The Maimie Papers*, written between 1910 and 1922 by a former prostitute to a Boston philanthropist; and an oral testimony of a contemporary rural woman living in South Dakota. Rose Kamel's essay traces Maimie's growth from self-contempt and isolation to self-confidence and involvement. As she gains in self-confidence, she gains in literary skills. Alice Gasque writes of Edna Anderson's oral testimony that "The spontaneous quality of the testimony and the frank, factual discussion of family life lend it a vitality that is difficult to match in either more traditional autobiographies or other types of nontraditional written literature."

The final essay in the first section, Annette Kolodny's "Captives in Paradise: Women on the Early American Frontier," uses captivity narratives by women to interpret the women's responses to the frontier experience. Kolodny concludes:

> For the women forced westward against their will, . . . the enduring popularity of the female captivity narrative, virtually unchanged for over a century, rested in the fact that it provided women readers (and perhaps the writers as well) a safe vehicle through which to confront the often unhappy experiential structures of their westward migration.

The concluding essays discuss the use of women's personal narratives in the writing and speaking classroom. Much research has been done in the last several years on writing as a process rather than as a product, but little has been done on the kinds of readings one can use in the writing course. Writing practitioners have discussed ways of using students' own writing as models but have not examined other types of readings in detail. Probably most writing instructors continue to teach the formal essays found in readers. Unfortunately, these essays may alienate students from the writing process rather than stimulate them to discover their own potential. Adrienne Rich's description of students' attitudes toward reading and writing in "Teaching Language in Open Admissions" still holds true: "My daily life as a teacher confronts me with young men and women who have had language and literature used against them, to keep them in their place, to mystify, to bully, to make them feel powerless" (63). Personal narratives, however, give students a sense that maybe they can write, too, and as a result they become far more concerned about preparing good papers. Nancy Porter, an institute participant, writes, "When a student transcribes a tape of an oral interview with a person the student has laughed, cried and deeply empathized with, the student wants to get the transcription 'right' because what she wants to do well by is a living voice, a life." This empathy applies to letters and diaries from the past as well. Students become involved with a real person who is very much like them in some ways—certainly in not being a public person, in being powerless. Because of these vital connections, students write, speak, listen, and read better.

John Schilb argues that students' writing improves when they read these texts. The personal narratives of ordinary women demystify reading and writing, thus alleviating students' anxieties. Because the texts are close to their experience, students can better understand concepts such as voice and structure and can analyze their own writing with these concepts in mind.

Dure Jo Gillikin's essay combines classroom use and analysis. The thrill of discovering diaries of unknown women motivated her students to become closely engaged with the text. Her own work with the record-keeping diary of Anne Rogers Minor enabled her to meet the demands readers encounter with these kinds of materials.

> This jotting-down-of-events diary engages readers, making them participatory authors as some avant-garde novelists deliberately encourage today. No longer solely spectator, the reader helps to create the story by adding in the details based on experience and on readings in literature, history, psychology, and sociology.

Judith Stitzel in "Hearing Voices: Oral History as an Aid to Reading," based on her experience in teaching a course on women's oral history, elaborates on Gillikin's point that reading these materials makes unusual demands. On a tape, students can actually hear the voice; listening carefully is a skill that they can transfer to reading when the voice appears on the printed page.

Susan Waugh in "Women's Shorter Autobiographical Writings: Expression, Identity, and Form" describes the inventiveness and creativity of her students when they write autobiographically:

> Even those who had lived for many years the fragmented lives of traditional women were not prisoners of a common subject, style, or form. The form of the life does not inevitably dictate the form of the autobiography. Not only did the women choose coherent, chronological, focused, logical, and consciously shaped forms over rambling, diarylike, or diffuse ones, they were also highly experimental.

Before one can use these materials in the classroom, one must locate and collect them. Susan Kissel's "Preparing a Collection of Regional Autobiographical Materials for Use in the Composition Classroom" describes the procedure by which she collected and then selected and edited local documents. What she accomplished in her region, northern Kentucky, and then published as *The Pewter Basin and Other Occasional Writings*, others can do in their regions. That students can participate in this process is demonstrated in Susan Ward and Joan Olsen Donovan's "Literature in Performance in the Place Where the Partridge Drums," a description of an oral-interpretation class in which Native American students in upstate New York brought in tribal stories, legends, and journalism. Elouise Bell's "Telling One's Story: Women's Journals Then and Now" is an overview of an actual course itself, beginning with the selection of topics and concluding with summaries of imaginative student projects. One interesting aspect of her article is the different uses older and younger students make of autobiographical and personal writings.

To facilitate the use of these materials in the classroom, we include a bibliography of published letters, diaries, and oral testimonies. In addition, we print two unpublished documents: "The Diary of Amelia Buss," written between 1866 and 1867, an account of a family's overland journey from New York to Colorado and their adjustment to their new home; and "The Letters of Delina Hopper," written between 1858 and 1865 from an Ohio woman to her husband in the Union Army.

Finally, of interest to scholars in preparing manuscripts for publication is Elizabeth Hampsten's essay on editing. She asks such questions as how much information about the social context a reader needs to understand the diary and what effect such public exposure has on the writings of nonliterary and nonpublic persons. Although some may disagree with her decision regarding standardizing spelling and punctuation, her essay raises important issues regarding the editorial process and historical accuracy.

OVERVIEWS

Women's Vernacular Literature

Teaching the Mother Tongue

Margo Culley

> It would be difficult to find a stronger example of
> conservatism than the steadfast resistance of educa-
> tion to the changes which have been going on in
> almost every department of human activity for the
> past century. (8)

The words are those of James MacAlister in an 1887 address to the
recently formed Modern Language Association, an address supporting
the study of vernacular literature in institutions of higher learning in
America. It is startling to remember that MacAlister was defending
the merits of Dante, Cervantes, Shakespeare, and Goethe against
those who thought the study of Greek and Latin literature a more
worthy enterprise. The establishment of departments of English studies in the 1880s and 1890s was a late and decisive victory in the
protracted contest—named by Jonathan Swift "The Battle of the
Books"—between the Ancients and the Moderns. In his description of
an earlier skirmish between volumes from the two camps, Swift reminds us of what was at stake:

> This quarrel first began . . . about a small spot of ground, lying
> and being upon one of the two tops of the hill Parnassus; the high-
> est and largest of which had, it seems, been time out of mind in
> quiet possession of certain tenants, called the Ancients, and the
> other was held by the Moderns. But these disliking their present
> station, sent certain ambassadors to the Ancients, complaining of a
> great nuisance; how the height of that part of Parnassus quite
> spoiled the prospect of theirs, especially towards the East; and

9

therefore, to avoid a war, offered them the choice of this alternative; either that the Ancients would please to remove themselves and their effects down to the lower summit, which the Moderns would graciously surrender to them, and advance in their place; or else that the said Ancients will give leave to the Moderns to come with shovels and mattocks, and level said hill as low as they shall think it convenient. To which the Ancients made answer: how little they expected such a message as this from a colony whom they had admitted out of their own free grace, to so near a neighborhood. That, as to their own seat, they were aborigines of it, and therefore to talk with them of a removal or surrender, was a language they did not understand. That if the height of the hill on their side shortened the prospect of the Moderns, it was a [sad] disadvantage they could not help, but desired them to consider, whether that injury (if it be any) were not largely recompensed by the shade and shelter it afforded them. That, as to levelling or digging [it] down, it was either folly or ignorance to propose it, if they did, or did not know, how that side of the hill was an entire rock, which would break their tools and hearts, without any damage to itself. That they would therefore advise the Moderns rather to raise their own side of the hill, than dream of pulling down that of the Ancients. . . . (360–61)

If the passage written in 1697 reads like a polite account of an English department meeting of the last decade, we must restore perspective. Swift has captured the essence of the contest between the seventeenth-century classicists and vernacularists in England, and he has prophetically rendered similar upheavals within the formal study of literature in American academies centuries later. We can identify three major revolutions in literary studies within American education: the introduction of literature in English and other modern languages, the introduction of American literature, and the introduction of women's literature. Each of these upheavals has been a struggle for territory and power, for legitimacy and authority. Each has brought changes beyond content and critical method, particularly changes in pedagogy. And the debates surrounding each have centered on the same issues and have been transacted in oddly similar language.

In his *Tradition and Reform in the Teaching of English*, Arthur Applebee convincingly demonstrates how quickly the summit of Parnassus won by the Moderns became an impenetrable rock of its own. In Applebee's words, the case against the study of vernacular literature was that "it was too easy—it had no substance, no organized body of knowledge, no rules, no theory, in short nothing to promote rigorous mental training, the discipline that was the justification of an education" (6). The study of English literature may also have been suspect because it was an enterprise women had access to. Largely prevented from learning Latin and Greek, literate women in the nineteenth century read literature written in English.

To organize and establish the discipline, teachers and scholars of English literature created a literary canon. As Applebee points out, the National Conference on Uniform Entrance Requirements in English, in an effort to regularize college preparatory work, published the first list of required books in 1894. Among the texts designated as immutable in that year were Scott's *Lady of the Lake*, Thackeray's *English Humorists of the Nineteenth Century*, Macaulay's *Essay on Clive*, and Irving's *The Alhambra* (Applebee 32). Graduate school reading lists that to this day dominate the training of teachers and scholars of English literature have their roots in this canon established by fiat.

When scholars of American literature began their own assault on the summit of Parnassus (firmly held by the English Moderns now turned Ancients), the scenario was much the same. America had produced no literature worthy of serious study, the cry went up. And Americanists, in the 1920s and 1930s, responded with a canon as immutable as any, with reading lists and sequences of required courses. Despite these tactics, American Moderns in many major institutions in this country have today only a precarious foothold on Parnassus: their courses are far fewer than those of the English Ancients, their "great books" tacked on to the end of the graduate reading list.

One need not question the worthiness of any particular text honored as canonical literature to understand the impact of such an approach to literary studies. Most simply, it creates a self-replicating system of study. One is taught particular texts, and in turn one teaches them to a growing pyramid of students. The base of the pyramid becomes the market of the publishing houses, who create anthologies of "touchstones" and sell in large numbers the relatively few titles kept in print. The teacher then operates in an arena where the control and mystification of knowledge become powerful temptations. The instructor's role as guardian of access to particular texts does much to create the aura of elitism that often taints literary study.

What is common to the canonical structures of Greek and Latin, English, and American literatures—as feminist critics have made us so well aware—is the virtual absence of women writers. (Eliot and Austen have always been exceptions.) "The best that has been thought and said in the world" has apparently been thought and said only by men. One list of the most frequently anthologized writers from 1917–1957 contains no woman writer (Applebee 278–79). Such complete invisibility is mirrored in all survey courses of American literature—courses, typically, in the work of eight great men.

Also absent from such courses is precisely what makes American literature so vital—its multiethnic character. The advent of black studies and ethnic studies in the 1960s challenged the Eurocentric view of American literature but did little to change its focus on male writers. The effort to bring the study of literature by women to the American academy owes much to the groundbreaking work done by scholars and teachers committed to multiethnic studies (though, ironically, it has taken those two decades for white feminist scholars to understand that the study of women's literature must have a multiethnic base). Like black studies, women's studies finds its roots in a social movement, insists on interdisciplinary scholarship and teaching, and challenges the academy to reexamine the very organization of knowledge based on a white male European model.

Fortified by the arguments of Virginia Woolf, Simone de Beauvoir, Kate Millett, Ellen Moers, Tillie Olsen, Adrienne Rich, Alice Walker, Florence Howe, and others, teachers of women's literature have achieved some height in their ascent of Parnassus. They are challenging an established body of literature at a time when certainty about the worth of literary study itself is eroding from within and without the academy; when an ever higher percentage of women are undertaking advanced studies in literature (ironically but not surprisingly just when the employability of the degree is in serious doubt); and when the profession is likely to become increasingly "feminized." In response to these realities, professors of literature—and humanists more broadly—are devising programs across the country to demonstrate the importance and seriousness of their work. The back-to-basics movement and the return to core curricula and required courses are efforts to firm up disciplines that have begun to be perceived as soft. The results in most cases have been direct assaults on the progress made in employment and curriculum reform by the feminist scholars and teachers of the last two decades. Not surprisingly, the feminist Moderns have rushed to establish the study of women's literature in the curricular mainstream and to create a canon of women's literature to rival established male turf.

These tactics are important, but we must go beyond them. If the revolution begun in the academies is to be anything more than a limited victory, it must be born in the anarchist vision of Virginia Woolf when she wrote,

Take this guinea and with it burn the college to the ground. Set fire to the old hypocrisies. Let the light of the burning building scare the nightingales and incarnadine the willows. And let the daughters of educated men dance round the fire and heap armful upon armful of dead leaves upon the flames. And let their mothers lean from the upper windows and cry "Let it blaze! Let it blaze! for we have done with this 'education'"! (65–66)

What feminist scholars must be done with if they are to replace dead leaves with a radical restructuring of literary studies is the exclusive allegiance to the idea of canonicity itself. Yes, we should continue to read, publish, and reprint the work of our most accomplished public artists. And, yes, we must insist that women's fiction, drama, and poetry become a central part of all basic, core, and mainstream studies. But we must also open our classrooms to the study of all forms of verbal art, no longer confining ourselves to those texts created for a public audience and a marketplace.

The literature of American women is vast. In releasing the word "literature" from a capital "L" and giving it the broadest possible construction—texts fashioned of letters—we may include women's diaries and journals, letters, memoirs, autobiographies, essays, speeches, stories, oral narratives, and songs. Texts are everywhere, and the limits to the sources for study are only the limits of our imaginations. Rhetoric courses might be constructed around the speeches of Susan B. Anthony and Charlotte Perkins Gilman. (Imagine how the world might be different if students read this material instead of "Self-Reliance" year after year.) The informal essay from Sarah Hale to Nora Ephron or the literature of the woman's page in American newspapers for the last hundred years could be the basis for courses in writing and social history. Such courses would naturally become interdisciplinary, as would the study of women's slave narratives, women's pacifist literature, and women's literature of the westward expansion, of the whaling industry, of abolition, or of the labor movement. Women's literature of the self would offer a comparative study of several genres: autobiography, memoirs, diaries, and oral history.

Such an approach to literary studies views culture as a process rather than an accumulation of products. It highlights the context and the individual imagination that generate the text as well as the context and individual imagination of the text's audience. The value of such texts is not assigned by tradition and passively received but created in the engagement between reader and text. Such literary studies will take those involved to the heart of the enterprise, an enterprise often obscured by received canons, prescribed reading lists, and required courses. The student of literature will confront the mystery of the human urge to create shape and give meaning in a multiplicity of arenas.

Research and teaching possibilities abound in all these fields. American women's diary literature, for example, is vast, and a surprisingly large number of these diaries have been published. Scores of well-known American women have kept journals; among those published in whole or part are those of Abigail Adams, Louisa May Alcott, Enid Bagnold, Ruth Benedict, Helen Bevington, Louise Bogan, Willa Cather, Kate Chopin, Janet Flanner, Charlotte Forten, Margaret Fuller, Lillian Hellman, Julia Ward Howe, Alice James, Helen Keller, Fanny Kemble, Meridel Le Sueur, Anne Morrow Lindbergh, Maria Mitchell, Sylvia Plath, Eslanda Robeson, May Sarton, Dorothy Thompson, and Laura Ingalls Wilder. The diaries of "ordinary" American women contain commentary on virtually every aspect of women's lives in this country in the last three centuries. We could, for example, easily group diaries of women as participants or observers in time of war. From the American Revolution onward, women have recorded how their lives have been touched by war, with numerous examples produced out of the Civil War and World War I. Women who became a part of the westward expansion, went to sea aboard whaling vessels, or traveled overseas as missionaries kept journals in large numbers. Women and spirituality is a topic that certainly could—and perhaps should—be based in the study of journals recording religious experience. Traditional aspects of women's lives—mothering, nursing, and all aspects of domestic life—find full expression in women's journals. Diaries of pregnancy have had a certain vogue since one was published in 1917. Even more compelling, because we know so little about them, are the women who recorded unusual, even eccentric lives in their journals. Women who were explorers, naturalists, miners, homesteaders, physicians, political activists, preachers, farmers, and prisoners of war have kept journals. Numbers of girls under ten have written of being young and female; women have written of being old, widowed, or confined to a nursing home. Virtually every aspect of women's lives in America—including some of the least pleasant aspects such as physical abuse and incest—has found its way into these journals. One important exception to that generalization is the topic of sexuality. But even the silence observed until recently on this important issue is a crucial lesson in the study of women's lives and the constraints of this literary form.

The study of women's diaries—like the study of other forms of personal narrative—involves a number of concerns appropriately literary. Formal concerns such as the evolution of the genre, structure, persona or narrator, repetition, "metaphors of self,"[1] and other imagistic patterns are all intrinsic aspects of such study. Particularly fascinating with regard to the study of "the recorded life"[2] are the writer's relation to time and her sense of audience, real or imagined. The diary is also a written record demanding a particularly active role by the reader in the creation of meaning.

My purpose is not to confuse the distinctions between different forms of art, between the forms sometimes unfortunately called "high art" and other forms. It is not particularly enlightening, for example, to say that a diary is really like a novel or "as good as" a novel. While a diary and a novel may contain some characteristics common to narrative forms, no purpose is served by forgetting that one text was created in private, usually without thought of publication, and that the other was self-consciously created to reach a public audience through commercial production. In fact, when clear distinctions are maintained about the contexts of artistic creation—intentionality, audience, and the material conditions of creation—we may see fascinating interactions between different forms of verbal art and, indeed, between the shaping of a text and the shaping of life itself, the ultimate text.

Helen Ward Brandreth, a young New York woman of high social class, kept a courtship diary and called it "Fanny Fern."[3] The diary echoes the romantic fiction she was reading: Brandreth has cast herself in its pages as the heroine of a Fanny Fern novel. The "episodes" of such a novel structure the daily entries in the diary and, perhaps, the life choices made as well. Similarly, a nineteenth-century New England woman who traveled south for her health and to be near her brother writes home to her family of this brother's death.[4] In a series of letters she writes in vivid and loving detail of his last hours and words. What is odd is that she was far from her brother when he died and has largely imagined the scene. Even more odd is that when her own death occurs some months later (a friend attending her writes of it in a final letter in this collection), she "stages" her own death according to the precise details created to describe the death of her brother. According to the friend, she even utters the same "last words." Ann Douglas writes of another such interplay between artistic text and lived text:

> Mrs. Sigourney's last recorded words were benignly all inclusive ones, "I love everybody." A few decades before, Mrs. Sigourney had published a sentimentalized biographical sketch entitled *Margaret and Henrietta* (1835). According to her account, Margaret had died with the same phrase on her lips. Could Mrs. Sigourney have mentally noted the appeal of such a last line, stored it up, and finally re-enacted a deathbed scene which she had in part invented? (206)

"Yes," of course, is the answer. To these instances we may add Alice James's (and a number of unknown women's) reluctance to die before her final journal entry was in order (James 232–33). These "final curtain" examples suggest that the interplay between verbal text and the shaping of experience itself may be lifelong. But we do not know as much as we might about the human urge to order, structure, create, and communicate meaning. Such provocative issues become obscured when we focus only on forms of institutionalized art, enshrined by the academy, the publishing houses, and other arbiters of taste.

The teaching of vernacular literature has important pedagogical consequences. Students often come to a class on women's diaries, for example, after years of avid journal writing. Even if they have not kept journals, they may be asked to do so for the duration of the course. Students may not begin with much self-consciousness about the forms of verbal art they already practice, but they will soon see features their own writing shares with the texts being studied. Strategic questions such as "Would I know you if I read your journal?" will lead directly to a discussion of the diarist's creation of a character (who both is and is not the self) in the pages of the journal. When student writers become aware that they select and arrange detail in their own work, concepts like "persona" and "narrator" are readily available. Further questions about editing material in this most private of genres will lead to an awareness of a real or implied audience: a future self, one's mother, future descendants. The audience functions here as it does in other forms of verbal expression—directly influencing every choice of form, content, and tone.

When students are able to make connections between their own texts and historical objects of study, they no longer consider literature an alien realm. They may place new value on their writing in seeing it as part of a cultural tradition. They may then find access to forms of verbal art they do not practice and may not be likely to practice, forms created in public arenas and for public purposes. Students no longer trying to conform their perceptions to accepted standards will value, no doubt, their own creative and critical capacities.

So, we feminist Moderns must resist the temptation to establish a canon of "great books" by women and to stop there. We must open our classrooms to the literature of all women, created in many forms and for many purposes. We must study the most exquisitely wrought villanelle written for publication and for the initiate few just as we must study stories told by grandmothers to granddaughters about the depression. The texts of women's literature, like energy from the sun, are everywhere and hence are not subject to control and mystification. Feminist Moderns newly established within the academy may be reluctant to embrace an approach that insists culture is a process, not a product, that value is created, not received. But if we are to do anything beyond replicating the classrooms of the masters and dons who have gone before us we must take the risk. Teaching women's vernacular literature, teaching in the mother tongue, may be the last best hope of the profession.

Notes

1. The phrase is from the title of James Olney's *Metaphors of Self: The Meaning of Autobiography* (Princeton: Princeton UP, 1972).

2. The phrase is from James Cummings' "Bookseller's Search for 'The Recorded Life,'" *AB: Bookman's Weekly* 6 Sept. 1982: 1427–40.

3. The unpublished diary, kept from 1876 to 1885, is housed in a private collection.

4. The letters are housed in a private collection.

The Languages of Oral Testimony and Women's Literature

Elizabeth A. Meese

All of us at one time have to address the question of what oral testimony has to do with literature and with us as critics of literature. The problem is particularly pressing for women's studies scholars since the only literature of many women in the world today is oral literature. Tillie Olsen, for example, notes in *Silences* that two thirds of the world's nonliterate individuals are women (184). If we are to understand the full range of women's cultural and artistic expression, we must extend the scope of our inquiry beyond printed texts. Here I attempt to construct some necessary bridges between oral and written material and to suggest some familiar criteria and methods for identifying the literary qualities of oral material. We can speak all we want of collecting oral testimony, but if we fail to establish its role within literary (or historical) study, such discussion will have been useless.

In an essay entitled "The Storyteller," Walter Benjamin maintains that "Experience which is passed from mouth to mouth is the source from which all storytellers have drawn. And among those who have written down the tales, it is the great ones whose written version differs least from the speech of the many nameless storytellers" (84). As teachers of literature, most of us are comfortable with the notion that literature emerged in the dark past from oral tradition. After the Greek epics, Old English verse, a few ballads, and comparable material, our interest in the literature of oral tradition ends, and we exhibit an almost exclusive orientation toward the printed word and the authority of the text. Oral tradition, however, continues today as the living and dynamic manifestation of expressive verbal culture for a significant proportion of our population—in fact, for the majority of individuals in certain subcultures—and it is the only mode of verbal creativity for members of some entire cultures in the world today. This may initially sound too anthropological and remote to be compelling for literature scholars, but I hope to suggest some relations that draw approaches and materials closer together.

It is important to begin with the terms themselves. We should, for the moment, speak of "oral testimony," a term more inclusive than those currently employed by individual disciplines. "Oral history" and "oral biography" imply specific limitations on the content of the spoken material and, in the case of "oral history," a consensus concerning its use—to corroborate, correct, or extend the traditional historical record. The terms "oral narrative" and "oral literature," as they are used by folklorists and anthropologists, presuppose evidence of three specific criteria. In her article "A Multidimensional Approach to Oral Literature," Heda Jason enumerates these criteria as (1) oral transmissibility, (2) artistic form (as in incantation, riddle, proverb, anecdote, and longer narrative), and (3) traditionality (that a story is perpetuated over time and sometimes space, being told and retold without continual reference to a fixed source). Obviously, traditionality need not be a determining feature for literary scholars, nor is artistic form a prerequisite for the value of oral history. Thus, at least in the beginning, the broader category of "oral testimony" will serve us better than those other terms that bring specific functions, methods and disciplinary value systems with them. Until we make our own differentiations, the broader category is the more useful one.

To approach the problem of the literary sensibility as it struggles with noncanonical forms of expression and with other users of language, I want to begin with the experiences of Virginia Woolf and James Agee—the first an encounter with written testimony, the second with the process of recording and interpreting the spoken word.

In a 1930 letter to Margaret Llewelyn Davies that stands as the introduction to *Life as We Have Known It*, a collection of memoirs by Cooperative Working Women, Virginia Woolf enacts the fundamental scene in an interpretive drama that continues today. Woolf's encounter with the written testimonies of working-class women remains instructive. When asked to write a preface for the volume, she begins by asserting her conventional position: good books require no preliminary apparatus; they stand on their own merit. She writes to Davies,

> But you left me the papers, and, turning them over, I saw that on this occasion the argument did not apply; this book is not a book. Turning the pages, I began to ask myself what is this book then, if it is not a book? What quality has it? What ideas does it suggest? What old arguments and memories does it rouse in me? (xv)

She thereby confronts and discards the first line of defense against this kind of material. She remembers a 1913 women's meeting in Newcastle and compares "ladies" and working women: "And though the range of expression is narrower in working women, their few expressions have a force and an emphasis, of tragedy or humour which the faces of ladies lack" (xxvi). Permitting herself no easy generalizations, Woolf grapples (not awfully successfully) with class differences as they affect women's lives, and her reflections bring her to language:

> One does not want to slip easily into fine phrases about "contact with life," about "facing facts" and "the teaching of experience," for they invariably alienate the hearer, and moreover no working man or woman works harder or is in closer touch with reality than a painter with his brush or a writer with his pen. But the quality that they have, judging from a phrase caught here and there, from a laugh, or a gesture seen in passing, is precisely the quality that Shakespeare would have enjoyed. . . . How many words must lurk in those women's vocabularies that have faded from ours! How many scenes must lie dormant in their eyes which are unseen by ours! What images and saws and proverbial sayings must still be current with them that have never reached the surface of print, and very likely they still keep the power which we have lost of making new ones. (xxvi–xxviii)

In this passage Woolf reveals her recognition of class barriers that come between women, and she sees her Newcastle experiences as a bridge to the voices of the Davies women. Words free both the speaker/writer and the listener/reader because individuals encounter one another outside their conventional role relations. Woolf explains,

> Thus if it were possible to meet [these women] not as masters or mistresses or customers with a counter between us, but over the wash-tub or in the parlour casually and congenially as fellow-beings with the same wishes and ends in view, a great liberation would follow and perhaps friendship and sympathy would supervene. (xxvii)

While this mutually humanizing capability is present in testimonies like these, just as it is in literature, the question of the material's intrinsic literariness is less easily approached. Woolf concludes that the testimonies she read would probably not mean as much to someone who is unable to visualize the scene and supplement it with the images and sounds of actual people:

It cannot be denied that the chapters here put together do not make a book—that as literature they have many limitations. The writing, a literary critic might say, lacks detachment and imaginative breadth. . . . Here are no reflections, he might object, no view of life as a whole, and no attempt to enter into the lives of other people. Poetry and fiction seem far beyond their horizon. Indeed, we are reminded of those obscure writers before the birth of Shakespeare who never travelled beyond the borders of their own parishes, who read no language but their own, and wrote with difficulty, finding few words and those awkwardly. And yet since writing is a complex art, much infected by life, these pages have some qualities even as literature that the literate and instructed might envy. (xxxvii–xxxviii)

From the examples she chooses to support her point, Woolf constructs a partial set of criteria for evaluating oral and written testimonies. She finds in these works an admirable identification with physical surroundings, precise observation, concise articulation, and the stark retelling of extraordinary content (the rape of a servant girl). After her rigorous and honest appraisal, Woolf arrives at a stalemate: "Whether that is literature or not literature I do not presume to say, but that it explains much and reveals much is certain" (xxxix).

Similarly instructive is James Agee's struggle in 1936 to give form to his understanding. His statements of intention and method in *Let Us Now Praise Famous Men* illuminate our immediate problem. He describes his and Walker Evans's work as follows:

Actually, the effort is to recognize the stature of a portion of unimagined existence, and to contrive techniques proper to its recording, communication, analysis, and defense. More essentially, this is an independent inquiry into certain normal predicaments of human divinity.

The immediate instruments are two: the motionless camera, and the printed word. The governing instrument—which is also one of the centers of the subject—is individual, anti-authoritative human consciousness.

Ultimately, it is intended that this record and analysis be exhaustive, with no detail, however trivial it may seem, left untouched, no relevance avoided, which lies within the power of remembrance to maintain, of the intelligence to perceive, and of the spirit to persist in. (xiv)

Agee's encounter with people's lives leads him to an awareness of the inadequacies of literary language. Even with Evans's photographs supplying visual images, the analogues of Woolf's firsthand experience that combines the knowledge of faces with that of words, Agee still feels the limitations of the language of art, the concept of "the book," when set to the purposes of oral testimony and the presentation of life for representatives of neglected classes and subcultural groups. He writes:

> If I could do it, I'd do no writing at all here. It would be photo-graphs; the rest would be fragments of cloth, bits of cotton, lumps of earth, records of speech, pieces of wood and iron, phials of odors, plates of food and of excrement. Book-sellers would consider it quite a novelty; critics would murmur, yes, but is it art; and I could trust a majority of you to use it as you would a parlor game.
> A piece of the body torn out by the roots might be more to the point.
> As it is, though, I'll do what little I can in writing. Only it will be very little. I'm not capable of it; and if I were, you would not go near it at all. For if you did, you would hardly bear to live.   (12–13).

Agee says, in effect, that he would substitute life for art if he could. He understands the power of his subject and his departure from tradi-tional forms and methods as he attempts to document the meaning of others' lives, the writer's experience of that meaning, and his effort to relate it through words. In addition to the inadequacies of language, the analytic and expressive methods of traditional disciplines are of no use to him. He explains,

> For in the immediate world, everything is to be discerned, for him who can discern it, and centrally and simply, without either dissec-tion into science, or digression into art, but with the whole con-sciousness, seeking to perceive it as it stands: so that the aspect of a street in sunlight can roar in the heart of itself as a symphony, perhaps as no symphony can: and all of consciousness is shifted from the imagined, the revisive, to the effort to perceive simply the cruel radiance of what is.   (11)

Somehow the problem of discussing oral testimony has been greater for the literary critic, who is one more step removed than the writer from the raw data of literature, the stream of life itself. In addition to the difference in field, there is a difference in method. Traditional literary studies are based on a fundamental principle: the opposition of art and life. Historically, critics have believed that lan-guage functions differently in literature than it does elsewhere, particularly in speech, and that characters and events—that raw material of life—are transformed into art, at which point they cease to be themselves and become fit objects of study.

What brought us to this point? In her book *Toward a Speech Act Theory of Literary Discourse*, Mary Louise Pratt unravels aspects of this traditional opposition in twentieth-century literary theory. She contends,

> Examples from literature are virtually never accompanied by data from extraliterary discourse. Instead, devices observed in literature were assumed to be 'literary,' to constitute 'literariness' (the term is Jakobson's) because non-literature was assumed *a priori* not to possess the properties of literature.   (5)

The Prague Circle of 1929 divided language use into two categories: language for the purpose of communication, which was directed toward the thing signified in the real world; and language "directed toward the sign itself" (8), that is, a message focused in on itself. According to this view, texts can be similarly classified—some are for communication, concerned with messages directed outward; others for art, self-reflexive, directed inward, calling attention to themselves. The limitations and effects of creating such a dichotomy are instantly apparent, particularly in the context of studying the literature of another sex, race, class, or political group—where texts often combine "art" that is about itself and fairly explicit messages that are directed outward to foster group solidarity or to provide a critique of the majority culture; hence, another dimension of literary-historical bias dismisses such works as polemical, didactic, and "not literature" (the fate of much leftist literature of the 1930s, for example). When power cannot be assumed as a privilege of life, powerlessness presents itself as an unavoidable condition of life and subject for art. The artist then feels compelled to direct messages outward.

I suspect that the problems of identifying the literary qualities of oral testimony are no different from those encountered when we examine any noncanonical or unfamiliar texts. (It parallels the reactions of many English department colleagues who are terrified at the prospect of teaching creative writing. "How," they ask, "will you know if the student works are any good?" And good or bad, "what in the world could you say about these unfamiliar pieces of writing?" Or, "One way we know how to recognize great literature is that it stands the test of time." What, indeed, I sometimes wonder, do we really know?)

The recent focus on "texts," as evidenced by critics schooled in deconstruction, will assist the readers of women's literature as well as students of oral testimony. Past understandings of what a text is and how it can be read are being challenged. The current preoccupation with structures encourages us to compare texts, asking questions about form, intent, effect. According to Pratt,

> all the problems of coherence, chronology, causality . . . plausibility, selection of detail, tense, point of view and emotional intensity exist for the natural narrator just as they do for the novelist, and they are confronted and solved (with greater or lesser success) by speakers of the language every day. (66–67)

In other words, we approach texts in terms of narrative strategies, and the discussion of such strategies is not in the least dependent on the kind of text under consideration, so that in theory one would approach an oral testimony with the same tools and questions one would employ with a printed book. Similarly, obscure works by women writers would not, by definition, offer greater resistance to analysis than do the works of Faulkner, James, or Emerson.

The linguist Labov presents us with two broad questions that we can apply to written and unwritten texts: "What is the speaker/writer trying to do in forming this discourse?" and "What does the hearer/reader do when receiving the discourse?" (qtd. in Pratt 73). To these basic questions we can add a number of others concerning context and function: Who is the speaker? What is her/his background? How is the story told? What is repeated and emphasized? What are the inherent contradictions? What is omitted? How does the speaker regard the material? the telling? the audience? herself? What happens when a person's life experience is made problematical, called to the foreground for examination or discussion? We may ask these questions of speaker/writer as well as listener/reader; furthermore, we may ask them of literary works that are familiar or obscure.

I do not mean that every speech act or text has artistic merit, but I certainly suggest that any work *may* have that value. I like to use a minimal standard, seeing art as an elaboration or shaping of experience that is rendered skillfully and possesses describable form. This standard asks us as critics and interviewers to know what is ordinary in order to distinguish some degree of extraordinariness; it requires us to understand culturally relative norms for competence in storytelling and to look at the maker and the thing made.

There are other dimensions of quality. An oral interview is a collaborative event, requiring both a good interviewer and a good informant. The quality of the resultant interview depends on the quality of the interaction between these two individuals. Together they produce a text that in one dimension is the dialogue between them and in the other (perhaps the more difficult one) is what Grele calls the dialogue between the informant and her own historical and cultural consciousness.

The meaning of an interview emerges as the interviewer and the informant engage in the communicative moment. While training and practice can improve interviewing skills, we have much less control over the informant's performance. The good informant is not unlike the good writer—each somehow performing beyond what can be taught and learned. The concept of the good informant derives in part from folklore scholarship and the notion of the "active bearer" of tradition. C. W. von Sydow in an article entitled "On the Spread of Tradition" makes the following distinction between active and passive bearers: "it is the active bearers who keep tradition alive and transmit it, whereas the passive bearers have indeed heard of what a certain tradition contains, and may perhaps, when questioned, recollect part of it, but do nothing themselves to spread it or keep it alive" (12–13). As with literary taste, circumstances may affect one's relation to material; for example, religious, social, or political revolutions may transform the concept of group norms, transforming an active into a passive bearer. Such shifts may be relatively temporary or permanent, depending on the conditions of the time. In addition, a person may be active in relation to one body of information and passive with regard to another; for example, an informant may be an active bearer of family lore and a passive bearer of labor history. Finally, von Sydow observes that both types of individuals are necessary for the spread of tradition:

> If there is no longer any active bearers of the tradition . . . alive, it may be possible to get information, sometimes fairly complete, but most often uncertain and fragmentary. Besides, the passive carriers of a tradition have the important task of giving it resonance. . . . Moreover, the passive bearers act, to some extent, as a check on tradition. If some deviation should be made, they can easily correct it, and they do so, which is of great importance for the unchanging survival of the tradition. (14)

The study of oral testimony contributes to the most fundamental questions of feminist criticism today. The evidence of women's oral testimony provides us with controls in discussions of female experience and aesthetics. Such controls are invaluable in a territory like women's culture that is mined with stereotypes, myths, and desires. Despite Agee's struggle to represent accurately the experiences of sharecroppers in the deep South, for example, one welcomes Emma McCloud's oral testimony in "Emma's Story: Two Versions" as a corrective to his version of her experience. Emma at sixty-two presents her own version of the story Agee recorded when she was eighteen. Agee saw a girl who, though naive and innocent, was flirtatious and "a big child, sexual beyond propriety to its years" (9). His chronicle is overwhelmed by male fantasies of Emma's seductive interactions with her brother-in-law, himself, and Walker Evans. Agee fancies that virtually all males are attractive to Emma, and his desire culminates in an image of her in bed with all three men. In the face of his blindness to his own projected desire, Emma's one direct and understated response conveys effectively her gentle, understanding sensibility: "The only thing that I do regret. I wish Jimmy hadn't wrote just like he did because now all the children's grown and can read and they'll wonder. I tried to explain to them it wasn't, but I don't know whether they believed it or not" (21). How limited would be our comprehension of her experience and of Agee's perception had Emma's own testimony not been collected and printed.

There are aesthetic parallels to this lesson as well. Woolf discovered, for example, that great themes appeared in the unwritten literature of working-class women. She found "the strength of the human instinct to escape from bondage and attach itself whether to a country road or to a sunrise over the hills"; for Woolf, this demonstrated "the fact that the highest ideals of duty flourish in an obscure hat factory as surely as on a battlefield" (xxvii).

Collections of such observations prepare us to address the largest problems of all: Do women speak and write out of a different experience of culture? Are their uses of language and their observations of the world different from those of men? Are there significant differences when we control for time period, region, and race? By means of oral testimony, we generate both the unwritten historical and the literary records, and, in addition, we broaden the standard of comparison for women's written tradition.

By confronting the words of the "other," the historically silent, the student of literature and culture learns to break away from what Woolf termed "fictitious sympathy" to form "real sympathy." Through those words, the "cruel radiance" of actuality finds embodiment. We can put a check on feeling that is "defective," as Woolf explained, "because it is not based upon sharing the same important emotions unconsciously" (xxix). Through oral testimony we are put in touch with those other emotions; we encounter a medium that individualizes the other. By constructing such bridges, Woolf believed, "the women would cease to be symbols and would become instead individuals" (xxix)—like us. In this change lies the fundamental cultural and humanistic value of oral testimony to the women's movement, to women's studies, and to the study of literature.

ANALYSES OF
SPECIFIC TEXTS

Letters as Literature

The Prestons of Baltimore

Virginia Walcott Beauchamp

When Madge Preston, wife of a prominent Baltimore attorney, complimented her husband on his charming and entertaining letters, he wrote back:

> That you should dub my letters bright scintilations of the morning while you characterize your own as dull and prosy is rather wicked. (1 Aug. 1865)

Calling on the supporting judgment of her niece Theodosia, who lived with them and helped to manage the duties of their household, Preston went on:

> Thede says and insists upon it that you are "the best letter writer that ever lived" I said "except Lady Mary Wortley Montague— Madam de Stael and Corinne" She says she "never received any letters from these persons but she has no doubt they couldn't hold a candle to Aunty"[1]

Probably Preston knew the epistolary achievements of Lady Mary and de Staël only by reputation. His blurring of the distinction between de Staël, the author, and Corinne, the character of her more famous novel, suggests unfamiliarity with the works of these celebrated ladies. Yet the allusion makes clear his assumption of possibilities for serious literary achievement in the epistolary form. And his compliment to his wife is not mere gallantry; among their circle of friends her reputation as a writer of letters of skill and charm seems to have been unequaled—except perhaps by his own.

Possibly some aspiration for posthumous acclaim prompted the Prestons to preserve their extensive correspondence. Lady Mary

29

Wortley Montagu's reputation, after all—gained from the spectacular success of those letters that she wrote from Turkey, where she had accompanied her diplomat husband—developed largely after her death (see Halsband). The Preston correspondence is most voluminous during the years 1847 to 1870, when travel in connection with his law practice or her social visiting or foreign touring drew them apart; but a major section also includes an extensive exchange with their only child, May.

May was drawn early into the family's appreciation of well-written letters. From their home on a farm estate near Towsontown (now Towson, a Baltimore suburb and county seat of Baltimore County), May had written to her father, away on business in the city. On 5 February 1855, he wrote the following reply:

> My dear May,
> I am delighted to see, that you are able to write to me, your letter has given me more pleasure than any letter I have ever received. You have improved wonderfully and I dare say in a very short time you will be able to write without difficulty to all your friends. What a pleasure this will be to you and how gratifying to all who take pleasure in well informed little girls. I shall not destroy your letter, but shall keep it to remind me in years to come, of what my dear daughter could do before she was six years old.
> —. . . . (MHS)

By the time May was sixteen and a student at St. Joseph's Academy in Emmitsburg, Maryland, she had become an accomplished artist in the epistolary form.

Her mother, Madge, viewed the writing of letters—the strengthening of the bonds of friendly association—as a major female responsibility, and she nurtured these skills in her daughter.

> I am glad Pauline wrote to you, and hope you will answer her letter; while on the subject of letters, let me give you a little instruction on that subject— Be sure always to *date* your letters distinctly—and *do not* begin them *so far down the page* as you do, a letter so commenced has an exceedingly awkward appearance— if you write on ruled paper, it is usually ruled so as to show you where to begin— let me see my child that you remember in future, what I have suggested. . . . (30 Jan. 1863, UM)

Before the thirteen-year-old May had gone to St. Joseph's, her mother had been her only teacher. When Madge at any time reassumed the role, she taught through encouragement and appreciation:

I dont recollect if I mentioned in my last letter, but if I did not, it will not hurt to repeat it again, my great satisfaction at your evident effort to please me in your hand writing and the beginning of your letter. Papa also noticed it and made satisfactory comments upon both. So you see my child nothing is lost upon us, and when you do not come up to our reasonable expectations, the pain is in proportion to the pleasure your efforts to improve give us. We are particularly anxious about your writing, as we class that, among the higher accomplishments; your letters also, are often read by our neighbours, and I do not like to see evidences of carelessness, though I must give you the satisfaction of knowing, that your letters are read with great pleasure and receive warm commendations from all quarters. (13 Feb. 1863, UM)

There we have it—the sense of an audience larger than the letter's single recipient, a letter passed lovingly and admiringly from hand to hand, scrutinized by many eyes. Madge's to May enchanted all May's schoolgirl friends and drew admiration as well from some of the Sisters who ran the school. For that larger audience, Madge knew that the letter's content must be well chosen and well expressed. Still the encouraging instructor, she made her views explicit in another letter to May:

. . . you have an agreeable faculty of catching at those little incidents in a somewhat monotonous life, that are pleasant and interesting to know, and a sprightly way of expressing yourself, which is well calculated by practice to make you, what is so desirable all should be, an easy and graceful letter writer. (13 Mar. 1863, UM)

Returning to the subject in a different context—this time aboard the steamer *Berlin* on an Atlantic crossing in 1868—Madge wrote to her husband:

My self love may have flattered my vanity and caused me to think you will be interested in these trifles, but I cannot help judging you by myself and I know that at this distance from you, the least word, look, or action of yours & our friends in America would be treasured beyond Gold. (Diary for 1868, p. 15, JHU)

Madge's diary entries show her concern with epistolary responsibilities—the noting of letters written and letters received—but also her special sense of audience and context: "I rose early this morning and wrote a long letter (14 pages) to May, giving her a funny description of my ride in the old stage &c &c . . ." (Diary for 1862, 9 Sept.). In a letter to May, Madge tells of the pains she has taken with her response to another juvenile correspondent:

> I rec'd a few days since, a very nicely written and well worded letter, from dear Charley Simmons. The boy wrote by his Mother's request having heard that you were away for the winter, she thought I must be lonely. . . . I have just answered Charley's letter. . . . I ransacked my brains for all the funny things I could find in them—to write to the boy and please him. (9 Dec. 1862, UM)

Madge's first letter to May at school established the former's reputation among the schoolgirls and Sisters at St. Joseph's. Concerned that the thirteen-year-old might suffer from homesickness, Madge, to entertain her, wrote a sprightly description of the return trip after leaving her daughter. At an Emmitsburg inn, where she spent her first night away from May, Madge had met an old gentleman who turned out to be a close friend of her relatives in Philadelphia. "It was so pleasant to talk over old times and old friends," she wrote,

> that I sat till nine oclock, and almost forgetting, that the barbarous stage driver, had told me I must be ready for traveling by four oclock the next morning. I tried to excite the sympathies of the old gentleman in my annoyance of getting up so early, but I found he was, like your father an advocate for early rising and only laughed at my distress. Of course I slept very little the first night away from my dear little daughter, and was not sorry to hear the rough voice of the driver, at three oclock in the morning, at my door telling me to "get up." We left Emmittsburg, before four oclock, too early, for me to hear, once more the sound of the old Convent bell and to know you also, were listening to the same sweet tones. There were no passengers in the Stage but myself, and the consequence was, that the great lumbering clumsy Stage, (which by the way, was sufficiently old, to have satisfied even a greater lover of antiquity than yourself) went jumping from side to side and pitching forward and backwards, heaving up and down for want of ballast, like a huge vessel in a storm at sea, or some mighty animal in convulsions. I tried to stay myself by seizing hold of the sides of the coach, and again by gathering together the soft cushions on the seats and lying down, but all to no purpose, the old Stage in its eagerness to get to its journey's end went tumbling about worse than ever, until I was forced to give in, and let the hysterical creature bounce me down at Union Bridge, only too thankful that none of my bones were broken, and that I still retained sufficient of

my senses to ask the good, kind old lady with the lump on her neck, for the breakfast, of which I stood so much in need, for be it remembered, that this long journey of sixteen miles, over these terrible rough roads were taken on an empty stomach and part of the time so dark I could scarcely see houses trees or even the fine barns so much admired by little Walter . . . (20 Sept. 1862, UM)

The letter's sense of the specific audience engages the modern reader just as it must have charmed the girl to whom the letter was addressed—the shared joke about the father's lectures on early rising; the documented impact on the writer (in her sleepless night, her longing for the convent bell) of the beloved recipient's absence; the reference to May's interest in antiques; the allusion to experiences shared on the journey north (the old lady with the lump on her neck, the exclamations of young Walter Abell, who had traveled with them). And its re-creation of an experience from the viewpoint of the writer is also compelling—the "barbarous" driver, his "rough voice," the passenger's desperate and unavailing efforts to cope with the vicissitudes of her travel, the references to her mental and physical state.

Yet other qualities in the passage appeal to us also. Madge's playfulness with language—the similes of a vessel in a storm, of an animal in convulsions; the metaphor of the hysterical creature—add to the reader's pleasure, as does the concreteness of detail. This is a letter worthy of any reader, not just the little girl for whom it was specifically intended. One can understand why May would have shared it among her companions. And perhaps, in so well re-creating a sense of life as lived long ago, its message is more precious to us—the unintended, unknown, unimaginable readers of Madge's posterity. If works of literature should transcend the circumstances of their writing, should appeal to universal audiences, this letter meets that test.

A letter on her sewing machine—similarly playful—re-creates for twentieth-century readers what has been outside our own experience, we who have grown up in a world dominated by technology: the excitement of new possibilities latent in the abstract concept of the machine. The letter is a paean of appreciation.

Rejoice with me my dear child in the good fortune that has just befallen me— Behold me the possessor of a Sewing Machine! — Yes! there it stands in all its beauty and all its usefulness, the very personification of all my wishes with regard to good household fairies, who are to sit cheerfully working and toiling for me, while I enjoy the delights of a book—a good bracing walk over the green fields, or a hunt in the dear old woods for chesnuts, or the more quiet pleasure of social conversation with a friend. . . . You would be amused to see us looking over it, examining all its simple yet wonderful machinery, and touching each different ingenious and useful little adjustment, as though they were the wings of the beautiful creature, and must not be handled too roughly!   (17 Oct. 1864, UM)

Madge's diary entry of that date is self-aware about the tone of her letter, and yet the tone of the diary passage reveals the underlying sincerity of the emotion expressed in the letter:

We . . . reached home at three, bringing with us our little fairy as we call the Machine. The dear, beautiful thing, we gave it a warm welcome and the seat of honor was at once awarded to it. I have written May a letter giving her a playful account of its advent to Pleasant Plains. I am so happy to think I am the owner of a Sewing Machine!

One instance of Madge's epistolary playfulness went astray, when her daughter—and even the school principal—misread the letter's arch intent. Madge had described the acquisition of a kitten (referred to in the letter as "our little pet") who repays by "her love and pleasant ways." Madge goes on to describe the family's visit to a recently vacated cottage on their property, where

they heard a plaintive little voice . . . which . . . they soon found proceeded from this poor little thing. . . . It was at once picked up and brought up to the house where warm and nourishing food, and a comfortable bed was at once provided and we soon had the pleasure of seeing our little foundling or rather our own Eureka open its eyes, stretch its white and beautiful limbs, spread out its soft arms as if to embrace and thank us for our kindness, look its love and then fall off to sleep again. And thus the little thing has been living with us since that time, and now it only depends upon you to say whether it shall for the future be considered as one of our household, share in its comforts pleasures and prosperities, or be given to some other person who will adopt it. . . .   (9 Feb. 1865, UM)

Since only the year before the Prestons had taken into their home an orphan boy, who was working as a farmhand and for whose education at a Baltimore school they were arranging, May's inference that the "pet" was an infant, whose adoption awaited only her approval, is perhaps not difficult to understand. ("Pet" is often also a term of endearment by Madge to May.) "How shall I begin to tell you the state of excitement your last letter has thrown me into!" May responded. "Did you mean that we have a real child at Pleasant Plains? . . . If it is a *real child by all means take it.*" After expanding on her often-repeated and sincere prayers for a sister, May asks that the supposed child be baptized with the name of Maud. Then she concludes: "I do not know whether I am talking about a person or an animal. Oh! Mama please never write that way again, be sure and let me know what you mean . . ." (13 Feb. 1865, MHS). Madge's diary entry for 15 February and a contrite letter the following day convey her distress over the confusion her metaphorical language had induced:

> My dear, generous, noble hearted little child! How can I ever forgive myself for the pain and anxiety my thoughtless folly has caused you! In my foolish desire of writing something to please and amuse you I forgot, that that, very "something" might produce a contrary effect. . . .   (UM)

Madge's self-consciousness, her attempt to be literary—to write playfully and by indirection—had disrupted her intention to communicate. Yet this set of letters may to other readers create the stuff of literature. The drama of human interaction that they convey is no less affecting because it is real.

If Madge Preston prized a sprightly style and minute, concrete details in letters she received, she also valued a certain degree of reticence in letters she sent out. On the first day of 1864, Madge recorded in her diary a new enterprise in communicating with May:

> I have begun to day a kind of Journal or daily letter for May, which I will send as opportunity offers, thus the child will be kept informed of the principle events of our home life, at least such as are pleasant—the unhappy ones I will retain for myself alone. . . .

The unhappy ones were intruding ever more into the record of the diary. Preston, suspiciously, was spending more and more nights in the city, especially when the obese German housekeeper of the townhouse where he kept his law offices could be prevailed on to visit the country. Notations about quarrels become frequent subjects of the diary. Madge was increasingly distressed over the continuing presence in the household of Theodosia and her older sister Rose and over Preston's apparent infatuation with Rose. By the next year he was striking Madge, who suffered a black eye, even a concussion. "I really think Mr Preston is insane," she confided to her diary.

Yet the letters to May reflect primarily the happy times. The troubling husband of real life moves through the letters as that pleasant character, "your dear Papa." His frequent and extended absences are attributed to the exigencies of his legal practice. Often the letters show Madge's daydreams about May's happy schoolgirl days—the happiest of her life, Madge counsels, before the cares and troubles of adulthood come to weigh her down. Madge almost encourages May to think of joining the communal group of the Sisters of Charity. Madge's pain is thus disguised and sublimated, the letters forming a kind of fiction that, with the accompanying diary entries, we are able to read.

Madge was the principal letter writer during this period. Preston had begun a letter to his daughter on Christmas Day, 1863, resumed it on 3 January with protestations of "how sad and depressed I am at times," and finally finished on 19 May, his daughter's fifteenth birthday. The fifteen pages of his letter set a precedent, followed in succeeding years, that the number of pages in May's birthday letter should equal her number of years.

The 3 January section of the 1864 birthday letter contains Preston's theory of the letter:

> At the foot of the last page I was interrupted and laid the letter aside, I now resume it, and at the hazzard of sending you a broken disjointed epistle jot down whatever thought presents itself. In fact letters ought not to be straight-laced—rule-and-square productions—the best are those that are written with perfect freedom— unshackled by conventional phrases in order to gratify arbitrary rules of etiquette.   (UM)

He was less tolerant, however, when his daughter found means to express herself with the same "perfect freedom."

Most of her letters are neatly written—in fact, carefully transcribed for the perusal of the Sister charged with the teaching of writing. Only two or three, written at Gettysburg or Emmitsburg inns, show the difference. There, where May was spending a night with schoolgirl friends and their visiting parents, May divulged secrets she felt compelled to withhold from the Sisters. (Her letters too held their reticences.) In such letters, she scribbled and crossed out, blaming the dim candlelight and the need to balance her page on her knee.

Preston found those letters appalling but expressed this opinion only to Madge; to May he wrote encouragingly:

> It affords me great pleasure to be able to say that your various letters have given evidence of your continued improvement. Your orthography is good—your selection of words satisfactory—and

the current of your sentiments, as well as the sentiments themselves indicate reflection and a very fair understanding. (3 Jan. 1864)

Preston's letters are full of literary allusions. This passage, in fact, follows immediately a disquisition on nostalgia for home as a source of literature of merit; he quotes a stanza from Byron, refers to Gray's "Elegy," and alludes to Scott, Burns, "Orators, historians, essayists &c."

Fictions or not (the frequent separations of the Prestons and the troubled passages in Madge's diary suggest that they are), the letters exchanged by the Prestons read delightfully like the effusions of a mutually enamored couple. His often assume a literary stance, a kind of elegant self-consciousness calling attention to itself (e.g., his playing with form in the number of pages of the birthday letters). A passage in one of his letters to Madge clearly values the epistle as one of our greatest treasures:

The pleasure of seeing you and May would be greater than that of writing to you. The pleasure of writing to our friends is certainly very great—whether we owe it to Cadmus the Phoenician or Palamedes the Greek matters but little, whoever may have been the inventor of letters, certainly was better entitled to divine honors than others whom the Greeks and Romans for very trifling services, or from ridiculous considerations made Gods of—but after all writing is not seeing—ten thousand things which we can personally orally convey to our friends are rarely communicated by letter. (4 Aug. 1865, MHS)

To Madge, the writing of letters was more an obligation, a woman's task:

. . . since my return from the North I have had so much to look after—seed planting—little chickens—house cleaning—and spring sewing, together with a number of letters to answer which had accumulated during my absence. . . . (to May, 26 May 1863, UM)

She encourages May to assume this responsibility:

If you can—I really wish you would answer the child's letter, as the whole family really seem hurt that you have not answered any of their letters, also, write to dear little Charley Simmons. . . . I think it no more than proper, that you pay the little boy that attention. (8 June 1863, UM)

But writing to May is also a major pleasure for Madge, and as we know from her diary, a primary psychological satisfaction and release:

> If I do not write you as long a letter as you wish you must scold
> Papa for making himself so agreeable to Thede and I to night— I
> have actually been trying to tear myself away from the little circle,
> ever since tea time, but each time I moved away, something pleas-
> ant and agreeable was said to call me back again. At last I jumped
> up, saying I would talk to no one for the next hour, or at least till
> after a short chat with my little daughter.   (11 Mar. 1866, MHS)

There is no posing in Madge's style. Even the arch letter on the kitten that was misread so disastrously was designed to delight and entertain the receiver, not—like so many of Preston's—to enhance the sender. Madge rarely tries to be clever (and then only to amuse). Primarily her letters are supportive and direct, vignettes of the life that teems around her and in which she participates.

One of my favorite passages depicts her in what was surely her most cherished role:

> Well my little Pet, I suppose you see in your "minds eye" if you are
> in a meditative humour to night, the vision of an old lady, seated at
> a convenient and comfortable looking writing desk, with papers
> and letters and envelopes, books &c &c scattered in an apparent
> wild confusion over it, and by looking a little closely you are made
> conscious, that old lady, is your own dear Mama and she is engaged
> in the pleasant task of writing to her darling child. The vision is a
> reality my little one, and here I am prepared for a good long talk
> . . . this stormy sabbath evening.   (3 Mar. 1867, MHS)

Here, in a private communication, is the motif so frequent in the works of our time—the interpenetration of art and life. Except for the autobi-ography, in no other literary genre is the self-portrait so appropriate—as Madge herself put it, "the least word, look, or action . . . that we treasure beyond Gold" (Diary for 1868, p. 15, JHU).

Madge claimed that she did not know how to entertain her corre-spondents with gossip (to May, 8 Dec. 1864, UM). She meant to criticize her epistolary style, yet her own instinct led her to put down in letters what, in fact, endures—a personal viewpoint that engages us. She provides a concrete and complex portrait of her own consciousness, not merely for the particular correspondents to whom she directed her letters, but for us all.

The gossip that she felt her correspondents preferred can be the material of social history. It can help us reconstruct the ways people of other times have lived and interrelated. (Stone and Cott, for example, rely heavily on such material.) To tell us what they did in the past— that is history. But to evoke the past or the present, to stir our imaginations and enrapture us—that is literature.

Note

1. From the William P. Preston Papers. The correspondence is held primarily in two repositories, the Maryland Historical Society and the Archives and Manuscripts Department of McKeldin Library, University of Maryland. There is no apparent order in the division of this correspondence between the two libraries. Maryland Historical Society (MHS) holds Madge Preston's diaries for 1862 and 1864. The University of Maryland (UM) holds her diary for 1865.

Madge Preston's 1868 diary, in the Rare Book Room of the Milton Eisenhower Library, Johns Hopkins University (JHU), is actually her careful recopying into a bound book of the letters sent to family members and friends describing the travels in Europe of herself and her daughter, May. The origin of this acquisition is not known; it was presented anonymously. Since Johns Hopkins himself was a friend of the Prestons, intimate enough that the young May embroidered the old gentleman a pair of slippers and spent several weeks with him and his sister on their estate at Crisfield, it is interesting to speculate that this carefully recopied volume of letters from Madge's and May's European trip might have been a gift to him personally.

Letters and Diaries

The Persona and the Real Woman—A Case Study

Virginia Walcott Beauchamp

Two documents, composed perhaps within an hour by the same woman, represent for me a kind of Rosetta stone for understanding the written expressions of nineteenth-century women. Both were written on 1 January 1867 by an upper-middle-class Baltimore woman, Madge Preston, wife of a well-known attorney.[1] Alone in her room just before midnight, she wrote a letter to her seventeen-year-old daughter, May, her only child, who was away at school. Minutes earlier, as the letter discloses, Madge had filled the first page of her new leather-bound diary. Then, having completed the letter to May, the mother again drew forward the diary page, and in the margin, where she was accustomed to record items of special note, she penned these words: "Wrote a short letter to May on this New Year." Then she put away her book.

The two documents are extraordinary for what—taken together— they reveal of a woman's life. The message disclosed in the diary allows us to penetrate the letter's language of silences. The diary, a record of pain and endurance, affirms an inner reality of the writer. The letter, a social contract of sorts, represents in its seemingly happy message the acceptance of responsibility and obligation between two human beings and with a larger society. It depends on reticence. Through what it withholds it creates an idealized image of a woman's life. It is a fiction.

Madge's niece Theodosia (or Thede) Smith had returned that day after a visit of two or three weeks with her own family north of Gettysburg. Thede had stopped in Emmitsburg, the town where May was attending school, to see her younger cousin. May, the daughter of affluent and educated parents, was a student at St. Joseph's Academy, the school founded by the sainted Mother Seton. Thede was a poor relation,

40

one of a large brood of Madge's widowed sister's. For most of the time since May had left for school—about four years earlier—Thede had lived with the Prestons, helping with chores, supervising servants and household slaves, acting as a companion to her aunt and uncle.

Madge's letter to May records both Thede's return and her report of the visit to St. Joseph's:

> You do not need to be informed that Theodosia did not reach here on Saturday as I wrote she would do, but came down yesterday. The most pleasant information she brought me, was, that she had spent an hour with you on Sunday—that you and Anna were looking very well, and were the happiest girls she had ever seen. Dear Sr. Raphael! Thede says, she was so sweet and lovely, she does not wonder you and Anna are so happy. How could they be otherwise with such surroundings. I rec'd your little curl, this morning as a New Year's gift.

The letter records also afternoon calls from Van McNeal (a young man who had been courting May and whom they all called "Vanity") and from his mother and sister.

> I believe there has been nothing new or interesting taken place that I am interested in since I last wrote you. Vanity called to see me this afternoon and asked kindly after you and Anna and desired to be respectfully remembered. Mrs McNeal and Ella also made me a New Year's call, and sent ever so much love to you. Ella seemes to be looking forward to your return with real pleasure as does Some one else.

The letter begins with a brief quotation and a mother-to-daughter message that, while light in tone, well describes the nineteenth-century moral view.

> "Better late than never" is a good old adage: for a modern version of it, let me suggest, "a Short letter is better than none at all."
> Though the day is almost spent, scarcely an hour left of it, I still must wish you A happy New Year, and to you, my dear child, it will be one, if noble and good resolves and an intention to perform faithfully your duties, go with you on your voyage. May you therefore be happy—may you never know a day less joyful, and may you never feel the cares of life press more heavily than they have done this day.

Why was Madge writing so late in the night? Since 1 January was a holiday, "of course Papa remained home: you will see therefore I could not take the time to do it." The family had sat up late—"to the latest possible hour." Madge had then posted up her household expenses for the previous year and penned the first page of the new diary, "and now," she wrote, "I am writing a few lines to my darling child, to assure her, I have not forgotten, but through every phase of the day her dear image has been before me."

Her letter ends with a formulaic closing:

> With love and good wishes to Anna and the girls, in the Happiest of New Years to dear Sr Raphael and Sr Genevieve, I am as you already know your loving Mama.
> With all the love imaginable from each member of the family to "dear May."

A holiday with Papa at home, a family member returned, cheerful news of the beloved daughter, afternoon callers, the year-end task done, the new-year's book begun, expressions of love, happiness, and contentment all around.

Now read the diary page, put aside by the same writer only moments before:

> Come here my diary, and thank God with me, that we are once more alone! What a struggle we have had to night and what a struggle we have had all day to be where the *eyes of intrusion* should not be upon us. Alas! Alas! it is even worse than I feared it would be, when those who have made the house pleasant by their absence, should return. How long, Oh how long is this fearful life to be endured— Something must bring about a change or I cannot live! How quiet, how peaceful, how happy the last three weeks, and how suddenly it has all ended, and what is the cause, can I doubt for one moment the cause? But enough— I had hoped we would have spent a pleasant and happy New Year, but how can happiness exist, where insincerity and deception are the ruling principles in a house? We did not rise as early as usual this morning though we wanted to begin the year right, consequently every thing has gone wrong to day. Mr Preston has remained home all day, *but has not "been at all well."* "Vanity" called on me this afternoon and immediately after Mrs McNeal and her daughter. While I was entertaining them Mr Preston and Theodosia amused themselves *playing cards!* It seemed to have put them both into an ill humour for the rest of the evening.

With Madge's vitriol thus dispelled, did a calmer mood replace the anger and anguish that must have been building throughout the day?

The letter itself and her sense of the function of such a letter suggest that it did not—though without the release of her fury, she could not have composed the letter at all. The letter reveals more of Madge's true state of mind than the intended reader could possibly have discerned, and the writer's need to disguise her true feelings fulfills what she sees as a social contract.

Exactly three years earlier, on 1 January 1864, Madge had written in her diary of her intention to keep an epistolary journal for May, recording events as they happened and sending off the accumulated pages from time to time. "Thus the child will be kept informed of the principle events of our home life, at least such as are pleasant—the unhappy ones I will retain for myself alone. . . ."

The unhappy events that Madge suppressed were not trivial. Preston had been spending more and more nights away from home. During the summer of 1863 he had become embarrassingly infatuated with Theodosia's sister Rose. Quarrels between the Prestons become frequent subjects of Madge's 1864 diary; by 1865 the quarrels have become more and more violent. Madge is struck across the face with an umbrella. She is knocked to the floor, with Theodosia looking on. During the period of mourning for President Lincoln, Madge lies prostrate in her bed at home, suffering with a concussion brought on by severe beatings to her head and face. Yet all such episodes are absent from the letters to May, which still contain messages from "your dear Papa." As Madge lies in pain after her husband's blows, May believes her mother to be suffering from an acute head cold.

In censoring out of her letters this dark side of her life, Madge seems to accept the prevailing child-rearing theory, in which the mother's example was paramount. Injunctions to cheerfulness on the mother's part were a staple of mid-nineteenth-century manuals. "The expression of the countenance, the tone of the voice, the theme of conversation, and every movement of the body . . . have their influence on the imitative little beings," wrote the author of *The Mother's Assistant* (qtd. in Kuhn 25). Mothers were enjoined to reflect a world of Christian benevolence and "gentle kindliness." Contemporary novels by the "female scribblers" reinforced such views by showing women's lives against a backdrop of home and its duties—that "wonderful place," as Susan P. Conrad characterizes the image this fiction projects, "never destitute of culture, sensitivity, and good company" (25). The home, thus romanticized, was seen and defined as women's sphere, and works like Catherine Beecher's best-selling *Treatise on Domestic Economy* codified both its space and its duties. But as Jessie Bernard has pointed out, since this "sphere did not define abuse as part of the female role, the solution to abuse . . . was secrecy." Victims of abuse felt "unique, alone" (90).

As an expression of one such victim trapped in a romanticized social role as serene homemaker and kindly mother, Madge's letter to May is a small masterpiece. Using the special vision the diary page has provided, let us reread the letter.

Madge may somehow have failed as wife and helpmeet, though she seems not to have considered this possibility, as she wrote once in her diary, "I have almost made up my mind to report Mr Preston as insane, and a dangerous person to be living with . . ." (23 Feb. 1865, UM). In her own eyes—confirmed by the approving expressions of the good Sisters at St. Joseph's—she amply fulfilled the good-mother role. How she must have clutched at that reinforcing image at the end of this horrible New Year's Day. And though the emotional storms of the day might have excused her, Madge still accomplished her household tasks. If she could somehow communicate this achievement to those who would most approve and appreciate it, her self-image might be reinforced against the crushing psychological blows of this miserable day. Madge well knew that her letters were always received as treasures, not only by the beloved daughter to whom they were directed but also by May's schoolgirl friends and at least a few of the Sisters of Charity—most particularly the school principal, the intelligent, cultivated Sister Raphael, and the warmly solicitous and courageous Sister Genevieve, whose nursing duties had taken her even to the Gettysburg battlefield.

"If noble and good resolves and an intention to perform faithfully your duties, go with you on your voyage"—these words to May surely characterize how Madge sees her own past behavior. Can it bring for her, as for May, promise of a happy New Year? "May you never know a day less joyful." Madge thinks of St. Joseph's—that serene haven of women, where she had also been a student and where she had first come to know of the Catholic way. "May you never feel the cares of life press more heavily than they have this day," as those cares had pressed down the writer on that joyless day.

Because of the holiday, "of course Papa remained home." His presence may have destroyed the holiday luster for those at home, but Madge's letter mentions only wifely sacrifice to the husband's needs: "therefore I could not take the time" to write earlier in the day. This message of self-denial is conveyed in later letters of 1867. On 14 April, for example, Madge accompanied the other members of the household on a picnic expedition that Preston had proposed. "Now you will readily understand," she wrote to May the next day, "as it was Palm Sunday, I had hoped and intended to have gone to High Mass at the Cathedral; but of this, I said nothing—but with the rest of the family *seemed* cheerfully bent on the country visit" (15 Apr. 1867, UM). The expedition was repeated two weeks later, and again Madge expressed to May, if not her real feelings, then the image of self-sacrificing wife that she wished to project:

My visit with Papa to the Mill yesterday was really one of great self denial but you know it is *part of my religion* to gratify Papa in all his little whims and wishes: very likely if I had told Papa my *reason* for not going to the Mill he would at once have yielded his wish to have me with him but then you know it would have been a great disappointment to him and the disappointment had better fall on me than on Papa. (28 Apr. 1867, UM)

But back to the letter of 1 January. "No one seemed disposed to go to 'Early bed,' but each one sat up to the latest possible hour." The image is of a family circle reunited and delaying the bedtime departures until they could be postponed no longer. Perhaps Madge was consciously evoking a picture she had painted in a letter to May the preceding March: "I have actually been trying to tear myself away from the little circle, ever since tea time, but each time I moved away, something pleasant and agreeable was said to call me back again" (11 Mar. 1866, MHS). There is no suggestion in the New Year's Day letter that Madge was outwaiting the others, desperate for time alone with her diary. Perhaps her totting up of the household accounts that she reports to May but omits from the diary was a strategy of delay and disguise if those intrusive eyes should reappear.

Thede's "most pleasant information" was surely of the dear daughter, since the messenger's mere presence again in the household is a source of such evident pain to the writer. Thinking of that report, Madge can focus again in her mind's eye on that pleasant vale near Emmitsburg, an image of serenity that must be a lifeline to the threatened woman.

Often in the correspondence Madge strikes the note of its crucial importance to herself: "What shall I do, when you and Anna no longer need my affectionate anxieties about you?" (11 Apr. 1867, UM). When Sunday callers interfere with her planned communication with her daughter:

nothing that is offered to me, can in any wise compensate for that deprivation. I feel the want of it, the whole week following and am not satisfied till the next Sunday gives me the chance of making up the disappointment. Independent of the pain to me, I would not unnecessarily deprive you my little darling, of what evidently gives so much pleasure and which I must say are appreciated from beyond their worth (my letters). (3 Mar. 1867, MHS)

Through the letters Madge can hold on to that life-saving, life-giving illusion of herself as the good woman whose virtue and dedication are to sustain and comfort the family.

The diary is also life-giving, but in quite another way. In the 1860 volume, the earliest that has been preserved (probably also the first that Madge Preston wrote, though the diary does not say so) appear long descriptions of the weather, which I read as a strategy for avoiding what she could not bring herself to admit. And among these passages Madge threaded comments on a housemaid, Clara, whose actions appear especially to engage her attention. She records Clara's coming and goings, often in the company of Preston. Madge's preoccupation with Clara contrasts noticeably with the absence of commentary about another young woman within the household—Miss Fanny, May's governess. In November Madge describes a trip to the city to talk with a woman she will not name about "a gentleman" who has conducted himself in "a suspicious manner" but about which Madge asserts she feels "perfectly convinced the conduct is innocent . . ." (14 Nov. 1860, UM). By 1862 she makes a series of oblique references to Clara's death in childbirth and to her surviving infant. Where the name of the man in the case should be recorded there are blanks (17 Mar. 1862, MHS). But a year later, as the fatal anniversary rolls around, the diary suggests that Preston was the man.

Madge apparently suspects that he has a sexual relation with his wife's niece, as he possibly had had three years earlier with Theodosia's sister Rose. At this distance the evidence is ambiguous, but that Preston used the niece to heighten his power over his distraught wife seems clear enough. Why on New Year's Day was Preston "not at all well"? The words are underlined. Was it just a New Year's hangover? Or was Preston acting with the peculiar evasiveness and nervousness that Madge's diaries often record after episodes with one woman or another? "Every thing has gone wrong to day." Apparently Preston was in one of his explosive moods. "Mr Preston and Theodosia amused themselves *playing cards*." The last two words are underlined, perhaps because a card game is an inadequate excuse for their failure to consort with the important callers, perhaps because Madge suspected that the activity and conversation in the other room were of quite another sort than playing cards. Whatever the truth of the matter, one sentence in Madge's diary passage puts a name to her affliction: "how can happiness exist, where insincerity and deception are the ruling principles in a house?" And one cry shows without disguise the depths of her pain: "How long, Oh how long is this fearful life to be endured—Something must bring about a change or I cannot live!"

Diaries are sometimes life-sustaining, when no one is near from whom one can draw support: Martha Martin, pregnant, injured, enduring a winter alone in Alaska; Anne Frank, cut off from girlhood companions, hidden from the Nazi hunters in that attic (see Moffat and Painter); all those westering women on wagon trains, meeting Indians, hunger, disease, fatigue, and the desperate loneliness. Fixing the unspeakable in words can be an act of survival. Charlotte Perkins Gilman understood the power of that urge to write, as her protagonist of *The Yellow Wallpaper* affirms: "I must say what I feel and think in some way—it is such a relief" (10). Implicit as well in these writings is the truth that the words may survive the writer, may report the unbearable circumstances that finally did her in.

On one terrible February day in 1865, Madge Preston must have thought it could be her last. "During this afternoon we have all been as unhappy as well could be owing to Mr Preston's humour which unfortunately for me, fulminated this evening and ended by Mr Preston striking to the floor [sic] almost senseless." Then, in the margin where Madge habitually designates events of special note, she wrote these words: "I record this fact, that it may, if necessary, be known to others in the future" (24 Feb. 1865, UM).

That victims of oppression live divided lives—hold a dual consciousness—is an oft-noted phenomenon (see Pearson and Pope 66, Du Bois 45). They enact a role required by the oppressor, in which they may even consciously collude, yet somehow the real person behind that role must find expression.

Madge Preston's letter belongs in that genre of loving exchanges among nineteenth-century women that Carroll Smith-Rosenberg explored in her now classic article "The Female World of Love and Ritual." Letters of love and concern from woman to woman seemed to flow across the land. How many of these were really lifelines to survival? What hidden horrors at home did they suppress? Madge's letter tied her to a female network of shared values and sustaining love; it encoded a reality she dared not express. The diary named for herself alone the monstrous circumstance with which she lived. Because both compositions have been left to us, we are able at last to break the code.

Note

1. The 1867 diary and the 1 Jan. 1867 letter are in the William P. Preston collection, McKeldin Library, Univ. of Maryland, College Park (UM). The 1864 diary is in the manuscript collection of the Maryland Historical Soc., Baltimore (MHS).

Writer Anxiety versus the Need for Community in the Botts Family Letters

Susan S. Kissel

Because written correspondence was an integral part of American life throughout the nineteenth century, we tend to assume that letter writing came much more easily and naturally to our predecessors of every position, age, and circumstance than to ourselves. I shared this assumption until I began to work with a collection of approximately one hundred letters, most of them written to Emily Botts in Boone County, Kentucky, from 1820 to 1880. The letters, composed by carpenters, farmers, and hardworking mothers and wives, formed the chief means of communication among family members divided by repeated moves west in search of better opportunity, moves that scattered them from Virginia to Kentucky and on to Missouri and Illinois. Their desire to stay in contact with one another was great, but so were their reluctance and their difficulty over the act of writing itself.

In the following pages I examine the evidence of that reluctance, (currently known as "writer anxiety"), some differences between male and female expressions of it, and the motivation of writers in this collection to continue their correspondence despite much negative feeling. Further, after considering the differences between an individual letter's effect on the original recipient and on the contemporary audience, I examine the ways an extensive collection of letters such as this one has impact on the contemporary reader.

The writers of Botts family letters offered many excuses for their delays in corresponding. The press of family and business affairs was an important reason then, as now, for putting off writing. A niece writes to Fannie Botts in 1812, "I have thought so often of writing to you all but for the last few years I seldom find time to write." She finds herself, at last, with the necessary time and space to write a reply when "Warford and his two girls have gone to see his mother and Fannie [who] is staying with me said she would tend to my little ones if I would write."[1] Lucy Maxfield implies that these same, never-ending responsibilities of child care, cooking, spinning yarn, and harvesting in her new Missouri frontier home have kept her from writing back to her Kentucky friend Julie Sherrill: "I know you have been looking for a letter from me for some time. It is such a task, for me to write that I have put it off untill now" (18 Jan. 1857). Men, too, blame work for the tardiness of their responses. Virginia farmer Eli McVeigh tells his Kentucky sister-in-law, Emily Hutchison Botts, "To day being a rainy day, I concluded to Answer yours of Feb y last. I have been waiting with the expectation that Jane [his wife] would, but Hutchison like [she] continues defering it" (12 July 1847). Mental as well as physical immersion in business concerns seems to have prevented William Botts from writing his brother and sister-in-law, Joshua and Emily Botts: "all the apology I can make is I have got out of the spirit of writing owing to the perplexity of mind, and difficultys I have to encounter" (29 May 1834). The work of the world delays the task of writing, as do conditions of the spirit and of the flesh.

Illness is the second most frequent reason for not writing. In 1875 Martha Jane Haydon writes from Missouri to her sisters in Kentucky a vivid description to account for her failure to write:

> I embrace the presant opportunity of trying to write a few lines though the wether is so cold that I can hardly write. Night before last and yesterday was the coldest wether that I ever felt things frose hard on the mantle when there was a fire burning all that time. I should hav written before this but was waiting for my health to improve until I got in bead first with pleurisy and then chills and then pneumony. I was confined to my bed three weeks and hardly able to go about the house yet. (Kissel and Rouse 68–69)

When well themselves, women write of the seemingly endless tasks of nursing family, neighbors, and friends. Lucy Maxfield, for instance, writes to her sister-in-law Hester that her daughter's illness has prevented her from writing, "Emma was so sick. I have been waiting for her to get better. She took a deep cold Christmas" (4 Apr. 1852). The day following Emma's death, Lucy writes that she has had to sit up with a dying neighbor's child as well.

"Sore eyes" especially inhibited writing, among both the young and the old, and failing eyesight would become a persistent problem for many of the latter. As Jane McVeigh explains to her sister,

Many weeks and even months have glided away since we received
your last kind and affectionate letter. I did not think that a week
would have elapsed and your letter remained unanswered this
long ever since August, my eye sight is very bad and by the time I
write a line or two, I can hardly tell one letter from another.   (2
Dec. 1849)

Jane is nearing sixty at the time she writes this and has had problems
with her eyes for many years, yet the young have similar difficulties,
as in this niece's complaint to her aunt: "I have been very near blind
with the sore eyes for a month and they are so weak I can hardly write.
You must excuse my poor letter" (1 Dec. 1872).

Apologies for the months and more often years that have elapsed
before the writers can find the time, occasion, or disposition to reply—
often to a letter from Emily Botts—open most of the letters in this
collection. Even the most fluent and capable of the writers postpone
letter writing, frequently referring to it as a "duty" and a "task." And
the letters usually conclude with yet another kind of apology. Those of
the men seem more qualified and restrained: "excuse this scrall as it is
written in somewhat of a hurry" (Eli McVeigh, 12 July 1847) or "excuse the awkward manner of this letter" (William Botts, 29 May 1834).
The women, however, seem to go beyond the merely polite and ritualistic to sound frequent notes of genuine embarrassment and humility.
Martha Jane Haydon makes a series of apologies when she concludes,
"I must bring my scribling to A close as I fear I have already tired you
with my unconected letter. . . . Excuse mistakes and bad spelling as I
am writing on my lap" (Kissel and Rouse 71).

Allusions to the writer's "poor scribble" and "poor letter" seem
both frequent and sincere in the letters of many of the women and help
to account not only for the reluctance of several to write but in some
cases for their periods of long silence and even their refusal to correspond. In 1848 Harriet Lee admits to her sister, Emily Botts,

It has been a long time since I wrote to you. I hope you will forgive
me. I am so little accustomed to writing it appears allmost like a
task for me to begin. . . . I have seen a great many ups and downs
trials and disappointments since I saw you [32 years]. I have had
ten children and only four are living. . . .   (Kissel and Rouse 27–
28)

Another of Emily's sisters, Jane McVeigh, must be badgered by her
husband into writing postscripts to his letters: "I had hard work to get
Jane to write what she has and as hard to get her to stop. The boy was
waiting for it" (12 July 1847). In 1856 Eli finally admits, when both of

them are in their early sixties and having increasing problems with their vision, "Jane will not write" (Kissel and Rouse 36). The clues to her reluctance appear in Jane's letters many years before this. It is revealing to contrast Eli's beautiful, confident, flowing script throughout the collection with her less practiced, more halting penmanship or his obvious pleasure in phrasing a line—"the salubriety of the climate and the improvable state of the soil" (Kissel and Rouse 32)—with her abbreviated, straightforward prose—"you must excuse me and I will do better in future" (28 July 1849). Nineteenth-century women's lesser opportunities for education and lesser participation in the affairs of the world clearly had the power to undermine women's confidence and enjoyment in writing.

Yet most of the correspondents in this collection manage to keep in contact with one another throughout the course of their lives. Admitting delays for reasons of illness, work, anxiety, or simple procrastination, they continue to write across the distances that separate them. Their motivation seems clear. As Emily Botts writes,

I wish some of you would come to see us. I get your pictures out every few days to look at . . . tell me if you ever hear from Brother Henry. I have not had a letter from him for ten years. We are so scatered that it seems I have no Brothers. I hope we will all meet on that bright shore some day where there will be no more parting. . . . This is a lonely Sunday for me.   (25 June 1882)

Loneliness—the need for family and community—is the motivating force. Eli McVeigh longs to be reunited with his sons and brother who have traveled on to Missouri. In 1865 Lucy Maxfield in Missouri writes home to Kentucky to her mother, Emily Botts, and mourns, "Mother I wish you would come out here and see us. You or one of the girls could come with Sanford this fall. It takes all we can make to pay tax so I never expect to be able to come to see you soon" (Kissel and Rouse 66). In 1848, after more than three decades apart, Harriet Lee writes from Virginia to her sister in Kentucky, "Emily I wishet you could summons up resolution enougf to visit your old native land once more. I suppose your children are all grown and out of the way and one of your sons could come with you. . . . Write to me as soon as you get this and dont neglect it as I have done . . . (Kissel and Rouse 29–30). Delay in writing clearly does not signify that these women lack affection for one another. As Martha Jane Botts tells her aunt, "I suppose you think we have forgotten you as we have not answered your letter, though it is not so, you are fresh in my memory all the time and I wish that I could see you to night though it is impossible, for now, to see you. I will try to give you some of the news of the day" (12 Nov. 1851). Finally, when her brother is planning to migrate to California, a woman named Zannie writes to her friend Jane McVeigh: "I would sooner follow a brother of mine to his grave than to part with them to go to California. . . . It is hard for us to be so far separated in this world" (13 May 1850). New friends, neighbors, and relatives cannot replace those earliest, deepest, most fundamental relationships of childhood and immediate family. Writing remained for all the correspondents their one connection. Eli McVeigh was never able to sell his farm in Virginia to move to Missouri. Emily Botts never returned to the Virginia home she had left in a covered wagon thirty-two years earlier. And Lucy Maxfield died, as did two of her daughters before her, expressing last wishes to see Emily Botts (her mother and their grandmother) and other relatives of their Kentucky homeland again. The movement west had separated this family forever.

Nowhere is it quite so clear as in such collections of letters that most often those who write—whether novels, essays, autobiographies, or letters—do so in order to receive a response. Thus the closing plea, "write as soon as you get this for we are very anxious to hear from you," is more than a mere closing ritual. Its refrain seems the central theme of this collection. The correspondents of the Botts family letters freely admit that they write in order to be written to. Joshua Botts in Illinois writes his cousin John Botts of Kentucky that he will "Scribble something to stir you up" to put an end, if he can, to his cousin's "long silence" (16 Apr. 1843). Similarly, Jane McVeigh, before she altogether stopped writing her short notes to her sister Emily Botts, apologized for her long delays, yet begged, "write soon as you get this I am anscious to hear from you" (2 Dec. 1840). When no reply was immediately forthcoming from her most faithful letter-writing sister, she would write another quick note:

> It has been a long time since any of us heard from you we have been anxiously looking for a letter from you for some time but have not received any. I hope it will be very soon when we shall hear from you as this is the only mode we have of communicating our thoughts to each other and we ought to be more punctual my eye sight is very bad or I would write more frequently I hope you will not wait for me, but write every opportunity, as it is one of my greatest pleasures to hear from you and your family. (2 Feb. 1849)

Short notes such as this, as well as a majority of the longer letters, are devoted in large part to motivating their recipients to respond immediately. And the responses are not to be like the letters received: writers ask for quick replies filled with news of their far-away families and friends as well as of local happenings, and they especially request "*great long answer*[s]," as Lucy Maxfield emphasizes in a letter to her sister-in-law Hester (4 Apr. 1852).

The letters the writers received, however, were, as might be expected, much like the ones that they themselves had written. The replies comprised apologies for the little news that could be offered and for the long lapse in time that had occurred, matters of family health, perfunctory reports of local church and neighborhood affairs, and, most frequently, reports on the weather and the current market value of crops. Yet these seemingly repetitive, uninspired, and ritualistic letters not only were eagerly awaited and longed for by their recipients but continue today to evoke intense feeling in readers. I would like to explore further the source of the letters' effect on readers both past and present.

It might prove helpful here to use Louise Rosenblatt's distinction from *The Reader, the Text, the Poem* between "efferent" and "aesthetic" readings of a work. Readers of the Botts family letters could approach the letters in order to gain information: the "news of the day" for the original recipient and the "news of the American past" for those today who look at the letters for information about social customs, economic conditions, sex-role stereotyping, historic events, psychological states, or (my concern throughout the article until this point) writer anxiety in nineteenth-century correspondents' remarks about themselves. These readings are all what Rosenblatt calls "efferent"—looking at writing as communication concerned with transmitting and storing information.

The letters may also be read, then and now, in an "aesthetic" way—in terms of the feelings that the words, style, structure, and subjects of the letters evoke. Certainly, the tear stains and evidence of continual creasing and recreasing suggest that many letters in this collection were read over and over again in just this way—for the emotions that particular lines and passages could arouse and, perhaps, purge. More complex and difficult to understand is the aesthetic response the letters arouse in the contemporary reader.

So many elements of the collection would seem to make such a response impossible for the modern reader. First of all, the sheer number of writers should only confuse and frustrate the reader who can glimpse bits and pieces but seldom entire lives. Further, the repetitiveness of the letters in both subject matter and form from one writer to the next should dismay and discourage contemporary readers who could rightly ask for more variety of subject and style to engage their interest. Further, in its present unedited form, the collection lacks structure, cohesion, conciseness, and even grammatical correctness.

Nonetheless, the Botts family letters tell a surprisingly moving story and create a powerful effect on the present-day reader, even without the aid of a single author or a shaping editor. Robert Manson Myers in his preface to *The Children of Pride: A True Story of Georgia and the Civil War* sheds light on how such collections engage the interest and emotions of contemporary readers. First, he alludes to the "immediacy" of letters—an immediacy that closely touches and involves the present-day reader:

> It is firsthand, not retrospective. It is the response to an event dashed off while it is happening, the sensation of an experience captured the moment it is felt. . . . Through such incidental glances we come to feel that we are present as events transpire, participating in the action and sharing the emotions of the characters. . . . Such immediacy is scarcely possible in an account of action already completed. With the elapse of time passions cool, animosities soften, perspectives blur: a memoir written months or years after the event is apt to be stale and distorted. (xiii–xiv)

Family letters such as these assume the reader's closeness in time and circumstances; they assume, as well, that the reader will be interested and concerned in the lives and events reported. To continue reading the collection, a contemporary reader must take this close, personal stance and become immersed in the moment the writer records. Such a close, active role decreases the modern reader's sense of emotional distance.

Further, Myers suggests that a collection of letters actively involves the contemporary reader in yet another way, since its

> [story] holds together, as it were, by continued splicing. At each new letter we must pause and adjust our stance: Who is speaking? To whom? Where? When? . . . The revelation is kaleidoscopic: character comes out in flashes, and plot develops not so much in conventionally ordered scenes as in glimpses. Gradually, we form a synthesis, and ultimately all the flashes and glimpses merge into one perfected vision. (xvi)

The variety of points of view in family letters engage the reader actively in putting together the puzzle that forms the collection's whole. As the voices become more familiar and individualized for the reader, they begin to form "a unit and create the synthesis" to which Myers refers. It does not finally matter that the pieces of the puzzle remain jagged and formless, that we are given only glimpses of individual lives, as the voices come together and take on the larger shape of the puzzle. The key word is "gradual." A collection's emotional power, like that of a piece of fiction or a drama, builds over time, slowly, as the reader becomes more and more immersed in the world that has been created.

At the same time, the contemporary reader brings to such a letter collection yet another perspective—that of the present day, its knowledge and values. The reader knows what Martha Jane Haydon guesses: the connection between "thick" water and neighborhood deaths. The reader is aware that the Civil War will alter the course of life in Virginia as Eli McVeigh outlines his ill-timed plans to sell his land there and move on to Missouri. There are both irony and pathos, as well, in Eli McVeigh's pride over his new son-in-law's family slaves on the eve of war and in the elaborate, sentimental deathbed scenes drawn out in great detail in these letters—scenes similar to those we have seen mocked in the fiction of Mark Twain. The present-day perspective—whether literary, historical, or scientific—adds another, deeper dimension to the puzzle and its emotional power for today's reader.

Further, the contemporary reader of the Botts family collection has access to even more letters and more information from the past than did any one of the letters' original recipients. Thus, although many of the Botts family letters were written to and saved by Emily Botts in Boone County, Kentucky, the collection contains many others that she never saw. There are, for instance, a number written after her death, including one that recounts the division of her quilts, clothes, and possessions among several of her daughters. The news about Emily Bott's death, too, allows the contemporary reader to balance the views of the letters with a larger world vision of both the past and the present. The contemporary reader's larger perspective not only adds intricacy and complexity to the art of fitting the collection's pieces together into a meaningful whole but also engages the reader more fully by demanding greater emotional and intellectual responsiveness.

Read in all these ways, the multiple perspectives of the Botts family letters come together to create a dramatically powerful and naturally structured whole. One voice adds to another; one life ends and another joins in. We read again and again of the daily wants and needs, of the same hardships and frustrations, as we move from one letter to another. The very repetition—itself a seeming weakness—becomes a unifying factor, an emotional refrain that charges the collection. Especially, we come to sense the importance of the words that speak of the writers' need for community, their longing for family and friends, for the value of old relations during the building of new ones. Despite the evidence of writer anxiety throughout the collection and despite the writers' lack of sophisticated rhetorical and stylistic techniques, the letters speak powerfully of the human experience in the lives of ordinary men and women in this country's past and of the need to share that experience within a community of family and friends. The paradox remains that the ritualistic quality of these letters—their evidence of writer anxiety, their reliance on formulaic openings and closings, their stress on completion of task over content, and their verbal understatement and simplicity—can nevertheless form so unified and so moving a whole.

Note

1. Nannie Warford, unpublished letter, 1 Dec 1872, Botts family letters, Cincinnati, OH. All quotations from the Botts letters are from the private collection of Shirley Beigel. Some have been reprinted in *The Story of the Pewter Basin and Other Occasional Writings*, ed. Susan Kissel and Margery Rouse.

The Pariah and the Author

An Analysis of *The Maimie Papers*

Rose Kamel

From about 1910 until 1922 "Maimie Pinzer," once a Philadelphia prostitute, maintained an intense epistolary relation with Fanny Quincy Howe, one of that special breed of intellectual, reformist Boston Brahmins whose name epitomized genteel America (see H. Howe). *The Maimie Papers*, scrupulously edited by Ruth Rosen and Sue Davidson, is a chronological ordering of this relation, transforming it into narrative within the context of social history. Although Maimie Pinzer did not intend to publish these letters, corresponding with a woman of letters proved cathartic. It also afforded the narrator a chance to mirror herself to another who was distanced enough geographically and socially not to intrude on her autonomy.

The narrative reveals a journey from isolation to selfhood and literary authority. Maimie's letters begin when she is a pariah, a Jewish prostitute friendless except for Mr. Welsh, a benevolent gentile philanthropist. They end with her sense of herself as not only a lovable and loving person but a writer capable of constructing a narrative. What accomplished this change? It happened largely because of the correspondence Maimie maintained with Fanny Quincy Howe, a correspondence that nurtured Maimie in a loving, maternal way. But Maimie had to place psychic distance between herself and Howe before she could reach emotional and literary maturity. This paper traces the stages of Maimie's maturation by describing first her isolation, then her reaching out to Howe instead of becoming an acolyte of Welsh, and finally her moving from a filial to a maternal perspective and achieving selfhood in both an emotional and a literary sense. Several extended narratives sent as letters to Howe illustrate these stages as well as demonstrate Maimie's emerging literary skills.

When the letters begin in 1910, Maimie is twenty-five; she has lived through a long period of alienation. Rejected by a loveless mother and shunned by parvenu relatives and neighbors, she could scarcely fare better dealing with WASPs who feared the mass migration of East European Jews to American cities.[1] Even the best-intentioned were becoming dismayed at the proliferation of foreign tongues and the wretchedness of slum life in immigrant neighborhoods.[2] Worse, the prosperous German Jews, earlier arrivals already assimilated into American society, also looked down on their East European counter-parts.[3] Moreover, the number of immigrant prostitutes was hardly conducive to assuaging native-born distaste. And since prostitution in the old country was rare, immigrant Jews reacted harshly against daughters lured from respectability or sold into white slavery. Com-munities ostracizing their "Maimies" believed that prostitutes rent the fabric of the Jewish household:

> Prostitutes did not occupy isolated sections of the ghetto, but the same streets where families lived and children played. Parents feared for their daughters, and were known to sit *shiva* [a period of ritual mourning] for those who became prostitutes. (Baum 115)

Indeed, from about 1890 through the era of *The Maimie Papers*, the white-slavery issue so worried the Jewish community sensitive to anti-Semitism that by 1906 the National Council of Jewish Women, sup-ported by exposés in *McClure's* and the *Jewish Daily Forward*, took over the management of a Home for Wayward Girls in Staten Island (107–75).

Toward the Philadelphia Jewish community that has both nur-tured and rejected her, she feels understandably ambivalent. At times she succumbs to ethnic deprecation, a form of self-contempt, turning up her nose at the smells of onions, garlic, and cabbage, stereotyping arranged Jewish marriages as motivated merely by money, attribut-ing the shortening of Jewish names to ignorance and communality to Orthodox parochialism, and regarding Jews and "low women" as equally her inferiors. The following quotations provide an example of the last point. "I don't think I ever met, to talk to the second time a woman who was publically known to live other than she should. I shun such people. Even girls who did no worse than I, couldn't claim ac-quaintance with me" (77). Compare the tone of this passage with that of her last letter, which sounds dishearteningly anti-Semitic. From Chicago, where she and Ira Benjamin have taken up temporary resi-dence, she writes,

> Bennie had selected this place before I came. It is desirable, inas-much as it is new and spotlessly clean, but it is patronized almost

entirely by big, fat, Jewish ladies and their thin, nervous husbands. However, I use the downstairs attractions very sparingly, so avoid contact. (416)

These outbursts, however, occur mainly during her sojourn in Philadelphia, the source of her isolation: "From my knowledge of Jewesses—or Hebrews of both sexes—they are very unforgiving, in fact much more so than the most conventional Gentile" (114). Despite this judgment, she cannot help but identify with the victims of patriarchal oppression, Jewish and gentile: Rachel, her sister, impoverished, ill, confined to the state asylum in Norristown; Caroline, her Protestant sister-in-law, subjected to the tyranny of Maimie's brother James; victimized neighbors; old people; even animals. Nor can she separate herself from the oppressive heritage fundamentally linked to the language of parents she still needs. She carefully describes and explains to Howe all the Jewish holidays—Rosh Hashanah, Yom Kippur, Shabuoth, Purim, Passover—as well as the *circus maximus* ambience of Jewish weddings and funerals, even the superiority of kosher meat (26, 39, 100, 121–26, 132). Especially significant is a description of a Yiddish play to which she "treats" her mother:

At any rate, I know they [Yiddish melodramas] play on the emotions much more than do English dramatists, and I couldn't stand to see a play oftener than once or twice a year of the sort we saw. *It was about a Jewish girl who had been betrayed and who was not forgiven by her parents until her death. It affected Mother very much, although I shook it off immediately we left the theater.* We went to a neighboring cafe, and Mother and I had some Jewish wine that sells for 35 cents a bottle and Jewish cake. We met some old friends of my father, and Mother had a really good time reminiscing. I stayed with Mother that night. (126, my italics)

Unfortunately, this kind of closeness to her mother is unusual. After "Morris Pinzer's" mysterious murder when Maimie was a child, which left his wife and orphans unprepared for financial vicissitude, Maimie was exposed not only to her mother's hostility but to the continued sexual abuse of an uncle, the end of schooling, prison, and ultimately the vagaries of a prostitute's existence. Because of the magnitude of the prostitution problem, Jewish and gentile benevolent societies were organized to reclaim "fallen women," even those who, like Maimie, deliberately chose to sell their bodies to survive. And survive Maimie did, until after thirty eye operations she permanently lost the infected one and through the ministrations of an inept doctor became addicted to morphine. At this desperate turn in her life Welsh took charge and introduced his client by letter to Fanny Howe. About him and another Christian caseworker, "Miss Outerbridge," Maimie had few illusions:

[Miss Outerbridge] has never had any of the real experiences of life and lives in the clouds. She has beautiful ideals and lives the life of characters in Sunday School storybooks. (22)

. . . since knowing [Welsh] and what a pure person he is, when I read his experience and advice, I don't feel as though they could mean anything to me, who is so totally different from him. He is so unselfish and pure. Reading his letters is reading books gotten up for Sunday School purposes, with the characters just such good Boys and Girls as no one ever knew. While I love him, *I can't imagine being like him.* He is so very very kind and sympathetic but so was Christ, and while everyone loves Him, they all don't do as He would have them do. (41, my italics)

Although Welsh serves as a surrogate for Maimie's dead father, whom she reveres, she resents his prescriptive efforts to elevate her status; arguments between them ensue. After Welsh insists that she stay married to Albert, a man she despises, Maimie sadly comments:

. . . I felt as anyone would . . . who was going to see their very own father. . . . When he returned from Lake Sunapee last fall, he kissed me and remarked about how I looked and was very intimate. . . . (66)

At the same time she knows that she cannot role-play indefinitely:

Don't I know, had I kept up a lively correspondence with Mr. Welsh, going to church every Sunday and detailing all the events, and reading a lot of stuff that bores me and pretending to be interested—Mr. W's return would have been as it was when he left and everything would have been lovely? But since I elected to be honest in all my dealings with him, I came out the loser in the end. (73)

Welsh sees perversity in Maimie's refusal to stay married to an inept husband for conventional reasons:

Why should I persist in living with him? When I married . . . I knew exactly what for—it was a sort of anchor. I was living more or less uncleanly; I had lost my eye, and weighed ninety-six pounds, which at that time I seemed to think was the end of all my attractiveness; I was mentally very low, and I reasoned it all out as one would a business proposition. I saw that he was not blessed with gray matter and that he was in awe of me, and I intended to always keep him that way. (51)

When she learns that Albert has stupidly spent some of her money without her knowledge, no amount of pleading from Welsh, his secretary Mr. Suiffen, or Miss Outerbridge can convince her to maintain the facade. When a former suitor, Ira Benjamin, now separated from his wife, seeks Maimie out to resume their relation, she is willing enough to live with him from time to time but will not consider a remarriage, despite Welsh's urging:

> . . . the worse lot of cant I ever heard. That is my honest opinion, and why bother about it? I could go deep into that subject to show why I have arrived at such an unusual conclusion; but I will simply say: because of the various marriage contracts I know intimately about—my own, my sister's, mother's and a host of others. (81)

Neither will she follow Welsh's directive that she replace her eye patch with a glass eye, because it would not have the accoutrements of "eyelids, or lashes, or anything that looks like anything that generally holds an eye in place" (65). Indeed, that eye patch, like the scarlet letter embroidered on Hester Prynne's dress, assumes metaphoric resonance, symbolizing both Maimie's separation from "respectable" women and a means of defying the middle-class code of respectability.

Maimie's correspondence with Howe is far more satisfying than her relation with Welsh: with Howe she can respond in a way less likely to violate her shaky sense of selfhood; she can express her anger directly rather than obliquely. For instance, furious about not being hired for sales positions because of the eye patch, she maintains that prostitution is less degrading than working for starvation wages: "I just cannot be moral enough to see where drudgery is better than a life of lazy vice" (4). In Howe, Maimie has found an ideal reader responsive to the validity of another's experience:

> I often wondered how an intelligent person of sound mind could keep a diary to record every small event, and thought. It seemed such a ridiculous thing, almost asinine. I think I have hit on the reason they do it. . . . It must be that, while they are the only ones that see them, they are unconsciously addressing another person, *a second self,* who is interested in the minutest details concerning the writer's life. . . . (9, my italics)

Written early in *The Maimie Papers,* this excerpt signals the narrator's consciousness that one's life story has a validity, an integrity, that goes beyond the randomness of daily experience.

Scholars have known for some time that women tend to write in fragmented forms (diaries, journals, letters) as structural counterparts of their disjointed lives. In a patriarchal society where men's life histories and opinions have public sanction, the male autobiographer does not question his right to write, to articulate fully, or even to vindicate himself for repudiating official assumptions; but a woman's private relational bond to others makes it rare for a woman autobiographer to articulate a sense of genuine selfhood. Thus, women sequester from public scrutiny the fragments that men use as raw materials for canonical life histories, preferring to invent second audience-selves with which they can share the experiences of their sex. In Mary C. Mason's words, "this grounding of identity to the chosen other, seems . . . to enable women to write openly about themselves" (Olney 210; see also Jelinek 1–20).

Fortunately for Maimie, she did not have to invent Howe: "For I have said all along to myself that I was writing you—my other self— just as I would write were I keeping a faithful diary" (32). Unjudgmental despite the gulf separating their disparate lives, sensitive to suffering, aware of the chaos lurking beneath the apparent placidity of everyday existence, Howe was an ideal audience.[4] Maimie also recognized that as an author who had published a novel (*The Opal*), Howe could play muse to her protégée's autobiographical apprenticeship.[5] Furthermore, Howe becomes the compassionate mother figure who can revive the narrator's flagging spirits and mitigate Maimie's chronic sense of maternal deprivation:

> Cousin Iris took a turn for the worse . . . she died in my arms at 4:25 p.m. . . . She had all her faculties to the end, and she begged me to forgive her some things she had said to me . . . that were not true. . . . I feel it all so keenly. . . . You are so good to me. (24)

> You see when I write you, I write everything, and mostly the things that trouble me, and that is because I love you and don't stop to think whether it would be better to write this or that, but just keep on writing what is on my mind—things that I have always had to keep to myself, for I never trusted any other woman—and then even if I did tell them, I wouldn't feel it has helped matters any . . . and while your letters to me are generally about myself, I felt that you told me the "real things" also. (49)

Howe's reassuring responses must have intimated the possibility of an epistolary self-analysis:

> For I found that which is the reason people keep diaries. It records these thoughts, and once they are carefully taken apart and written, you can follow the lines of your thoughts more clearly; and then it is a clearinghouse, and from one writing to the next, one's brain is . . . ready to follow the line of thought or perhaps start a new line. . . . (12)

In such a climate of acceptance, Maimie can order tumultuous daily life and use language as a vehicle for change. Two lengthy, pivotal episodes suggest that, having "internalized" Howe, Maimie moves from a filial to a maternal perspective, and that having absorbed Howe's literary values, Maimie can improve her writing skills until, like the Colonel's Lady and Judy O'Grady, Howe and she are literary sisters under the skin.

The "Brownie Episode" illustrates the first point. Maimie alludes so often to Miss Poke, her dog, and to Potsy, James and Caroline's little girl, that we can assume her penchant for mothering helpless creatures. Unlike Potsy, though, Miss Poke cannot be declared off limits to a former prostitute and follows her mistress devotedly. The episode begins innocuously in an early letter written as a response to the pictures Howe has sent of her children:

> I was glad to get your kiddies' pictures. How very much Helen looks like you. . . . They seem so affectionate toward each other. . . . you have such sweet babies and could spend your time entirely with them. I believe I wouldn't be so kind to you if I was happy and the positions were reversed. . . . (68)

She then mentions Miss Poke: "You and she are the only two in my life who seemed to thoroughly understand me. She is as human as anyone, only she can't speak with her mouth" (69).

Two months pass before Howe alludes to a new cocker spaniel, Brownie, inspiring Maimie to recall a time when wandering brought her to Memphis, Tennessee. There, relieved to have left Albert behind, she and Miss Poke found shelter at Mrs. Frey's guest house where two other dogs, Buster and an appealing spaniel, Brownie, clamored for Maimie's attention:

> I moved in; and long before we womenfolk got so we exchanged confidences, the three dogs were fast friends, romping all the time

together. . . . After tea the ladies would bring their chairs out on the gallery [porch]; and the moment Poke and I appeared the two dogs would be up and ready. (116)

A graphic description follows of the run-down neighborhood with its shabby houses inhabited by kindly blacks who fed Poke and Brownie, always neglected by Frey. At the local restaurant the blacks would provide gunnysacks for them to tug at, attracting many stray dogs. Nearby was another boarding house run by a "maiden lady" "who did not love anyone—dog or human. Instinctively, our dogs did not go near her grounds." One day this woman appeared warning Maimie and Frey that she was setting out "buttons" of poisoned meat, ostensibly meant for the strays. Maimie decided to move eight blocks away to ensure Poke's safety, but Brownie would materialize every afternoon, crying and scratching on the door. Since the landlord would not allow him in, she would have to feed Brownie and walk him home, a practice that soon became untenable. In desperation one evening, she ignored Brownie's yelps, and Frey phoned the next day to declare that his poisoned body had been found stiff and cold near their kitchen door:

and to this day have never forgiven myself that I did not feed him, before sending him home. That is all. We buried him in Jones' Restaurant yard, which was very large. And Mrs. Frey did a lot of crying, and of course placed the blame on me. . . . And to this day, at the mention of Brownie's name, Poke will run around in a circle, and bark, and seem to remember that he was her playmate. (120)

Childless, Maimie has received snapshots of "her other self's" children, a reminder that but for Miss Poke she has lived a rootless existence without the compensatory freedom from middle-class restraints that real vagabonds enjoy. Later she learns that "Brownie" lives on in the shelter of the Howe household, spared the ignominy of an unloved stray. In re-creating the dead dog, then, Maimie does more than yield to a momentary overflow of pathos. She is telling Howe that but for a reversal of fortune, hers would be a secure existence without the need to scratch at a door in order to be allowed in. This episode shows a certain emotional assurance or confidence that she hasn't exhibited before. Furthermore, this extended narrative demonstrates both to Howe and to herself that she can manipulate fictive strategies—foreshadowing, effective description, economy in the depiction of characters, climax, a stark denouement. Maimie is growing up and becoming less a daughter to Howe than a mother herself.

A second lengthy, pivotal episode suggests that Maimie can become Howe's literary sister by developing her writing skills. Early in

The Maimie Papers she confides, "I wish I could write you about the story that goes in my mind with each of your pictures. That is, my relation to you in each of them" (24), a statement disclaimed in the same sentence as something too "silly" to pursue. Basically, the enormous disparity in both correspondents' lives must have made open competition between them untenable. Much more plausible, then, for Maimie was the strategy of projecting competitiveness on to another woman writer—Jewish, parvenu, and eminently successful to boot. Such was Mary Antin, celebrated author of *The Promised Land.* Maimie's brilliant depiction of their sole meeting reveals more, perhaps, than she knows.

Familiar with Antin's immigrant experience, reprinted in the *Atlantic Monthly,* which she received every month from Howe, Maimie resists Howe's suggestion that she meet the celebrity.

> Instinctively, I feel like sending her about her business. Doesn't that prove what a sweet disposition mine is? I must explain that I wouldn't do such a thing, and only admit it to you so you will know me as I am and not think I am as amenable as I should be. That she is of my own race and from humble origin should make me feel she is really the sort I ought to like—but I'm afraid that she is not like "Mrs. Howe." . . . You know her only from her writings; and while one's writings are generally supposed to reflect oneself . . . some are very clever with the pen and would trick one . . . suppose you do not tell her *all* about me—leaving out the ugly part until you feel sure she would not condemn me.   (114)

Howe persists, but Maimie continues to procrastinate, pleading for more time to read Antin and to acquire the proper dress for a formal visit. Finally, accompanied by Ira Benjamin, whose mother Antin knows, Maimie finally arrives at the writer's front door. In White Plains, New York, Mrs. Grabau (Mary Antin) lives amid clutter, oblivious to good taste. Maimie's description is virtually Dickensian:

> Choked up with furniture [the parlour] seemed to represent the various changes in Mrs. Grabau's fortune. . . . I'm sure some of it was bought when she thought plush furniture was the "fashionable" thing. Then came the intensely simple mission—that suggests the installment house—and if you'll excuse this, I will say that I'd have to be built square in the seat to enjoy the hour spent on the chair I selected to sit my visit out in.   (160)

Frowsy and eccentric, Antin seems oblivious to civility, offering no refreshments to her guests, running about to attend to household business despite the presence of servants.

Now her face—as I said it might have been a very youthful person's except for the many lines in it, and the extreme hardness of the eyes, that seemed entirely unsympathetic . . . shifty, thru not being entirely sincere. Her hair is very much curled; in fact, it has a kink like the Negro head, and as is sometimes seen among Jewish children of the lowest order. . . . (160)

An apparently innocuous attempt to flatter Howe follows, as Maimie unfavorably compares Antin's hair with Howe's golden curls; once again Maimie's insecurity engenders ethnic snobbishness. The attention to detail is masterful:

Her smile seemed to break her face all up, and did not seem real— and one felt instinctively that the smile would not just fade away naturally, but that as soon as she released the string, her features would snap back to the same sharp look we saw at the door. And sure enough, it did. (161–62)

Needless to say, theirs was not a meeting of hearts and minds. Maimie's attempt to draw out Antin's reminiscences by discussing her own childhood in a bewildering Christian America fell on deaf ears. Antin's impatience with the plebeians inhabiting White Plains rankled:

As in every place—where there must be shops and business houses—an element of working people like myself creep in; and then persons like Mary Antin become annoyed. I wonder whether the town she was reared in as a child in Russia was exclusive enough to suit her? (163)

Only when Maimie exaggerated the number of her personal visits with Howe did Antin show a fleeting interest. Otherwise, all conversational gambits were rebuffed. Expecially irritating was Antin's insistence that her daughter not speak Yiddish (the language so passionately evoked in Antin's *The Promised Land*) to the servants. Small wonder that the guests refused the hostess's barely civil dinner invitation and made a hasty exit:

And I must say I never saw such conceit, especially in a person of her intelligence. She is cocked up about Mary Antin to such a degree that she is sickening. . . . According to [Ira] I am just as capable as she—only that because I was pretty, I was not permitted to think and work in solitude. . . . I say he is wrong. She is really a genius—for a genius anyone must be to write as she does, and yet be a person quite different from anything her writings would indicate. (167)

Howe probably got the message: that for them to have a closer relation might well have exposed Howe's feet of clay. The self-consciously literary thrust of this extended narrative suggests that Maimie prefers geographical distance the better to explore the remnants of her past. "To think and work in solitude" entails enough distance for the author to use herself rather than Howe as a sounding board.

To that end, Maimie takes a bookkeeping job in Montreal. She must prove to herself, her family, Welsh, and Howe that she can make her own way in the world without reverting to her old life. She must remove herself from Philadelphia, which "stands for the old life," so that she can probe into her past. In short, she wants to be independent from Howe, her family, and her old habits. In Montreal, together with Jean Holland, an educated but eccentric translator, she tries and fails to run a multigraph business. The failure lies not only in Holland's financial ineptitude but in sexual discrimination. "It seems all the forces of the business world in Montreal are against a woman developing a real business" (219).

Despite the setback, her letters to Howe show increasing bravura, the result not of fleeing isolation in order to disguise the past but of a willingness to make choices and incur risk. Always curious about other places and human foibles, her wanderlust wars with a contrary need to put forth new roots:

> I wish I were born a man. I know what I'd do this morning. I'd button up my coat and jump on the tail end of a train and steal a ride to wherever it was going—and when I'd get there, I'd stop to consider "What's next." As it is, in the first place I couldn't steal the ride: and even if I went the regular way, how could I manage without "things"—which would mean a trunk; and then Miss Poke—Oh, I guess I couldn't think of such things! (50)

In spite of her adventuresome spirit Maimie does take root in Montreal. First, though, she must recover rather than bury the past. A third extended narrative illustrates her growing emotional and literary maturity. In response to Oscar Wilde's "Ballad of Reading Gaol," Maimie recalls the most harrowing experience of her childhood. The resulting narrative can match Moll Flander's account of spiritual deprivation suffered at Newgate:

> I had left school directly after my father's death, and was put to work in the house, doing the sort of work I despised, because I had

never been taught how, and, too, because I loved school and books and things that school meant. I was thirteen in July, and in September—my second term at the Phila. high school—I was not permitted to go back. Prior to my father's death, we had a general servant in the house, and a laundress and scrubwoman who came, each two days a week. After his death, I was given it all to do but the laundress's work—and I did it poorly, and always only after receiving severe whippings.   (192)

"Julia Pinzer" did not even permit Maimie to read at home and once threw an overdue library book into the fire, preventing the child from using the library and forcing her to tell the librarian why she couldn't.

Soon afterward Maimie found work in a department store where girls were often solicited by pimps. Because she was earning five dollars a week, she could come home after dinner with few questions asked. Then she spent three days at a young man's room and on her return was arrested:

Of course I was terribly frightened—but imagine my horror when I was placed in a cell! It was a horribly filthy, vile-smelling hole. I cried and begged they should send for my mother—and though they did, after awhile, she refused to come. It was night time, and there was no light; and I could hear the rats, which I feared more than death. I was terrified and pleaded to be taken out of there. It was only after I permitted one of the men, who seemed to be in charge at the time, to take all sorts of liberties with me, that I was permitted to come out of the cell; and I sat up for the rest of the night where he, too, sat all night. The man was fifty, or even older.

In the morning, there was a hearing. My mother was present; and my uncle was with her—and he was acting with her to persuade the "Commonwealth" that I should be sent to some house of refuge as being incorrigible. This uncle is the same one who did me the first wrong, when I was a tiny girl, and any number of times since then. It seemed that in order to prove me immoral, so that I should become a public charge (without excuse to my mother), it would have to be proven that I had committed a crime, and the man produced.   (193)

After the terrified child gave the name and address of the youth she stayed with she was again led away,

pleading to my mother, in shrieks, to take me home. It was morning and not as bad as at night; but as I had nothing to read, and the terrible fear of spending another night there seemed imminent, the hours seemed years. There was only a bench and an exposed toilet in the cell, and it was, as I thought, terrible. At noon, there were footsteps and the jangling of keys, and the cell was opened. I thought for sure my mother had relented and was so grateful. I put on my hat and coat, and came out to the large room—and though I did not see anyone I knew, I was laboring under the delusion that I was being taken home. I saw some men in line, and I was told to get behind the last one. Still, I had no suspicion of what was coming. The line moved, as did I. And oh! what a lot they were . . . the dregs and scum of the earth. (194)

Dragged to the Black Maria, taunted by men who told her she would be sent away for years until she came of age, "the ride was probably the worst of the whole harrowing experience" (194). At Moyamensing, "this same prison that my father had given a library of two hundred books printed in the Yiddish language," Maimie "was overcome with the thought of what my father would think of my being there" (195). Her clothes were taken away, and a kindly matron brought her a Bible and promised her "a real book" the following day, comforting the prisoner until she was able to fall asleep.

I awakened in the night, and then it was that I became panic stricken. I beat on the bars of the cell and cried until someone came. This time, it was a woman and a man. The woman was of the grim-visaged sort, entirely without compassion, and threatened me with all sorts of dire things unless I was quiet. I cannot remember how I passed the remainder of the night, though I do know I did not get back into bed. (196)

The next morning the kind matron returned bringing stale chocolates and "a book which I think was *Robinson Crusoe* or *Pilgrim's Progress*"; shortly thereafter she received one of Shakespeare's plays: "I found when reading, it did not seem so terrible to be there" (196).

The reader cannot help but notice that throughout this narrative the hunger for books takes precedence over all needs but that of maternal sustenance. If anything, the two are intertwined. Couched almost in the language of allegory—the forsaken pilgrim, the dark night of the soul—the texture of this episode expresses not only a dichotomy between maternal bonding and prison bondage but signals a way to survive through reading and writing. In prison, Maimie learns of the enormous gulf between her father's bookish centrality and the vengeful anti-intellectualism of her mother. Degraded by the perverse sadism of maternal rejection, she clings to a matron like a lifeline, because that woman provides a way to transform insupportable reality:

"I recall that I was ashamed of the fact that I didn't seem to mind it so much, and that I rather enjoyed the privilege of reading undisturbed" (196).

Undoubtedly believing that she had not been punished enough, Mrs. Pinzer had Maimie transferred to a reform school for wayward girls:

> Though I was the youngest . . . then by four years, still I taught the ones who had little or no schooling, during our school hours. I received absolutely no school training there whatever—except what I derived from teaching girls of seventeen and eighteen their alphabet and the simple sums.
>
> I did not think to tell you this story so thoroughly; but I felt when I began, I just wanted you to know; then, as I wrote it, it seemed to be as though I was writing that particularly ugly part of my life *as though it were a narrative*. Somehow I feel now . . . perhaps I wrote you this before. (196–97, my italics)

Positioned about halfway through the text, this passage demonstrates that for Maimie Howe has become the book-supplying matron, with one significant change. The supplicant is not only grateful and imitative but selective. In accordance with the writerly way she perceives Howe, she crafts the prison episode to establish narrative as well as emotional distance. Consequently, she can begin to depict her mother more dispassionately—a prodigious feat given their history and the mutual antagonism that still erupts from time to time.

> My mother is a woman of fifty-four years of age; smaller than I am, but a bit stout—though not ungainly. While not a smart dresser, still she doesn't look like a frump . . . doesn't annoy me with mannerisms as do so many other members of my family.
>
> Now then—why can't I like her? It must be because of the woman which is under the skin . . . she never seems to be anything but froth; she only hits the bare outside of things. . . . We get along most serenely because we never scratch through the veneer.
>
> And when I look on this woman, and I force myself to keep in mind that I was born of her, that I lay in her arms as a baby, nursed at her breast and was at one time her chief interest, I listen for a cry in my heart for her—and there isn't any. I look at her and feel . . . only coldness. (250–51)

Secure in the epistolary mothering received from Howe, Maimie turns her attention to the Montreal prostitutes denied the love and respect she herself was denied in old Phildelphia, denied especially to Rachael Pinzer, a victim-prisoner at Norristown State Hospital. Now autonomous, Maimie finds sisterhood powerful. In the same letter that bewails the Pinzers' alienation, she tells Howe about Stella, a beautiful prostitute desperately in need of attention:

> When I act in anything for her, I see a composite picture of Stellas, Maimies, etc.—their number is legion. I know so well her every thought and action. And even better than she does, I know her hopes. You will hardly be able to grasp this, not having lived through it, but my recollections of the same thing when I was seventeen are very fresh and readily brought to mind . . . somehow—Stella is Maimie. Do you get the idea? (274)

This excerpt pointedly declares Maimie's independence from her "second self," now a needy girl whose role Maimie has shed as one sheds an old skin. Once the Stella-self even had a name, "Mimi," living manipulatively, dishonestly:

> And I got so that I found it quite convenient to heap on "Mimi" all the *dirty,* contemptible things that Maimie did. . . . And now I realize that was all ballyrot. "Mimi" never did a thing that Maimie didn't want her to do. And as I never did anything weakly—even did my evil in strength—I decided that "Mimi" was a sloppy excuse for a week-kneed individual. And I've never stood for another one of those silly excuses for wrong doing. . . . *I am what I am.* It sticks in one's throat at first to admit it, but it gets easier. (373)

Dismissing narcissism, she forthrightly approaches the Stellas, Lillians, Alices, Margarets, Sharons, and Joanies to rehabilitate them in a way different from that of the missionary—from Welsh's way. She offers peer counseling "fully fifty years before the development and adoption" of that social-work practice (xxxv). Maimie knows that she can fully understand a prostitute's experience as Howe never can. Identifying with Stella's syphilitic condition, she finds medical care for her in Philadelphia. With extraordinary courage, considering the recurrent financial crises and drains on her energy, she undertakes managing a home for former prostitutes, replete with fireplace, family photographs, a communal kitchen, clean beds, victrola, and books. She responds indignantly to the caseworkers' proposed name for the shelter, "The Montreal Mission for Friendless Girls":

> I thank God you are not friendless; but if you were—you would no more admit it than any girl does. . . . The kind of girl—the hu-

man jellyfish—that is willing to be classed as "friendless" I haven't much time for. . . . I couldn't possibly lend a helping hand to all. And as I can work best with the kind that I believe I was most like—as a young girl—is it not likely to do the "greater good" to devote my time to them? And I'd like to see the place I'd have walked into, when I was a young girl, that was known to be a haven for "friendless girls"! (340)

The lady may be protesting too much, but she's streetwise enough to know that a Salvation Army prescriptiveness can lead only to Shaw's *Major Barbara* dilemma. The mission would attract those who wanted a bowl of soup and shelter from the rain and who would be willing to mouth any pious platitude before filling their stomachs and returning to the streets. Hence, a sisterly commitment is made to victims who still possess the strength to choose, the will to survive.

She might well have pioneered the reclamation of Montreal's prostitutes, but World War I intruded on these plans:

Nearly every building that has heretofore been used for charitable purposes . . . have been taken over for military purposes—barracks, recruiting offices, this or that league. . . . What of those who benefitted thru these other and original lines? They must manage as well as I will have to. (293)

Because of the suspicion heaped on foreigners and pacifists during the war, not to mention Maimie's constant need for financial support of the halfway house, the increasingly brief, businesslike letters in the last third of the text reflect impatience with jingoism, sympathy for the suffering of German soldiers, scorn for churches professing peace while preaching war:

I can't believe that God who is omnipotent wants man on earth to be killed by us—for no matter what cause. And I can't follow the clergy who have the congregation sing "Peace on Earth, good will to men"—and then conclude the performance with sermons intended to incite men to kill. . . . So why should I keep up the farce that I believe these places the houses of my God. (388)

Furthermore, she still finds the institution of marriage repellent. Aware of both Welsh's and Howe's suggestion that she divorce Albert and marry Ira Benjamin, Maimie solicits their financial aid to implement these procedures and then arrives fifteen hours late at the wedding ceremony. In trying to avoid even the appearance of wifely dependency, she sometimes goes too far. Once, after dousing herself with boiling lye water, she tells Ira a tale calculated to exclude him from the problem. To Howe's friend Miss Huntingdon, Maimie writes:

> I always invent fables so as not to call his attention to my lack of sight. This I do mainly because he persists in treating me like a cripple. If he knew the truth about this, I'd have him pouring my tea and coffee. . . . Sometimes we have fearful rows because he wants me to play "sweet old lady" and I don't fancy the role. (389–90)

If an assertive declarative "I am fully able to cope with the best of them" (233) signifies her independence from Howe, "I always invent fables" acknowledges the narrator's assertion of the right to write about experience earned and craft consciously fabricated. In two culminating narratives Maimie indicates that the self-recovery begun in Montreal has fashioned an autobiographer.

The first begins, as do all the pivotal episodes, in response to a powerful fictive stimulus. Howe's daughter, Helen, has written revealing a child's lack of confidence about the worth of writing poetry. Recreating a haunting childhood episode, Maimie's letter to Helen, an exemplum, evokes her hoydenish past as leader of neighborhood rowdies, contemptuous of a "poor little rich girl," Annie Moore, who lived nearby and used to peer longingly at the less privileged children scampering back and forth before the white gate that sheltered her.

Occasionally, Mrs. Moore invited Maimie in because Annie had no other friends. Walking past the Moore house one day, Maimie carelessly dropped some lump sugar meant for the horses at a stable close by. Glancing back, she noticed Annie using a stick to propel the sugar under the gate. Discomfited, Maimie retraced her steps and handed Annie what was left of the soiled and sticky lump.

> Annie ate greedily of the sugar, jamming her mouth so full there was no chance for conversation. And not until the last piece had disappeared . . . did I say a word, and when I did, it was on the basis that I spoke to my other girl friends—for by eating that dirty, sticky sugar Annie had qualified and was one of us. (368)

Because Annie's mother did not allow candy in the house, the child continued to eat the huge packets Maimie gave her in order to keep the strange friendship alive. Invited to Annie's playroom one day, Maimie discovered "fat books with stories and pictures."

> Pretty soon, I was stretched out full length on the floor, with Annie beside me, apparently having forgotten about her pretty cloth-

ing—and we turned the leaves and Annie was explaining the pictures and short stories. (369)

Seduced by literature, Maimie was hardly prepared for the depth of Annie's devotion, manifested in writing and dedicating a poem to her, which Mrs. Moore, much to the embarrassment of both children, coaxed Annie to read aloud "for at that time, to figure in anything meant having done something that was not allowed . . . and I was downright mad about being tricked. . . ."

Shortly thereafter Annie died of some unspecified lung disease:

> Often I . . . wished I could have understood her better. . . . I also think of that poem . . . Annie wrote almost on the eve of her death. Would it not be wonderful to read that now. After all those years to read of the love of a sweet little girl who loved me for some reason which I did not understand then, and I still find it a mystery. (370–71)

Despite the sentimentality characteristic of turn-of-the-century writing, this letter valorizes Maimie's use of narrative strategies to manipulate an audience. To be sure, she has done so before in order to impress Howe, but this letter is more a self-confident way of reordering the past through skillful fable making. Moreover, the fables do not merely circumvent the "ugly" and "dirty" (consistent adjectives) aspects of the past. Helpless young girls in danger of dying constantly loom on the terrain of the autobiographer's consciousness. Annie's story allows Maimie to identify with the dying and to imagine her own demise, a motif powerfully developed in a stark unsentimental account of Caroline's death. The wife of brother James, Caroline succumbed to the flu epidemic that followed World War I. Maimie's terse description of returning to Philadelphia is a journalistic masterpiece:

> She was taken ill on Monday—this during the heart of the epidemic—and Thursday, 4 p.m. she died. I was not here of course. The entire family were flat in bed and not a servant or nurse on the premises. . . . I received the wire Friday night, and was in Phila. Sat. at 9 a.m., having made a special that was bringing doctors and nurses to the East for the epidemic. . . .
>
> Arriving, I found the door open. . . . And opening the door, I smelled the stench of mortification. . . . In a small room which they call the parlour, James was stretched out on a cot; and against the other wall, on a couch, was my mother.

The exact location of the children and other relatives follows in detail.

> Caroline was dead, her body lying there with no more attention
> than is given a cat.
>   Such a wailing and crying as was set up when I came in. I
> thought James had lost his reason and that my mother would
> never survive. I did not cry. I didn't dare to. I saw what I had to do
> and I wish to report that I did it.
>   I tended the living first. Sarah [Potsy] got my attention to begin
> with. Words cannot describe the chaotic condition of that house.
> Though Caroline had been sick but four days, . . . the place was
> filthy. Everything that was handled was left where it dropped.

Maimie managed to get Caroline's body to a mortician:

> I had to wash and dress the body at home, and I even opened her
> arteries, my assistant being a boy of eighteen whose only knowl-
> edge of the undertaking business was learned in driving one of the
> [undertaker's] auto carriages. . . . The body was taken away in a
> grocery truck loaned by the wholesaler where James buys his mer-
> chandise, and I had to put her in a clothesbasket. The boy and I
> carried her out, and . . . I came back in the truck; and I had all
> sorts of fumigation things and antiseptics. All that night I labored
> to remove that terrible stench. And then for three days and nights
> I never stopped treating Sarah. It was seven days after my arrival
> that I took off my shoes and outer clothing.   (412–13)

Only after being assured that Ira would not be exposed to unnecessary
danger did she allow him to help build Caroline's casket and dig her
grave:

> and Bennie and I had the sad duty of placing Caroline in her coffin.
> I dressed her in my wedding dress. Needless to say, she was no
> longer our beautiful blonde Caroline,—but oh, how I loved her . . .
> and I kept up the thought that the roses were Caroline and not
> what we put in the casket.

Not until then does she dwell obliquely on the death of her own child:

> When I lost my baby last year, Caroline, who wrote to me secretly
> (for James had forbidden it), said she felt so badly for me, and if she

were able, she'd send Sarah to me to stay awhile to comfort me. *I
can recall now that I thought that I'd rather have Potsy than even
my own baby.* And now I have her and love her, but how it hurts
me; for she loved her mother, and it is so sad for her. (413–14, my
italics)

The prodigal daughter has at last returned to bury the past and
mother the future. The episode also reveals that no one in the family
but Caroline, the gentile sister-in-law, would have done the same for
Maimie. Only sisterhood, that constantly reiterated leitmotif, can in
some measure compensate for the pariah's primal deprivation of a
mother.

And what of the apparently uncharacteristic line "I'd rather have
Potsy than even my own baby," surely not merely a momentary conces-
sion to grief? A temporary responsibility, Potsy could stimulate the
narrator's imagination without exacerbating her ambivalence toward
her mother, laden with feelings of loss and pain. Thus, when we compare the climactic death episodes with the "Brownie" and "Mary
Antin" narratives that culminate Maimie's sojourn in Philadelphia,
we discover that a writer's sensibility has begun to displace the symbi-
otic relationship with Howe.

An autobiographer must achieve psychic distance from relational
bonds, for a woman writer inevitably a costly achievement. Despite her
attempts to justify not undertaking the formal autobiography Howe
urged her to attempt, Maimie might well have harnessed herself to the
writer's trade: "I really feel I could write it—if I could write a bit at a
time. And maybe I will try it; and if it goes easy, keep on with it" (199).
It is disheartening, to say the least, that when approached by Mark
and Fanny Howe, Ellery Sedgwick, editor of the *Atlantic*, decided
against publishing Maimie's memoirs. Of course we have no way of
predicting whether recognition would have disciplined her enough to
ignore countless interruptions, welcomed, perhaps, as an antidote to
the writer's inevitable solitude. Finally, the possibility of partaking in
the notoriety given to Mary Antin and indeed of surpassing Howe's
literary achievement may have divided Maimie against herself,
thereby turning her political-social skills to the oppressed sisterhood
clamoring for her attention.

Those obstacles notwithstanding, how much more edified might we
be today had "Maimie Pinzer" sustained the literary centrality needed
to author herself. For us it would mean a gain in our insight of social
history and the autobiographical experience. For Maimie it would
have signified the worth of a personal history, the invaluable closure of
her life's journey.

Notes

1. On turn-of-the-century native-born biases against Jewish immigrants, see "From Henry Adams to Henry James" and "Legal Right, Social Rebuffs" in Irving Howe, *World of Our Fathers* (405–13). Even a heretic-feminist such as Charlotte Perkins Gilman, author of *Women and Economics*, spouted bigotry: "Twenty-two years in that unnatural city [New York] where everyone is an exile, none more so than the American. . . . One-third of the inhabitants . . . are now Jews. . . . What must any people think of another people who voluntarily give up their country—not conquered—not forced out—simply outnumbered and swallowed up without a struggle" (*The Living of Charlotte Perkins Gilman* 316).

2. Sol Gittelman quotes from a sociological survey published in 1930 by Madison Grant and Charles S. Davidson: "In ignorance and illiteracy, in coarseness and low standards of cleanliness, a large part of the Slavic world remains at the level of our English forefathers in the days of Henry VIII" (198). Hapgood Hutchins, a sympathetic journalist, wrote disparagingly of Jewish women who "lack the subtle charm of the American woman, who is full of feminine devices, complicated flirtatiousness, who in her dress and personal appearance seeks the plastic epigram, and in her talk and relation to the world an indirect suggestive delicacy" (qtd. in Baum, *The Jewish Woman in America* 190).

3. See Baum 53; I. Howe 139–41; and Neidle 109.

4. Quoting from Helen Howe's memoirs, the editors of *The Maimie Papers* observe that "a deep pessimism and sense of tragedy" characterized this unusual woman's daily perceptions of the human condition. Although nominally a Unitarian, Howe tended toward a "deeply ingrained agnosticism," perceiving "the only reality in life as unhappiness—the stretches of happiness being only parentheses" (xvii).

5. For references to *The Opal* see *The Maimie Papers* 32, 37, 39, 172, 317, 349.

An Analysis of the Oral
Testimony of Edna Anderson

Alice T. Gasque

The value of oral testimony as nontraditional literature is apparent when we are able to identify outstanding examples of the form and as we refine the methods of evaluation and analysis. Recognizing literary merit in oral testimony and responding to it within an aesthetic framework are difficult tasks; nevertheless, recognition of and response to this literary form can yield valuable insights into how we view ourselves and the world around us. The oral testimony of Edna Anderson[1] is valuable because it extends our understanding of our own lives and of the world.

Edna's story begins with her life as a child and later as a teenager in a relatively poor farm family. She recounts her experiences as a young farm wife, struggling for financial improvement by selling eggs and other produce and by taking in schoolteachers as boarders. She tells us that she and her husband were happy, the parents of two girls and a boy. Their major disappointment was that their only son was severely retarded as a result of a difficult birth. They were well on the road to financial security and had moved from the farm into town when Edna's husband died unexpectedly, leaving her a widow at the age of thirty-one.

For five and one half years after the death of her husband, Edna managed to support herself and her three children, with some help from neighbors and relatives, by purchasing and renting property, selling valuables, and supplying rooms for schoolgirls of farm families during the winters. Finally, after being courted by several men, she married a gentle, undemanding man against the objections of her oldest daughter. Her attempts to care for her son at home led to difficulties in the family resulting in two miscarriages during her second marriage. After the birth of her third daughter (the only live birth of

78

the second marriage), she consented to institutionalize her son permanently. Her story concludes with her concern about the care that her son has received at the institution.

Edna Anderson's oral testimony differs from hundreds of other oral histories and narratives because it is an introspective account of the life of an ordinary rural woman, revealed in an intimate monologue. The student[2] who interviewed her disappeared from the original narrative, serving as a passive catalyst for Edna's review of the private joys and sorrows of her life. Edna's self-revelation is driven by her identity as a daughter, wife, and mother—an identity reflective of her ideals of domesticity. Her testimony is a rich display of the values and emotions of a contemporary midwestern rural woman. She tells us something new about the ideal of domesticity in conflict with the changes in the family produced by economic conditions, physical and mental health, social-class distinctions, and various other internal and external stresses.

The spontaneous quality of the testimony and the frank, factual discussion of family life lend it a vitality that is difficult to match in either more traditional autobiographies or other types of nontraditional written literature. Furthermore, Edna's story is artistically structured. Telling a life is not identical with living it. In reordering the events, Edna selects and rejects detail, characterization, setting, plot, and dialogue and rearranges these elements in a pattern of contrasting images that ultimately serves to unify the entire testimony.

The circumstances of Edna's life were narrow, and her knowledge of the rest of the world was restricted by midwestern farm economics and the social condition of her family. She was the middle child and only daughter of a strict German father and of a mother whom he intimidated. The farm family was severely afflicted by the drought and depression during the dustbowl years in South Dakota. At the most intense period of the depression, the family moved from the outskirts of Willow Lake, a community of nearly four hundred people, to a farm outside Bradley, a village of only one hundred people, located approximately thirty-five miles north of Willow Lake. Both towns are in Clark County in the middle of an isolated flat prairie in eastern South Dakota.

Life for nearly all South Dakota farmers during this time was extremely difficult; the conditions of Edna's family were not unique.[3] Nevertheless, Edna makes only oblique references to the most widespread economic disaster of the region: the dustbowl years. Her failure to discuss the depression as a historic event coincides with the similar silences about historic events in more formal written autobiographies by women:

They emphasize to a much lesser extent the public aspects of their lives, the affairs of the world, or even their careers, and concentrate instead on their personal lives—domestic details, family difficulties, close friends, and especially people who influenced them. (Jelinek 7–8)

Edna discusses the economic conditions of her family in her references to picking cobs while other children participated in school and community events and to her first job after high school as a domestic helper for a professional family that required seven clean white collars a week. These experiences parallel the lives of many single farm girls who moved into town as household workers.[4] She escaped from domestic hard labor and low wages when she became ill from working long hours in the basement. She returned to her own family as her mother's helper until her marriage.

Edna's moving north to Bradley with her family initially hindered her courtship by a poor young farmer; a more severe difficulty was the prospective bridegroom's move from Willow Lake to Iowa, where the best-paying farm jobs were located. The combined obstacles of the long distances, infrequent meetings, and travel expenses between Bradley and Iowa contributed to the frustrations of the young couple as they attempted to save enough money to begin farming on their own. When the farm rental arrangement and the planned marriage on Thanksgiving Day fell through, the disappointment of the couple culminated in their engaging in premarital intercourse—a step that led to pregnancy and marriage when they had almost no means of support.

Edna's forthright description of the details leading to her marriage displays an unusual frankness in revealing private emotions. Edna feels that she had somehow failed her ideals by submitting to sexual relations before the wedding. She supplies us with several compelling reasons for her sense of failure: a tradition of chastity before marriage, a strict father, her overriding love for her husband, the force of disappointment when the farm fell through, her strong religious background.

Despite the narrow circumstances of Edna's life and her limited range of experience (she recalls only two trips outside the state during her first marriage: one to Iowa and the other to Minneapolis), the story that she tells illustrates universal emotions of love and grief, joy and sorrow.

Edna's narrative structure is not in logical, linear, or chronological pattern; it does not begin with an abstract, build to a climax, reach a resolution, and finish with an epilogue. Instead, the testimony moves like a camera's shutter in time, flickering among the far-distant past, the nearer past, and the present and among the identities of Edna as daughter, wife, and mother. The narration juxtaposes contrasting images that enhance the veracity of the account and provide the tension that unifies the entire narration. The strongest emotions are those most often found in comedy and tragedy and in dramas of love and death—the emotions of joy and sorrow.

While Edna at one stage characterizes herself as "sort of a clown," the joy she conveys is always tempered by sorrow. She succeeded in marrying the man she loved, but she did so under unhappy circumstances. She succeeded in moving from a depressed farm economy to a house in town and a busy filling station, but her beloved husband died within six months of the move. She succeeded in marrying a second husband after the death of her first, but she had several problems with her oldest daughter as a result of the marriage. She succeeded in raising four children, but she had two miscarriages and severe difficulties with her only son, who was eventually institutionalized.

Edna most effectively conveys her joy in her first marriage in a memorable scene of the couple sitting by the furnace during an evening blizzard, listening to the Lone Ranger on a small radio, and eating homemade ice cream. As a narrator, she has a fine ear for detail. We remember the scene because she has juxtaposed images of hot and cold, isolation and connection, fantasy and reality, comfort and danger.

She conveys her sorrow at his death in much the same way. She introduces the scene by depicting her daughter's response to her husband's death—a headstrong tomboy who loved her father and loved the filling station, she wept for him in the closet rather than in front of Edna and the rest of the family. Not until Edna parks the new car (one of the nicest in town) in the garage after a social event does she realize that she too has suffered a severe blow in the death of her husband. She is alone, bereft of his companionship and his financial support, and she immediately sells the car that represents advancement, wealth, success, and the ultimate realization of a happy domestic life. When the children cling to her in fear, she realizes that she, like her daughter, can never cry openly in front of them again. The conflicting images here are the ideals of domesticity and of female independence; financial success and failure; a growing status in the community and its collapse, leading to her dependence on the charity of others; the pain of grief and her frustration in expressing it.

Edna's understanding of the difficulty in embracing the values of domesticity is most apparent when she reveals that those ideals were not enough. She says, "I thought that the fulfillment of life was to have a home and a family." Somehow, the circumstances of her life betrayed those ideals.[5] While women in the upper middle class could afford to hire domestic help for such mundane chores as washing, ironing, and cooking, Edna had to do those chores for her family and for others in order to support her family when her husband died. In the same section of the narrative, she blames her father for his shortsightedness in preventing her from going to college because she had a boyfriend. Of course, the economic conditions of her family may have been the chief deterrent to a college education, but since she has suffered through her attempt to support her family without specialized training, Edna rejects the ideals of passivity and female dependence.

She has similar difficulties with the domestic ideals of motherhood and nurturance. Throughout her narrative, her most significant encounters with her children are with her first two—her daughter and son. Her first daughter's birth was easy and almost idyllic. She describes her activities in helping her husband in the field the day before the birth, and she remembers the sun shining on a beautiful fall day. The birth of her second child, which closely follows the first birth in the narrative, contrasts sharply with the earlier account. Her labor lasted for about two weeks, and the child was injured at birth. The juxtaposition of these births repeats the pattern of contrasting images apparent in the organizing structure of the narrative.

The rest of the oral testimony concerns her relations with these two children. Her relationship with her daughter offers the best opportunity for her to impart her own values through motherhood. She and her daughter, Deb, share personality traits—a sense of independence, close kinship with their fathers. Edna showed some independence in engaging in premarital sex against the values of her parents, though she later regretted not waiting until after the marriage. She also clearly indicates that she was her own father's favorite: "he always cuddled you, you know, and he especially preferred me to the boys."

Unfortunately, these shared characteristics do not result in a closer mother-daughter relationship. Like Edna, Deb maintains an uneasy truce with her mother, believing that their lives have no connection. This alienation shows up fairly early in Deb's clash with domestic ideals in remaining a tomboy, her private grief after the death of her father, her pursuit of leadership positions at school (she was voted class president), but her rejection of Edna's choice of a second husband displays it most clearly.

Edna's use of dialogue dramatizes the conflict between mother and daughter. There are only four places in the oral testimony where dialogue appears. Three of the four are individual remarks made by Edna's first husband. All four fragments involve crises in Edna's life. The first describes the circumstances of the premarital intercourse; the second depicts her first husband's delight at the birth of his son; the third (the longest exchange) depicts the difficulties between Edna and Deb about the choice of Maynard as a second husband; and the fourth is an agonizing question raised by Edna's first husband about institutionalizing their son.

Deb's disgust with her mother in her second marriage reflects some of Edna's uneasiness toward the values of womanly submission and domestic bliss. Repeating the pattern of contrasting images, Edna claims that her second husband was nothing like her first. While her first husband closely resembled her father in his leadership of the household, Maynard "always had to do just like his mother said." Edna confesses:

> I did miss the man part of it because my first husband was the boss. I never did anything without asking him. But with Maynard, it just seemed like, you know, what I said went. I didn't like that at first. It terribly bothered me. But it's probably a good thing. . . .

Maynard's deferring to Edna ironically allowed Deb more freedom than she might have been permitted under a more traditional domestic authority, but the second marriage effectively prevented the possibility of a close mother-daughter relationship.

Edna's feelings about her son conclude the testimony. Her joys and sorrows in mothering this child create the climax of her story. The difficulties of his birth, the joy of her first husband when Alvin was born, the importance of bringing Alvin home after her second marriage, the resulting two miscarriages, and the grief in permanently institutionalizing him all contribute to the texture of this climax. Edna's failure to keep Alvin at home is perhaps the greatest sorrow of her life. She recognizes the problems caused by the unwillingness of the neighbors to accept Alvin as he is. She also recognizes her own inabilities to cope with him as he runs off down the icy street in winter, following a tractor. Her only consolation and chief joy is that Alvin can occasionally visit her at home on weekends.

This oral testimony gives us an intimate view of the life of an ordinary woman who had no unusual educational experiences and who did not change history in a traditional sense. Nevertheless, her testimony has rare introspective qualities, and the structural form of the interview is similar to that of poetry. Most spontaneous oral testimonies do not share the richness of this piece in both content and form. The value of this work lies in the artistry of the narrator, Edna Anderson, and in her perceptions of herself and the world around her.

The form of oral testimony as a literary document presents particular problems for preservation, analysis, and interpretation. Audiotapes as literary artifacts are more difficult to maintain, disseminate, and use than the printed word. For the purposes of analysis, it is easier to use a transcript than to review an audiotape. It is also more difficult to provide listening facilities than to keep a book on a shelf. However, transcribing the audiotape is, in fact, a transformation of no lesser importance than the transformation of a spoken, spontaneous performance into symbolic, static images. In the transformation, an editor may attempt to reconstruct the rhythms of the narrator's speech patterns—the intonations, the nuances, the dialect, the laughter, and the tears.[6] These attempts often fail. In addition to punctuation, a carefully edited transcript will always vary at least slightly from the audiotape. Most oral testimonies require more creative interference from the editor than Edna Anderson's interview demanded.

Second, publishing literary textual analyses of oral testimonies necessitates reproducing at least some of the edited transcripts. Ultimately, the transcript may replace the audiotape as the literary artifact. For the literary critic, the question of analysis involves accepting or revising the transcript as the text. In the case of longer oral testimonies (those extending over several days or months or years), the critic must make artistic rather than strictly editorial decisions about which details to select and which to omit.

Although these problems are formidable, there are impressive rewards for those who persevere. Oral testimonies allow us to hear voices that would otherwise go unheard and help us understand oppressed or submerged cultures. The spontaneity of the narratives has a fresh and stark truthfulness seldom found in more studied literary forms. Finally, the intimacy of introspection found in a few oral testimonies, such as the Edna Anderson interview, gives us a clearer knowledge of the human condition.

Notes

1. The narrator's name has been changed to protect her privacy and that of her family. She has, however, consented to release the audiotape for the purposes of research and publication. A copy of the tape may be obtained by writing the author of this paper.

2. Susan Sherman, a student enrolled in the Literature of Women's History on the Plains course at the University of South Dakota, interviewed Edna Anderson in the spring of 1979 as part of a project on the lives of South Dakota wives and mothers. Although Sherman's interview techniques contradicted the advice of most manuals and the advice offered to her in class, they obviously worked. She kept entirely silent during long pauses, waiting for Edna to resume her narration. When the taped transcript was edited, Sherman's initial questions were omitted since Edna obviously assumed control over the interview, turning it into a monologue.

3. A full account of the effects of the depression and the dustbowl years on the farmers of South Dakota appears in Schell 342–66.

4. One remembers the life of the main character of Willa Cather's *My Ántonia*. The tradition of this type of employment for young, single farm women has endured from the opening of the frontier to the present. Julie R. Jeffrey discusses the demographics of women's employment in the west (94–95).

5. See Myres (1–11) for an extensive discussion of the ideals of domesticity and their effect on the images of western women. The values, interestingly enough, even permeate the lives of contemporary western women who consider themselves to be the female counterparts of the cowboy. See Jordan's *Cowgirls*.

6. There have been several anthologies of oral histories of rural contemporary women. Some, like Sherry Thomas's, attempt to reveal the speaker's dialect by variant spelling. Too few of them attempt any sort of literary analysis.

The Oral Testimony of Edna Anderson

Susan Sherman and Alice T. Gasque

[This oral testimony was edited from a transcript of an audiotaped interview by Susan Sherman, a student in a course entitled The Literature of Women's History on the Plains at the University of South Dakota. Sherman interviewed Edna Anderson in the spring of 1979 for a paper on the role of wives and mothers in South Dakota. The questions have been edited out of the transcript to allow Edna Anderson to tell her story in one voice.]

When I was little, I had two brothers and my mother and dad. My dad was strictly the boss. My mother was always sort of the—you know, she did whatever he told her to do. Once in a while, she'd get excited and there'd be an argument, but she always would submit to him. My oldest brother was about five years older than I and my youngest brother was just seventeen months younger than I was. And we went to church together. And we always went to school together. We always had to walk, but it wasn't far. When I had Debra, she had to walk a good half a mile. And then we moved and she walked two and a half miles and we hardly ever took her. That would be about 1941.

I was married in January 1935 and then I had Debra the first year, or in the fall. As I said, we had her at home.

My youngest brother and I always had to go pick cobs because we burned cobs you know. Every night we had to see how all the cobs were and I always remember my brother said he sure hated the fact we'd been with cobs. But it was just a job. We were always busy. He wasn't able to participate in any sports because we had to get home and help, you know, with the chores. And we lived on the edge of town, but my dad farmed in Willow Lake.

After I was married, I remember the day before Debra was born; I was out with my husband all day. I was supposed to exercise. He was out fixing fence, so I went with him and I handed him the hammer, the pliers, or whatever he needed and then, the next day, she was born in the morning.

With her, the water broke at six o'clock in the morning, and of course, I hadn't—the only thing I knew was I had been to the doctor a few times and he told me what to expect. So, when I woke up in the morning, the whole bed was wet. I figured that this is what happened. Then, about eight o'clock, I started getting pains, so my husband called his mother and he called the doctor and the doctor got there a little before ten, and she was born at 1:15. Everything went kind of beautiful; it was a beautiful fall day. The sun was shining, I remember.

I had a teacher came to live with us. She paid me twelve dollars a week—or twelve dollars a month, to stay with us; three dollars a week, it was. That was her room and her board, everything. I furnished the towels. Of course, we didn't, you know, have a lot. I had no bathroom. We had to go outside to the toilet. She was a real nice girl, this lady was. And she stayed with us several years then. But when Deb was in first grade, we had a teacher because we were half a mile from the school. Of course, I gave her the pot to take upstairs, and she would never empty it herself. So I tried leaving it a couple of days, but she wouldn't empty it. Finally, she couldn't stand the odor anymore so she had to take it out herself.

I remember when I sent for dresses from Montgomery Ward. I still have the paper. They were called Hooverettes and they were sort of a wraparound dress and they cost forty-nine cents each. And the top of the dress, or whatever they called it, that was forty-eight cents. I look through it sometimes.

When I had Alvin, I had a severe birth with him. I went into labor off and on for about two weeks. And of course, then, he was injured at birth. It was the most violent birth. It was fast and he was laid wrong. Then, I had him at home. That's the last child I had at home. I had the next one in the hospital. Then, everything went all right. It was because of injuries I had when Alvin was born that I was so torn apart.

I remember, too, that I sent for a pair of shoes and they were one dollar. Of course, I suppose that they were just once on special. I know that then I wore size five and one half, but now I wear a size seven. I don't know, but I suppose I got heavy or something. I only weighed about ninety-nine pounds when I was married.

I thought the fulfillment of life was to have a home and family. I did want to go to college when I got out of high school, but my dad wouldn't let me go because I had a boyfriend. And he claimed that there's no use. Well, he died eleven years later, and if I'd had that education, I could certainly have used it. Instead, when my husband died, I had to stay home with my kids. See, I had Alvin who was retarded, you know, cerebral palsy, and Louise was a baby. Deb was ten. All I could do was stay home. I cooked for schoolgirls. They used to live with us. I got four schoolgirls to come live with us. We had a nice home. I could always make a lot of good food for our family too. I guess that's why Deb's heavy.

That was when I used to make angel food cakes—you know, people ordering some cakes, and then I'd make anything I could do at home. Then, when Deb got a little older, she stayed home and took care of the kids. On Saturday nights and Wednesday nights, I could go to the store and work and then I could earn a little more. My mother came and stayed with me for about two months one summer and took care of the kids and then I earned fifteen dollars a week.

When I was a girl right out of high school, I earned three dollars a week working on housework. I had one afternoon a week off. I had to do all the washing and the ironing. The man worked at a white collar job. He had seven shirts every week and they were hard to iron. We had to do everything. If she had a party, we had to serve the meal and prepare it beforehand. Sometimes the lady would help with. But I had to do so much stuff in the basement that I got sick. I got pleurisy so bad that I quit working. I just stayed home until I got married—helped my mother.

I had a blue crushed velvet dress, a long one with white crushed velvet sleeves. We went to the minister's house (my husband and I and my brother and his girlfriend) and then we went home and had a big dinner. The next day we went to Watertown and had a picture taken. That was our wedding. We never got to go on a vacation.

About ten years after we'd been married (we'd been married eleven years when my husband died—eleven years and one month), when we had been married ten years, we took my husband's mother to Iowa, and that's the only trip we ever got. Except, we went to Minneapolis six weeks before my husband died and we bought a car.

We farmed for nine years and in that nine years, the first three years we went in debt further each year, but then things kind of picked up. So, we had enough money to buy a filling station in town which had a little house beside it where we could live. And we made as much in the next year and a half at that station as we did in the nine years we were on the farm.

We bought us a nice house away from the station in the south part of town. My husband only lived six months after that. He died of an appendicitis operation. They said it wasn't broke. It was just seeping a little and penicillin was new in those times. So they just gave him penicillin and it seems like it just turned into peritonitis. He must have been allergic to penicillin. Anyway, he lived six days. He never was sick before in his life. That was kind of a shock.

I was a widow at thirty-one and I had, you might say, two babies with Alvin and Louise and then this ten-year-old girl that was kind of bratty, you know. I mean, she was always her dad's girl. And she loved him. She wanted to be with him all the time. She loved the station and she was always running after him. And I would find her a lot of times in the back of the closet crying. She would never cry in front of me. I know, one time, I had gotten this nice car, you know, and it was one of the nicest cars in Willow Lake at that time, and I drove the car in the shed one night after we'd come home from some place and I had a girl staying with me then; she was a high school girl. She had taken the kids in the house and I drove the car in the garage and it just hit me that I was all alone. I know I went in the house and I was crying. And the kids just hung on to me so, that I never dared to cry in front of the kids. I never did either. I tried to keep up, you know.

Well, the people in Willow Lake were very good to me. I had to sell my car. I rented out the filling station. I got one hundred and twenty-five dollars a month and that's what I had to live on, besides, you know, taking care of these girls and feeding them and you didn't get much for that. But my husband had a one thousand dollar insurance policy that paid for the funeral. That was about nine hundred dollars, and then I had sixteen hundred dollars in insurance that had accumulated and I bought eighty acres of land with them. So that kind of helped me to have a little extra.

I got along that winter without a car, but that was awfully hard with Alvin. He liked to be in the car so well. My husband used to take Alvin in the gas truck. The fellow that would bring us the gas would stay in the station sometimes and then Bill, my husband, would take Alvin and then he'd go deliver the gas, so that Alvin could have a ride in the truck. That's what he liked. Of course, when I didn't have a car, he didn't get out at all and he didn't like that.

Anyway, I guess, life was pretty lonely in those days. He died in February and that fall, I got the flu and I just prayed I'd die because I felt so alone. But the people in a little town are good to you. And his brother was real good to me. The neighbors across the street, they sold us milk. They had been friends of ours. We used to go roller-skating one night a week. They always took me along; that was kind of nice. And of course, we always went to church. I played the organ when I was eighteen years old in church and I taught Sunday school. But then we moved. My folks moved to Bradley on a farm. After, when I was eighteen, I got away from all that and we went to a little Baptist church in Bradley then. I was so glad to get back to Willow Lake when my husband and I were married a couple of years later.

We couldn't hardly get married. We had nothing to get married on. My husband went to Iowa to pick corn. And he'd get, seems to me that he got, ten dollars a day. And he thought, boy, if now, he could pick corn for a while, then we could get married. So, there was a lot of little things. I mean, we ate a lot of rice and beans and stuff like that. We had a few chickens. I would go in to buy groceries with my three pails of eggs that were gallon pails and I would figure out my grocery list rather exactly, from those many dozen eggs and eggs were not very expensive either then. I used to like salmon so well and that was about thirty-nine cents a pound, or can, I guess, but then most of the time, I'd have to come home with mackerel that was fifteen cents a can. Oh, how I hated mackerel, but that's what you could afford.

I guess I've been naturally a contented person. And of course, when you loved your husband, why, you were glad just to be with him. I remember in the evening we would hurry and get the chores done. We had a radio, you know, a little thing. And we'd hurry up and get through so we could listen to the Lone Ranger. I remember, we had two cows and on winter nights, we made ice cream just about every night. We always had ice cream. We had a little two-quart freezer and an electric churn. And we'd sit by the furnace and eat ice cream—that was our enjoyment—and listen to the radio. I remember one time, we were six weeks that we didn't get off the place when we had a big blizzard. We were just there all the time. But I can't ever say that I was discontented because of that.

I was a much happier person than my mother was. I'm sure I was. And even though my mother, of course, she was not expected to live when she was about fifty. She had a large cancer they said that was hooked to her pancreas gland. And they opened her up and when they saw what was there, they just closed her up. And here, she's alive today. So they don't always know. But I think I've been basically a happy person. When I was younger, I was a nut. I mean, I used to be sort of a clown. I guess I thought that was the way to be, you know, have a lot of fun.

But my dad was terribly strict. There was one fellow when I was sixteen, I liked to go with. He was really a nice guy, but there was TB in his family. So my dad absolutely forbid me to go with him. Here, my brother got TB; my youngest brother got TB. And this other fellow is alive today and well. He lives in Rapid City. Dad was strict with all of us. He was a typical German dad, is what he was. Still, when I'd get sick, I always wanted him. He was big and he always cuddled you, you know, and he especially preferred me to the boys. I always thought he worked my oldest brother too hard.

I just dreaded it so when we moved to Bradley because Bill didn't have the money to come very often to see me. I just hated to have him go. When another couple got married, he said, "Well, if they can get married, we can get married." In the fall, he had rented a farm. And we were going to get married on Thanksgiving Day. Then the deal fell through with the farm. And we weren't able to get married then, because they backed out on the deal. I know my husband said, "Why do we have to wait for that little piece of paper?" He said, "Oh, we'll feel so much better if we can just be together." And the pressure of trying to stay apart from each other. I don't think anybody in today's society knows what it's like. I really don't. But, you were brought up—you didn't dare, and you tried your best not to. But after Thanksgiving, we did have relations. Of course, we had to get married then in January. Then we moved in with his folks for two months. That bothered me terribly. I just felt so guilty. But it never seemed to bother my husband. He was just tickled that he was—.

I remember when we had Alvin. We didn't know that there was anything wrong with him right away, and he was so proud of that little boy. And he went around and you know, like, "I got my hired man," you know. He was so proud of that little boy. It was really a heartbreak when we found out that he wasn't right. He was about three or four months old. So there was heartbreak in our family, but I was happy with my husband. I've been happy with Maynard too, but I didn't have the exciting love like you have with your first marriage, I think.

As time went on, I went with a Catholic fellow for a little while but that didn't pan out too good. When Maynard came along, he was so good to my kids. Of course, Deb really fought that. She was sixteen then. So, she was not about to have anybody take her dad's place. When he came that day and asked me to go to the show that night, and then I said to Deb, "Will you stay home with Alvin and Louise?" and she said, "Who're you going with?" And I said, "With Maynard." She said, "With him?" I never will forget that. She was so disgusted, and she just hated hearing that. She went her junior year to school here and then her senior year we let her finish at Willow Lake. Then she got to be class president, and you know, she was a big wheel.

After that, one of the first things I did was buy me a really good Bible after my first husband died and I really started studying. That helped me a lot. In 1951, Maynard and I were married. Then began a whole new type of life.

I had lived alone five and a half years. I had run my own business. I had the farm and I rented it out and everything, and Maynard had always had to do just like his mother said. So, he was not a hard man to live with. But I did miss the man part of it because my first husband was the boss. I never did anything without asking him. But with Maynard, it just seemed like, you know, what I said went. I didn't like that at first. It terribly bothered me. But it's probably a good thing on account of Deb, because she was pretty headstrong, and of course, she was sixteen years old then. And Maynard was the most patient person in the whole world with Alvin. And of course, we had him home then for a long time.

My first husband said one time, "Do you suppose that we should take Alvin to Redfield?" I felt so hurt. I just felt so bad. I just cried and cried about that. Well, Maynard and I had him home. We bought the first house down there because it was good for Alvin. But one day he got on another lady's lawn and she reported it to the authorities or somebody. She said that they shouldn't have anybody like that around. And this same lady said that Alvin liked to feel different kinds of fur and stuff. And she walked by with her fur coat, and he reached out to feel it—the coat, you know. And she said that he was trying to attack her. And she had two little girls. I suppose that's what she was afraid of. I don't know. But he never hurt a soul. It got harder and harder to have him home.

I had two miscarriages before I had Marie; I'm sure it was because of Alvin. One time, it was icy and he got away from me. He'd see a tractor and he liked to go run behind it. And so I had to go about a block and a half to get him, you know, push him home on that icy street. And when I got home, I just laid on the bed and just sobbed, and I prayed that the Lord would help me because I just couldn't hardly do it anymore. You know, he was a big kid then. He was about seventeen then.

On account of this reporting stuff, we had a hearing then and Dr. Reed said it would probably be better for me if we took Alvin. I had had those two miscarriages then. I thought I might be pregnant with Marie, and so we thought it would be better if we took Alvin and we did. We had him in Redfield for about a year and then we had Marie and she was fine. Then, we felt (or I felt) I should like to have Alvin home again. That was not a wise idea, but we had him for about a year then. Marie would mimic everything he did. She was a bright little girl, and it wasn't right at all. So, we permanently took Alvin to Redfield when he was nineteen and he's been there ever since. So, I'm grateful that there is such a place. Really, there's a time when you don't want to part with them, but there's a time when you know you can't do it alone. I think it's wonderful that there are young folks that are working there now.

I do worry at times that so many times he has an accident or fall. The last time he was home he had three stitches right across the end of his nose and he looked like—. But if he was home, I don't know what I could be doing and you know, I couldn't handle him anymore. But we loved having him home for the weekend or something; so we do that. He was home four days the last time and he liked the weekend. We went back to that same house. He enjoyed that.

Captives in Paradise

Women on the Early American Frontier

Annette Kolodny

In contrast to the wealth of descriptive documents composed by male explorers, promoters, and the founders of early settlements, little remains to tell us how women regarded their new environment once they, too, began to cross the Atlantic for these shores.[1] Some years after the event, Anne Bradstreet confided to her children that when she first "came into this Country," in 1630, she had "found a new world and new manners, at which my heart rose."[2] In 1645, another Massachusetts woman confided to her minister that when she first arrived in New England, she had felt "shut up for a long space of time . . . in the woods."[3] But such brief and scattered hints of at least initial antipathy toward the translation from civilized England to the rocky and wooded coast of Massachusetts record only the confidences of private moments. They were never intended to become part of that growing body of literature in which New World immigrants set down for future generations the story of their conquest of and accommodation to the new continent. The public record of women's responses to the New World landscape must properly begin in 1682 with the publication of *The Soveraignty and Goodness of God . . . Being a Narrative of the Captivity and Restauration of Mrs. Mary Rowlandson*, the first printed New England Indian captivity narrative.[4]

Although first published some years after her death in 1678, Mary Rowlandson's text had nonetheless to confront Puritan resistance to public statements by women (the same resistance that motivated reaction against Anne Hutchinson). It did this by proclaiming itself a document of orthodox Puritan piety and by declaring that it had been released for public view only *"for the Benefit of the Afflicted."* An anonymous "Preface to the Reader" corroborates the claim of the title page by assuring readers that "this Gentlewomans modesty would not thrust [the manuscript] into the Press, yet her gratitude unto God, made her . . . perswadable to let it pass, that God might have his due glory, and others benefit by it as well." That the narrative applied at least symbolically to the larger community was strongly suggested, in most early editions, by the sermon appended to it ("A Sermon Preached at Weathersfield, Nov. 21, 1678. By Mr. Joseph Rowlandson," her husband; its text taken from Jeremiah 23.33).

At the time of her captivity in 1676, Rowlandson had for some years been a full member of the Lancaster, Massachusetts, congregation and the wife of its chief minister. Her narrative of her "eleven weeks and five days" (29) among the Narragansetts thus understandably seeks to reveal in that event "the works of the Lord" (11). After all, what sustained her during her captivity—despite real physical suffering, the death of one child, and separation from two others who were also captured—was her capacity to perceive her situation as a token of God's just chastening of the faithful and a promise of ultimate mercy in seeing them through. This meaning, she suggests, became clear to her when, on receiving a Bible from an Indian who had plundered yet another Massachusetts outpost, she opened it "to read, [and] . . . the Lord brought that precious Scripture to me, *Jer.* 31.16. *Thus saith the Lord, refrain thy voice from weeping, and thine eyes from tears, for thy work shall be rewarded, and they shall come again from the land of the Enemy*" (8). What was essentially private experience, however, also easily translated into a story with symbolic significance for the larger community. The basically analogic character of the Puritan mind, trained to interpret present experience through a grid of biblical types, would have understood Rowlandson's captivity as a symbolic extension of the state of the larger community, which in turn represented a suffering and embattled Old Testament Israel. Rowlandson's chastisement thereby signaled the chastisement of the entire community, a community then finding itself, in fact, in "the land of the Enemy," its border towns constantly threatened by Indian attack. Noting Rowlandson's frequent "resource to jeremiad texts" (Bercovitch 117), most scholars have concentrated on this aspect of the work. What has attracted less comment is that Rowlandson's narrative also constitutes the first detailed account of a white woman's journey through what she termed a "vast and desolate Wilderness" (4).

At the outset, to be sure, the physical and religious journeys are almost indistinguishable. Indeed, as Richard Slotkin points out, for "Rowlandson . . . time is marked not in temporal days but in 'Removes'"—or relocations from one Indian encampment to another— which constitute both "spatial and spiritual movements away from civilized light into Indian darkness" (109). Each successive remove away from the Massachusetts settlements thus pits Rowlandson against not only the physical wilderness of the Connecticut River valley but also an all-embracing "Wilderness condition" (6). Nonetheless, as the narrative continues, the spiritual and physical journeys grow increasingly distinct (though they never wholly lose their symbolic interconnections). The Indians, who had earlier been characterized as a "company of hell-hounds" (3), gradually take on individual personalities; and within their society, Rowlandson manages to carve out an economic niche for herself with her knitting skills. As the extra food or special favor she receives in exchange for her stockings and caps enables her to negotiate the often-treacherous political terrain of her captivity, so too her Bible helps her to negotiate the spiritual desolation of her "Wilderness condition," serving as a "guide by day, and my Pillow by night" (18). The only terrain she can never negotiate on her own is the landscape itself.

Repeatedly, Rowlandson records her admiration for the "*Squaws* [who] travelled with all they had, bag and baggage, and yet . . . got over this River" with an ease she cannot imitate (9). The several crossings and recrossings of the Connecticut River and its tributaries leave her "so weak and feeble, that I reeled as I went along, and thought there I must end my days at last" (20). Weakened by cold and hunger, burdened by her pack, and further weighed down by fears for her children, Rowlandson finds the winter journey unremittingly difficult. At times, the landscape reflects back images of her fears, as when a "Swamp by which we lay, was as it were, a deep Dungeon" (10). At other times, her description of the geography mirrors her physical state, as when she recalls passing "over tiresome and wearisome Hills" on the eleventh remove. "One Hill was so steep," she explains, "that I was fain to creep up, upon my knees: and to hold by the twigs and bushes to keep my self from falling backward. My head also was so light, that I usually reeled as I went" (14).

Never does she suggest that the landscape has any beauty, and only once does she record that it provided her sustenance directly— that is, without the Indians' intercession. On the twelfth remove, "so hungry I could not sit," she ventures away from the encampment "to see what I could find." "Walking among the Trees," she writes, "I found six Acorns and two Chestnuts, which were some refreshment to me" (15). This one instance notwithstanding and although complaints of hunger echo like a refrain throughout these pages, Rowlandson never acquires more than a rudimentary knowledge of the wilderness fare that allows the Indians to survive (especially after the English have destroyed their corn). "Their chief and commonest food was Groundnuts," she recalls; "they eat also Nuts, and Acorns, Hartychoakes,

Lilly-roots, Ground-beans, and several other weeds and roots that I know not" (28).

Rowlandson acknowledges that she "never saw one [Indian] die with hunger" (28), but she attributes that survival not to the raw wilderness's capacity to sustain life or to the Indians' woodcraft, but to "the wonderful power of God, in providing for such a vast number of our Enemies in the Wilderness, where there was nothing to be seen, but from hand to mouth" (29).

On her own, Rowlandson's narrative strongly hints, she could not survive. The landscape into which she has been taken is one she believes cannot sustain her and whose physical hardships can destroy her. Crossing its rivers, she finds herself in "Water . . . up to the knees, and the stream very swift, and so cold that I thought it would have cut me in sunder" (20). She cautions another woman, a more recent captive, against making an escape attempt on the grounds that "we were near thirty miles from any *English* Town . . . and bad rivers there were to go over" (7). And later, when her own ransom seems imminent, she begs her Indian captors to take her by horseback to Albany for the exchange rather than return her the way she has come, because "I was utterly hopeless of getting home on foot, the way I came" (12). Harsh though the landscape may be, however, it is even more threatening as a place in which she is easily lost—with all the emotional and symbolic baggage that word held for the Puritan. At one point, learning that her son is "about a mile from me," she asks permission "to go and see him." "They bade me go," she continues, "and away I went; but quickly lost my self, travelling over Hills and through Swamps, and could not find the way to him." In the end, she is forced to "turn homeward again," whereupon her Indian "Master . . . shewed me the way to my Son" (13). In what was no doubt an unconscious slip, Rowlandson here quietly suggests that while she has adjusted sufficiently to her life among the Narragansetts to consider their encampments at least a temporary home, she is incapable of any analogous accommodation to the wilderness itself.

Thus threatened by both her Indian captors (and what appear to her as the vagaries of their intentions toward her) and "the vast and howling Wilderness" (10) through which they take her, Rowlandson meekly submits before what she accepts as God's rightful chastening and consoles herself by recalling—in her mind's eye at least—the settlements on which she has been so rudely forced to "turn my back" (4). By the sixth remove, still "mourning and lamenting, leaving farther my own Countrey," she says she "understood something of Lots Wife's Temptation, when she looked back" (9–10). Notwithstanding the apparent aptness of the comparison, the destroyed habitation for which Rowlandson yearns is no Sodom or Gomorrah but, quite the opposite, one of the many fledgling Bay Colony townships that represented Puritan hopes of raising Jerusalem anew in America. The analogue appropriate to that dream—and, as her minister husband may have pointed out, to the entire Puritan enterprise—was the Old Testament type of *Judea capta,* the image of Israel suffering in Babylonian captivity. This image, like an undercurrent, governs much of the narrative, becoming explicit in Rowlandson's depiction of her eighth remove, when she is taken by canoe across the Connecticut River to a large convocation of Indians at the camp of "King Philip." Here she is "amazed at the numerous Crew of Pagans," many of whom soon "gathered all about me, I sitting alone in the midst." In this situation, she writes, "I fell a weeping," noting that this "was the first time to my remembrance, that I wept before them." "Although I had met with so much Affliction," she repeats herself, "and my heart was many times ready to break, yet could I not shed one tear in their sight" (11). She dwells on the scene and on her unusual crying there, I think, because she wants to render as fully as possible the type she is about to invoke. For whatever her weeping among her captors beside the Connecticut River may have meant to her at the time, once reunited with her family (both her children were also rescued) and resettled in Boston, Rowlandson attaches to it an interpretation that is at once intimately personal and communally resonant: "Now I may say," she writes, "as in *Psal.* 137. 1. *By the Rivers of Babylon, there we sate down, yea, we wept when we remembered Zion"* (11).

Ever attentive to local rhetorical possibilities for exemplum and exhortation, New England divines were quick to seize on the emblematic, "typick" features inherent in the increasing incidence of captivity. For general theological purposes, experiences like Rowlandson's were invaluable for teaching congregations that, during times of trial, "we must rely on God himself, and our whole dependence must be upon him" (36). For more immediate theocratic (and essentially political) purposes, the pattern of capture and suffering followed by redemption might signify a promise that New England's current problems—Indian wars, crop failures, epidemic disease, or even bad weather—were similarly a divinely mandated "scourging," justified by the community's momentary backsliding but essentially temporary.

The dramatic wilderness journeys of the captives, moreover, allowed—indeed, demanded—a renewed appreciation of the conflicting images guiding the physical removal of the Puritans from the spiritual Babylon of England to the uncharted forests of New England. On the one hand, entry into the New World wilderness called forth the types of Moses and John the Baptist, essaying the wilderness both to test and ultimately to revitalize their religion. On the other hand, what ap-

peared to many as the untamed savagery of the New England landscape—an image comprising both the terrain and its native inhabitants—suggested that perhaps they had simply abandoned one Babylon
for another. The dark forest recesses, controlled by the very "bond-
slaves of Sathan,"[5] thus easily suggested themselves as yet another
type through which to signify the notion of spiritual wilderness. As a
result, Babylon, a favored Puritan signifier for human corruption and
spiritual wasteland, was symbolically transposed from a desert city-
scape to a forested landscape.

In the Puritan sermon's rhetorical emphasis on this Americanized
Babylon, the captivity story—especially when its protagonist was a
woman—proved repeatedly useful. Nowhere in American experience
would the authors of these jeremiads find a more affecting image of
New England as *Judea capta* than in the languishing figure of a Puritan woman held captive in the rugged wilderness retreats of the Indian. Cotton Mather, in particular, sought to exploit these possibilities—even where, as in the case of Hannah Dustin, the story applied
imperfectly, at best, to his intended purpose.

Nonetheless, in the spring of 1697, Cotton Mather delivered in
Boston a "humiliation" sermon that relied for its dramatic impact on
"a Notable Deliverance lately Received by some English Captives,
From the Hands of Cruel Indians."[6] Composed near the end of a decade
of almost uninterrupted warfare between New England and the newly
allied Indian and French troops (called "King William's War"),
Mather's text emphasizes the French and Indian threat as one among
several justifiable "*Scourges* of Heaven" sent to punish and humble the
chosen "for our Delinquencies" (4–5). The persuasiveness of his closing
admonition that the congregation confess its sins and, in so doing,
humble itself before God, therefore, rests on Mather's ability to induce
in his listeners a felt perception of the implied cause-and-effect relation between the "*Spiritual Plagues* whereto we are abandoned" and
the community's being "*Humbled* by a Barbarous Adversary once and
again let loose to *Wolve* it upon us" (33, 34). The emotional, if not the
logical, link between the two was embedded in Mather's earlier para-
graph-long rumination on the image of *Judea capta,* which, imagina-
tively at least, prepared the audience for the captivity story to follow.
He invites his listeners, in effect, to experience their community's spiritual vulnerability through the biblical type and then, more dramatically, their own individual vulnerability through identification with
an actual captive woman who exemplifies the type.

In exploring the implications of his chosen image, Mather suggests
that New England's problems bear out the prophecy in Isaiah concerning the Daughter of Zion: "*She being Desolate, shall sit upon the
Ground.*" "When *Zion* was *Desolate,* by the Roman Conquest," he reminds his audience,

there were Coins made in Commemoration of that Conquest, and on those Coins there was a Remarkable Exposition of this Prophecy. On the Reverse of those Medals, which are to be seen unto this Day, there is, *A Silent Woman sitting upon the Ground, and leaning against a Palm-tree, with this Inscription* JUDAEA CAPTA.

Mather first repeats his description of the figure on the Roman coin and then redesigns it to make it explicitly applicable to New England: "Alas, if poor *New-England*, were to be shown upon her old Coin, we might show her *Leaning* against her Thunderstruck *Pine tree, Desolate, sitting upon the Ground*" (31). The full impact of the image, however, is meant to take hold retrospectively, as listeners recognize its resonances in the captivity story that Mather introduces as an "*Example* . . . Subservient unto the main Intention" of his "Discourse" (40).

But Hannah Dustin's story cannot, in fact, consistently correspond to his design. Supposedly taken down by Mather from the woman's own recounting of the events, the narrative opens with a detailed description of the Indians' intrusion into the Dustins' Haverhill, Massachusetts, household. A week-old infant is slain and the house set on fire. Hannah Dustin, still recuperating from childbirth, and her nurse, Mary Neff, are taken captive.[7] Within a few days of their captivity, Dustin and Neff are forced to travel on foot more than a hundred and fifty miles and are then given over to the charge of an Indian family that had earlier been converted to Catholicism by the French. Thereafter, they travel with this family, who have in their charge, as well, "an English Youth, taken from *Worcester*" some months before (45). Approaching "a Rendezveuze of Salvages, which they call a *Town*" (probably somewhere north of what is now Concord, New Hampshire), the women are told by their captors "that when they came to this Town, they must be Strip't, & Scourged, and Run the *Gantlet*, through the whole Army of Indians" (45). One night, Mather informs his listeners, while still about a week's journey from the rendezvous, Hannah Dustin "took up a Resolution, to Imitate the Action of *Jael* upon *Sisera*." Rousing from sleep "the *Nurse*, and the *Youth*, to assist her" and

> furnishing themselves with *Hatchets* for the purpose, they struck such Home Blowes, upon the Heads of their *Sleeping Oppressors*, that e're they could any of them struggle into any effectual Resistance, at the Feet of those poor Prisoners, . . . *there they fell down Dead*. . . . Onely one *Squaw* Escaped sorely wounded, and one *Boy*.

The brief narrative then ends with an acknowledgment of the former captives' presence in the audience: "But cutting off the Scalps of the *Ten Wretches*, who had Enslav'd 'em, they are come off; and I perceive, that newly arriving among us, they are in the Assembly at this Time, to give Thanks unto, *God their Saviour"* (46–47).

At one point, just before describing the slaughter of the sleeping Indian family, Mather interrupts the flow of the narrative to ask his audience, parenthetically: "Syrs, can we hear of these things befalling our Neighbours, & not *Humble* our selves before our God!" (46). Clearly, that aside was meant to remind the "assembly" that they were to interpret the story in a specific way: as an exemplum of God's chastening followed by merciful deliverance, not as an instance of Amazonian determination and effectiveness. The danger, of course, as Mather well understood, was that stories of "captives who escaped from the Indians by [their individual] strength or cunning might suggest that man could rely on his own strength for salvation" (Slotkin 114). To curtail that response—a response that the narrative certainly invited—Mather did what he could to emphasize some features of Dustin's adventure while suppressing others. To heighten the story's correspondence with the *Judea capta* type, he underscores Dustin's feminine vulnerability by stressing her convalescence from the recent childbirth. Playing on the Puritan identification of the Babylonian captivity with Roman (or papist) conquest, he somewhat embarrassedly acknowledges that the Indian family is faithful in its daily prayers but insists that "these *Idolaters*, were, like the rest of their whiter Brethren *Persecutors*, and would not Endure that these poor *Women* should Retire to their *English Prayers"* (44). Mather then attempts to justify the dramatic center of the narrative—the captives' slaughter of the sleeping Indian family—by comparing it to Jael's slaying of Sisera in Judges 4.21. That biblical precedent has the effect, also, of suggesting images of Israelite captivity, since Sisera commanded the army of a king of Canaan into whose hands the Israelites had fallen. Finally, though, he has to justify the sheer brutality of the act—an act particularly unusual for a woman—by claiming that "she thought she was not forbidden by any *Law*, to take away the *Life*, of the *Murderers*, by whom her *Child* had been butchered" (46). He does not mention that such a rationalization echoes Hammurabi's code more than it does any Christian ethic or that, "notwithstanding her present Condition," Dustin survived the forced march into and return journey from the wilderness. What he cannot so easily suppress—if only because the evidence was there for all to see—is that Dustin and Neff managed to keep "up with their New Masters, in a long Travel of an Hundred and fifty Miles . . . without any sensible Damage, in their Health, from the Hardships, of their *Travel*, their *Lodging*, their *Diet*, and their many other Difficulties" (43).

Mather was attempting to exploit material inherently intractable "unto [his] main Intention" (40). He might edit the story, but substantially revise it he could not. Dustin's spectacular escape, followed by her appearance before Boston's General Court, scalps in hand, to collect her bounty, was simply too well known. And not a few of his audience, Mather may have suspected, were attending the lecture that day in order to hear the story again and to view firsthand the former captives. Having thus risked losing some control over his material and all too aware that precisely those aspects of the story that had so riveted public attention tended to subvert his purposes, Mather closed his sermon with "An Improvement," a clearly articulated interpretive comment. In it, he enjoined congregation and returned captives alike to perceive in these events "a Surprising *Providence*" (48), and he called on the three redeemed captives, in particular, to "Become the sincere *Servants* of that Lord, who by His *Blood* has brought you out of the *Dungeon*, wherein you were lately Languishing" (49).

Still, Mather apparently did not rest secure that his message was clear enough. A few months later, when he prepared the sermon for publication, he appended to it "A Narrative of *Hannah Swarton*, containing a great many wonderful passages, relating to her Captivity and Deliverance." Somewhat tempering the subversive implications of Hannah Dustin's captivity story, Hannah Swarton's first-person narrative returns readers to the pattern begun by Rowlandson: it exhibits the traditionally feminine—and typologically useful—response that John Seelye has termed "passive forbearance in the face of adversity" (289). Additionally, it restores what Mather had excised from the Dustin account: the captive's detailed recollection of what it was like to be "hurried up and down in the Wilderness" (52). Such material was retained in the Swarton narrative because it served yet another of Mather's purposes: it helped to dramatize the dangers of removing from established towns. Because Swarton saw her captivity as a just punishment for her family's decision to leave "the Publick Worship . . . to Remove to the North part of *Casco-Bay*, where there was no Church, or Minister" (55), her story thus tended to discourage the growing atomism of the Puritan settlements, an atomism against which Mather himself so often inveighed.

The Indian raid on the Maine coastal fort at Casco Bay, in May of 1690, resulted in the death of Hannah Swarton's husband. She and her children were taken captive, but, like Mary Rowlandson, Hannah Swarton was quickly separated from her children and granted little "Liberty to Discourse with them" (51). Again like Rowlandson, Swarton appears not to have cried before her captors, reporting "that they would threten to kill us, if we cryed each to other" (51). The physical hardships of her sojourn with the Indians similarly repeat Rowlandson's. She complains of unremitting hunger, which left her "pined with want" and "faint for want of Food" (52, 53), and of exposure due to inadequate clothing. The *"Indian Dress"* into which her captors have put her, she protests, provides "no Stockings, and but one pair of *Indian Shoes*, and . . . Leather Stockings for the Winter: My Feet were pricked with sharp Stones, and prickly Bushes sometimes; and other times Pinched with Snow, Cold, and Ice" (53).[8] The terrain through which she travels offers another kind of hardship, confronting her with "steep and hideous *Mountains* one while, and another while . . . *Swamps* and Thickets of Fallen Trees, lying one, two, three foot from the ground, which I have stepped on, from one to another, nigh a thousand a day" (59).

Although Swarton follows Rowlandson in establishing the spiritual barrenness of this landscape and bewailing her lack of *"Bible* or *Good Book* to look into, or Christian Friend to be my Counsellor in these Distresses" (56–57), her narrative for the most part stresses its physical discomforts. Indeed, as she feels compelled to explain, "being continually in danger of being killed by the Indians, or pined to Death with Famine, or tired to Death with hard Travelling, or pinched with Cold. . . . I was so amazed with many Troubles, . . . that I had not time or leisure so composedly to consider of the great Concernments of my Soul" (56). The apologia, no doubt, was directed at an audience she knew to be familiar with Mary Rowlandson's best-selling and often-reprinted narrative. For if Swarton had not read that text before her own captivity, we may be certain she read it on her return, recognizing it as a model that could organize the meaning of her experience and that had already molded her readers' expectations.

Like Rowlandson's, Swarton's captivity narrative is about "the great Concernments of [her] Soul." And what comes to concern her most in this regard is not surviving the physical hardships of the woods—though this struggle is certainly difficult enough—but surviving incarceration among the French in Canada, "for fear lest I should be overcome by them, to yield to their Religion" (59). Thus, on her arrival in Quebec, "after many weary Journeys, through Frost and Snow" (59), Swarton's narrative swerves from one kind of spiritual testing to another. If her time in the woods has renewed her appreciation of God's justice and mercy in punishing her and then sustaining her through physical trials, her more comfortable captivity among the Catholic French tests her capacity to hold on to that newly won faith. Whether consciously or not, the passage that enunciates this transition symbolically summarizes her past sufferings while, at the same time, it prepares readers for those about to begin. Walking away alone from her Indian master to approach the outskirts of French settlement, Hannah Swarton leaves behind her a trail of blood on the otherwise pristine winter landscape: "The Snow being knee deep, and my Legs and Hams very sore, I found it very tedious to Travel; and my sores bled, so that as I Travelled, I might be Tracked by my Blood, that I left behind me on the Snow" (60). Suggestively an *imitatio* of Christ, and thereby an anticipation of the events to follow, the image also reminds readers of Swarton's physical frailty in an inhospitable landscape. More ominously still, that she may "be Tracked by my Blood" associates her with a vulnerable and hunted prey. In either interpretation, however, the landscape is literally marked by the sign of her suffering; and at a deeper, perhaps unconscious level, that marking betokens how inappropriate is her presence here: it stains the whiteness.

The second half of Swarton's narrative details her three and a half years among the French at Quebec. Invited, cajoled, and even threatened into adopting Catholicism, Swarton successfully resists these pressures and moves, instead, toward a fully articulated Puritan conversion experience. What she comes to in her resistance to the priests, in other words, is the "Ravishing Comfort"—or the firm assurance—that "God was my God, and my Sins were pardoned in Christ." Tellingly, the only sin to which she specifically refers, "that Sin which had been especially a Burden to me, [is] namely, *That I left the Publick Worship and Ordinances of God, to go and Live in a Remote Place*" (67–68). This act stands in her mind as the figurative abandonment of the faith to which she has now, at last, returned. Having "turned our Backs upon *Gods Ordinances*" thus "Justif[ies] the Lord, in all that has befallen me" (56). And assured as much as any Puritan might be by her experience of "the Lord . . . by His *Spirit* . . . come into my Soul, and so fill[ing] me with Ravishing Comfort" (67), she, like Rowlandson, now perceives her captivity as both a deserved and a religiously educative experience: "So, tho' I had deserved all this, yet I knew not, but one Reason, of Gods bringing all these Afflictions and Miseries upon me, and then Enabling me to bear them, was, *That the Works of God might be made manifest*" (70).

All that remains, then, to complete the multileveled pattern of redemption is her return "to the Country *from whence I had been Scattered*" (70). She refers here, of course, not to the Maine outpost but to Boston, the center of New England's Puritan way, where she arrives "in Safety . . . in *November*, 1695" (72). And even though this captivity narrative is unusual in that it does not end with a reunited family group (since Swarton's children remain in captivity), it nonetheless asserts a return to "our Desired Haven" (72). The physical return to Boston, in other words, underscores and reinforces the earlier spiritual return. The point was at once religious and political: if the scattering of God's chosen "*far off among the Heathen*" follows on their decision "*to go to live in a Remote Place, without the Publick Ministery*" (69, 68), then, at least by implication, Swarton is suggesting to her readers that without that ministry—and the orderly planting of towns that it represents—the frontier is no more than an extension of the wilderness, at once spiritually desolate and militarily vulnerable. That this implicit linking of the frontier with the dangers of the wilderness had the further effect of restricting the kind of landscape on which readers might, with comfort, imagine themselves, Swarton herself probably did not consider; and Mather, if he did, approved. For, unquestionably, this admonitory effect was precisely what he wanted the narrative to have and may, in part, explain his decision to print it (rather than some other available narrative) as an appendix to his humiliation sermon.

Still, what needs to be understood is that Mather was not really interested in landscape per se, any more than he was interested in captivity as a catalyzing event in an individual's life. His interest, instead, was always on the iconographic content with which he might invest the landscape and the typological significance of the captivity played out against it. Thus, it is not difficult to understand why— despite the popularity and piety of many male captivity narratives— Mather (like so many other Puritan ministers) utilized, whenever possible, the stories of female captives. *"The Fearful Sex,"* as Mather phrased it,[9] more perfectly accommodated the interpretive type because female captives (with the possible exception of Dustin) were more easily identified with the shrinking, passive vulnerability that was at its heart. In the *Decennium Luctuosum,* for example, he offers a number of captivity stories involving both men and women (including an expanded version of Dustin's narrative). But when summarizing "the Condition of the Captives"—and presumably here he meant all of them—he insists that its meaning may only "truly . . . be Express'd in the Terms of the ancient *Lamentations . . . The Daughter of my People, is in the Hands of the Cruel"* (50).

However unintended, the result of these interpretive strategies was a popularized image of a meek and frightened woman, linked in the public imagination not with the symbolic wilderness alone, but with the actual forested landscape of the northeast. At the end of the seventeenth century, Mather had easily transferred the symbolism of the Roman coin's *"Silent Woman sitting upon the Ground, and leaning against a Palm-tree"* to a New England *Judea capta,* "Leaning against her *Pine tree, Desolate, sitting upon the Ground."* By the end of the eighteenth century, it was a relatively easy task for Ann Eliza Bleecker to tap her readers' sympathies by exploiting that same image on behalf of her 1790 captivity novel, *The History of Maria Kittle.* The seventeenth century's passive *Judea capta* had simply been recast as the eighteenth century's passive sentimental heroine, "sad and benighted," wandering with her Indian captors "through almost impenetrable" wilderness. Finally, "overcome by sorrow and fatigue,

[Maria] immediately sunk helpless at the foot of a tree" (25). Thus had the sermons and sermonizing of the Puritans succeeded in crystallizing possibilities first hinted at by Mary Rowlandson. Rendering them familiar by repetition, Mather and his brethern effectively codified the imaginative constructs through which later generations of Americans would identify the dangers of the wilderness with the vulnerability of the frontier and, on either landscape, conjure up lurid notions of the suffering and helpless white woman.

Despite the decline of Puritan influence, the captivity narrative— first perfected in New England—retained its popularity throughout the eighteenth century and well into the nineteenth. But now, whether authentic, a sensationalized redaction of some earlier text, or wholly invented, the form began to shed its original controlling religious significance and responded to the changing needs of a different generation. Understandably, those who declared their independence from the crown (in part because of what they perceived to be inept British administration of the western lands) and those who crossed the Alleghenies through the Saluda-Cumberland Gap required different imaginative constructs than ever the town- and church-centered Puritans dreamed of. Reading narratives like *The Adventures of Col. Daniel Boon*, Richard Slotkin has demonstrated how, in the hands of men, the captivity narrative began to evince not only an increasing sympathy for the Indian but also an increased appreciation for the possibilities of experience in the wilderness (268–367). The avatar of that transition, of course, is Daniel Boone, passed down to us in later versions as Cooper's Leatherstocking, Faulkner's Boon Hogganbeck, and A. B. Guthrie's Boon in *The Big Sky*.

The most enduring figure in the myth of America's westward expansion, Boone first came into literary prominence when John Filson appended to his 1784 *The Discovery, Settlement and Present State of Kentucke* a first-person narrative entitled *The Adventures of Col. Daniel Boon, One of the First Settlers*. Supposedly taken down by Filson from Boone's dictation, *The Adventures* comprises autobiography and reminiscence, a history of the Indian wars, a promotional tract, and incidents of captivity. The character of captivity, however, has changed radically: no longer the event that structures the narrative, Boone's two captivity experiences are subordinate to the larger design, which is essentially about the conquest of the wilderness. Additionally, the experience itself has changed from one of unwilling captivity to almost compliant adoption. The Indians' "affection for me was . . . great," Boone boasts. "[I] was adopted, accordin to their custom, into a family where I became a son, and had a great share in the affection of my new parents, brother, sisters, and friends" (Filson 64–65).

Immediately and enormously popular, Boone's *Adventures* was quickly reprinted as a separate text, sometimes whole but more often in edited versions. Among the most famous (and often reprinted) of these editings was one produced in 1786 by the Norwich, Connecticut, printer John Trumbull. In *Regeneration through Violence*, Richard Slotkin is particularly acute in detailing how Filson's more complex original became in Trumbull's hands a portrait of Boone as a man of the wilderness rather than the settlements and, as he has ever after been known, as a man of action rather than contemplation (323–24). Slotkin fails, however, to appreciate Trumbull's bold stroke of genius in choosing to bind with his shortened Boone *Adventures* "A Narrative of the Captivity and Escape of Mrs. Francis Scott, an Inhabitant of Washington County, Virginia."

Having considerably trimmed and edited Filson's original and selected a smaller typeface, Trumbull ended up with too few pages to be sold profitably as either book or pamphlet; he thus decided to bind the Boone narrative with another text and took the Francis Scott narrative from current newspaper accounts. Trumbull chose the Scott narrative, as Slotkin suggests, "to satisfy his audience's demands by . . . combin[ing] two major forms . . . , the Indian war narrative" which, in Trumbull's version, had come to dominate the Boone text, "and the captivity narrative" (324). But in so doing he placed side by side those patterns through which Americans were coming to image male and female experience at the edge of the frontier. Precisely this contrast, I think, caught readers' imaginations and accounted, at least in part, for the book's success.[10] For, by being juxtaposed to the newly emergent narrative of male westward conquest, the now familiar female captivity narrative helped readers locate what was essential to that developing myth. By the same token, the radically revised male narrative helped readers recognize the enduring features of the corresponding female text.

The Scotts settled on the edge of the frontier that Boone himself had earlier helped to open. But where Boone, in 1769, happily chose to "resign my domestic happiness . . . to wander through the wilderness of America" (3), Scott, in 1785, is forced into that wilderness against her will. Boone, when captured, easily adopts Indian ways, "often . . . hunting with them, and frequently gain[ing] their applause for my activity at our shooting matches" (9); Scott, when taken, is always "anxiously looking for an opportunity to make her escape" (18). Boone escapes and returns expeditiously to the settlements; Scott escapes only to find herself "without any provisions, having no kind of weapon or tool to assist her in getting any, and . . . also knowing that a vast tract of rugged high mountains intervened, between where she was and the inhabitants eastwardly, . . . and she almost as ignorant as a child of the method of steering through the woods" (19–20). Exhausted and close to starvation, she is quickly "reduced to a mere skeleton" (22). The abundant wildlife that sustained Boone appears to her also, but it cannot provide her with food. Instead, "from the tenth of July to the eleventh of August, she had no other subsistence but chewing and swallowing the juice of young cane stalks, Sassafras leaves, and some other plants she did not know the name of" (23).

If Daniel Boone was seduced by "the ample and beauteous tracts" (5) of the wilderness, Francis Scott finds herself abandoned to it, at once its victim and prey. In contrast to the solitary Adamic Boone who "esteemed" Kentucky "a second paradise" (6), Scott is rather a hapless Eve, bitten on the ankle by "a venomous snake" and characterized by the third-person narrative as "a forlorn creature" (22, 23). At the end of his narrative, Boone looks back on his years in Kentucky and exults over the "Peace" that now "crowns the sylvan shade," characterizing himself as "an instrument ordained to settle the wilderness" (15). At the end of hers, Scott continues "in a low state of health." And she looks back on her experience on the Virginia-Kentucky border only to "remain inconsolable for the loss of her family" (24), all of whom were killed when Indians attacked their frontier cabin on the Clinch River and dragged Scott into the woods. Read together, the narratives state as clearly as is possible that the self-same landscape might be experienced as a place of either "astonishing delight" (5) or "inexpressible affliction" (21), depending on one's sex.

Clearly, despite instances of white women who, when given the choice, preferred to remain with their adoptive Indian families and despite the shift in male narratives from captivity and suffering to adoption and acculturation, certain features of the women's captivity narratives remained stubbornly resistant to change from the seventeenth century through the end of the eighteenth. To explain that resistance, we have to go beyond the observation that the Puritan *Judea capta* was easily adapted to the literary conventions governing an eighteenth-century fiction like Bleecker's *History of Maria Kittle*. We have to understand, as well, the particular historical and experiential contexts in which these narratives were composed.

The second half of the eighteenth century was a period of steady and persistent movement westward, interrupted only briefly by the Revolutionary War and later renewed on the very roads that had been built to support that war. Once peace was declared, Americans once more pushed across the Alleghenies, even as President Washington invited "the sons and daughters of the world [to] . . . *Increase and Multiply*"—especially on "the fertile plains of the Ohio," which, he boasted in a letter to Lafayette, "we have opened." It was, he assured his correspondent, a "Land of promise, with milk and honey."[11] And so it proved to many of the men who made or recouped their fortunes there. But for their wives, often enough, removal to the frontier meant only "enduring the hardships incident to the emigrant life."[12]

A case in point is the Gilman family of Exeter, New Hampshire. Joseph Gilman had been a partner in a dry-goods business from which, out of his own pocket, he helped supply New Hampshire's Revolutionary Army forces with ammunition, blankets, and clothing. The promissory notes and paper currency issued him by a provisional congress as partial payment proved worthless once hostilities were over; and, much to his chagrin, the once comfortable Gilman found himself suddenly, at age fifty-one, impoverished and in debt. Having tentatively "speculated in Ohio land" at the close of the war, he decided, in the autumn of 1788, to remove there permanently with his wife and son. It was obviously a precipitous move, and one for which his neighbors (and, presumably, his creditors) were unprepared. Recalling that sudden departure many years after the event, an Exeter friend of Rebecca Ives Gilman wrote that "one night, unknown to everybody, . . . she and her husband with all their moveables left the town on their way to Ohio. AND THE MORNING SHOWED ONLY A DESERTED HOME. Had an earthquake happened it could not have occasioned more consternation." A little neighbor boy reported "that his mother [had] cried all the day after they left Exeter," his mother being "very fond of Mrs. G. who was idolized in Exeter." Clearly, it was a close and affectionate circle that the Gilmans left behind them when they departed for the Ohio, and a circle that, had it known of their financial difficulties, would have acted to keep the family in their midst. "Friends said, if they had known their intention they should not have gone," remembered the woman from Exeter. "Thirty or 40 years afterwards," when the two met again in Philadelphia, the old friend "reported this to" Rebecca Ives Gilman. "Would to heaven they had known it, she replied."[13]

Joseph Gilman apparently found the land of milk and honey promised by Washington. Despite continuing depredations by the Indians and some initial financial uncertainty, he was nonetheless soon writing relatives in the East that he was "fully satisfied" with the "goodness" of the land (21 Aug. 1789). Of his wife we read little in his letters beyond an occasional greeting that she sends to relatives in New England and scattered comments on the state of her health. Only once, in a letter of 1790, does Gilman share anything of his wife's responses to their Marietta home: "Mrs G admires this country," he writes, "the temperance of the Climate and Singing of birds in Winter charm her" (23 Feb.). That fond assurance notwithstanding, the forty-two-year-old woman who had been so unceremoniously ushered out of her beloved Exeter home to begin the long trek over the mountains had not happily or easily adapted to life in the fledgling Marietta settlement at Fort Harmer. Years later, Rebecca Ives Gilman, now "an old lady bowed by affliction more than by years," confided a description of quite different experience to her old friend from Exeter. As the friend later recalled,

> She told me that she had learned to milk the cow and used to sit with the pail and looking up to heaven, say "are these the stars and the moon I used to see at Exeter?" And sob and cry as loud as a child, and then wipe her tears and appear before her husband as cheerful as if she had nothing to give her pain.[14]

The stars and the moon, of course, were the same, but nothing else on that frontier held their familiarity. Still, like every captive from Rowlandson on, Rebecca Ives Gilman went meekly westward and held back her tears before those who had brought her, against her will, into the wilderness.

Leslie Fiedler has written that "the male imagination . . . tends to transform the tale of captivity into one of adoption, to substitute the male dream of joining the Indians for the female fantasy of being dragged off by them" (90). Fiedler fails to acknowledge that, for the first hundred years or so, narratives of female captivity (and especially those actually written or dictated by women) generally contained neither overt nor covert allusions to the kind of sexual fantasizing he somewhat leeringly suggests here.[15] Indeed, in Francis Scott's narrative, captivity and its delineation are rather brief, serving less as a major event and more as a pretext for precipitating Scott into the central drama of her story: her suffering in the wilderness. The narrative of female captivity functioned not as any wish-fulfillment fantasy but, instead, as the only available literary form to mirror back some aspect of contemporary women's frontier reality. To Rebecca Ives Gilman, removal with her husband and son from the established and cultured town of Exeter to the edge of the frontier at the wooded confluence of the Ohio and Muskingum rivers, surrounded by hostile Indian tribes, must have seemed like removal to a desolate wilderness. Women like her could feel at least a poignant familiarity in Rowlandson's description of "turn[ing] my back upon the Town, and travel[ing] with them into the vast and desolate Wilderness, I know not whither. It is not my tongue, or pen can express the sorrows of my heart, and bitterness of my spirit, that I had at this departure" (4). The anger such a woman felt (but dared not express) toward the husband who had staked the family's future on the availability of rich lands on the frontier might thus, through the captivity narrative, be vicariously displaced onto the dusky figure of the Indian, a projection of her husband's darker side. And the anguish they dared not demonstrate may have seemed less burdensome when they read of other women, similarly "afraid of dropping a Tear" before those who had forced them into so inhospitable an environment (Mather, *Decennium* 50). Those women who came from the towns and small cities, especially, would have recognized echoes of their own bewilderments in the captivity heroine's lack of wilderness skills, empathizing with Francis Scott in her being "almost as ignorant as a child of the method of steering through the woods." At the very least, however, these narratives offered models of the passive forbearance that some readers were themselves practicing—and on a recognizable terrain. For the women forced westward against their will, in short, the enduring popularity of the female captivity narrative, virtually unchanged for over a century, rested in the fact that it provided women readers (and perhaps the writers as well) a safe vehicle through which to confront the often unhappy experiential structures of their westward migration.

Notes

1. Research for this essay was conducted during time made available to me by grants from the Rockefeller and Guggenheim foundations, for which I remain grateful. Mary Beth Norton first alerted me to the Gilman family papers in the Massachusetts Historical Society; my persistent research assistant, Patricia Riley, was indefatigable in helping me track down others in archives all across the country. Finally, I wish to express my deep appreciation to Robbins Gilman, president of the Exeter Historical Society (New Hampshire) and descendent of the Gilman family discussed here, for his generosity in giving me access to privately printed materials and miscellaneous family holdings.

2. "To My Dear Children" in *Works* 5. This antiquated usage means her heart rose in rebellion against what she first encountered on these shores.

3. In his notebook entry of 10 Feb. 1645, the Reverend John Fiske of Wenham, Massachusetts, gave an account of the conversion declaration of "Joan White from the church at Salem" (30).

4. No copy exists of the first New England edition of *The Soveraignty and Goodness of God, Together with the Faithfulness of His Promises Displayed: Being a Narrative of the Captivity and Restauration of Mrs. Mary Rowlandson.* A second edition, with the same title, appeared in 1682 (Cambridge, Mass.: Samuel Green), but extant copies are damaged and incomplete. All quotations here are from *A True History of the Captivity & Restoration of Mrs. Mary Rowlandson, a Minister's Wife in New-England; Wherein Is Set Forth, the Cruel and Inhumane Usage She Underwent amongst the Heathens, for Eleven Weeks Time; and Her Deliverance from Them. . . . Whereunto Is Annexed, a Sermon of the Possibility of God's Forsaking a People That Have Been Near and Dear to Him. Preached by Mr. Joseph Rowlandson, Husband to the Said Mrs. Rowlandson: It Being his Last Sermon* (London: Joseph Poole, 1682). The title for this first English edition was used for many subsequent American editions and is the title by which the work is more popularly known.

5. Francis Higginson, "Some brief Collections out of a letter that Mr. Higginson sent [from New England] to . . . Leicester" (1629), quoted in Carroll 11. Carroll's discussion (7–25) has been especially helpful to me here.

6. Cotton Mather's "Humiliations, follow'd with Deliverances," was first preached "At Boston Lecture . . . 1697. The Week before a General FAST" and that same year was published as *Humiliations Follow'd with Deliverances. A Brief Discourse on the Matter and Method, of That Humiliation Which Would Be an Hopeful Symptom of Our Deliverance from Calamity. Accompanied and Accommodated with a Narrative, of a Notable Deliverance Lately Received by Some English Captives, from the Hands of Cruel Indians. And Some Improvement of That Narrative. Whereto Is Added a Narrative of Hannah Swarton, containing a Great Many Wonderful Passages, Relating to Her Captivity and Deliverance* (Boston: B. Green and J. Allen, 1697).

7. Alerted to the Indians' presence in the neighborhood, Thomas Dustin was able to flee with his seven other children to a hiding place in the woods.

8. Although Swarton's time in the wilderness stretched from May 1690 through mid-February 1691, her narrative almost exclusively details the winter hardships.

9. *Decennium Luctuosum, an History of Remarkable Occurrences, in the Long War, Which New-England Hath Had with the Indian Salvages, from the Year 1688. to the Year, 1698. Faithfully Composed and Improved* (Boston: B. Green and J. Allen, 1699) 220. With only slight alterations, *Decennium Luctuosum* was later incorporated into Mather's *Magnalia Christi Americana; or, the Ecclesiastical History of New England from Its First Planting* (London, 1702).

10. It was a contrast for which American readers seemed eager. That same year, a Boston printer, E. Russell, paired the Scott narrative with yet another male narrative in his *A True and Wonderful Narrative of the Surprising Captivity and Remarkable Deliverance of Mrs. Frances Scott*, to which he added "A True and Faithful Narrative of the Surprizing Captivity and Remarkable Deliverance of Captain Isaac Stewart, Who Was Taken Prisoner by the Indians near Fort-Pitt, in the Year 1764."

11. Quoted in Henry Nash Smith 236.

12. Mary H. Emery, Exeter, New Hampshire, to Hon. Nicholas Emery, 14 Jan. 1852. Typescript. Gilman Family Papers. In this letter, Mary Emery is recounting the experiences of an elderly unnamed aunt.

13. Mary H. Emery, 14 Jan. 1852.

14. Mary H. Emery, 14 Jan. 1852.

15. An exception is "A surprising account of the Discovery of a Lady who was taken by the Indians in the year 1777, and after making her escape, she retired to a lonely Cave, where she lived nine years," attributed to the pseudonymous "Abraham Panther" (and popularly known as the Panther Captivity), which first appeared in *Bickerstaff's Almanack, for the Year . . . 1788* (Norwich: John Trumbull, 1787). In this fictional captivity, the heroine is threatened with death if she does not agree to engage in sexual relations with her captor; unwilling to comply, the maiden kills her captor and takes over his cave.

USING PERSONAL NARRATIVES IN THE CLASSROOM

The Usefulness of Women's Nontraditional Literature in the Traditional Literature-and-Composition Course

John Schilb

It seems appropriate to begin an essay on women's nontraditional literature with an excerpt from a letter, not in this case by a woman, but by a male friend of mine. I had spoken at his college on the potential roles of both composition and women's nontraditional literature in a curriculum. The following summarizes his response:

> Stay with the composing and inventing stuff. It's in vogue, and you present it energetically. Your feminist interests frankly depress me. If it gains you some interesting distaff friends, fine. If not, drop this tiresome subject. You don't even seem to have (as I do) the saving grace of refreshing irony in approaching the matter. I suspect you may even believe what you say.

I chose this passage as an introduction because I suspect that it represents more than my friend's intimately cranky advice. I think he speaks for many in our profession who would also identify writing as a matter of justifiable concern while scorning women's studies—imagining a man committed to it as an adroit seducer or a pompous fool. Of course, veteran teachers of composition will remember their own battle for intellectual status. Even now, tension persists within at least a few English departments between those who teach only upper-level classes

in literature, perhaps with dwindling enrollments, and those who
teach freshman writing classes, with enrollments substantial enough
to permit the first group the luxury of doing what they do. Yet overall,
composition has gained recognition as a legitimate field. Women's
studies has won numerous advocates and curricular berths, but it remains much more likely than composition to suffer derisive remarks of
the sort I have quoted, along with tangible forms of the sentiments
they reflect: exclusion from university policy making, denial of tenure,
budget cuts. It can fill every chair in the classroom and still emerge an
unwelcome guest in the halls of academe.

Explanations for the resistance have filled entire volumes. The
waste of educational resources it produces, however, demands more
study than it has received. Here I would like to argue the value of a
specific component in women's studies—women's nontraditional literature—for a specific component in a traditional curriculum—the literature-and-composition course. The one ought to play a part in the other
because, quite simply, it can help students read and write better. I
could launch additional defenses of women's diaries, journals, letters,
autobiographies, oral testimonies, and previously neglected contribu-
tions to poetry, drama, and fiction. The call for social justice might
have grown louder than it will in the subsequent pages; but the prag-
matic approach, the focus on sheer usefulness, may convert English
teachers armed with irony, whereas anything that smacks of ideology
might renew their assaults. Besides, personal experience compels me
to extol the benefits of using this material in courses designed for the
freshman struggling to acquire mastery of language.[1]

A definition is in order, because I realize that the term "literature
and composition" might embrace a stunning variety of meanings. Indeed, to write of "the" literature-and-composition course would prove
highly misleading if the definite article were taken to signify a species
that exists without variation in every English department throughout
the land. For some people, the term will conjure up images of students
examining an anthology of essays, usually divided into the classic
rhetorical categories, and then proceeding to undertake similar essays
of their own. For others, it will mean the introduction of students to
one of the hallowed genres, coupled with practice in writing literary
criticism. For still others, it will evoke two or three syllabi, corresponding to the tracks in which students have been placed as a result of
proficiency tests. All that I am thinking of when I refer to it is a course
assigned major responsibility for the development of first-year students' power to read and write. Even though I would like to see every
version of it employ the type of works I have in mind, I am hardly
asking for enslavement to a standardized model. I do not believe that
the texts dictate a special pedagogical technique or that their use pre-

cludes resorting to any of the so-called traditional literature. Plurality
has reigned in literature-and-composition courses, and I would have no
wish or need to weaken it.

I see four main advantages of using women's nontraditional literature in the traditional literature-and-composition course. They have a
common element that enables me to group them under the rubric of
one overriding advantage: this literature can demystify the acts of reading and writing for the student. Reading and writing no longer appear
the formidable, dreary tasks a person must complete to achieve reputa-
ble grades and success in the job market. (Not every student imputes
such a sinister mystique to them, but the least cynical among those of
us who have toiled for the cause of literacy will acknowledge the weary
suspicion that often pervades our classrooms from the first day of a
semester. While we may feel confident about our verbal expertise, we
too may begin with a lack of enthusiasm, for the art of teaching reading and writing may strike us as hopelessly esoteric.) Most of our
students will have to learn that these acts in which they will repeatedly
engage over the next several weeks are worth engaging in, that their
merit justifies sweat.

Women's nontraditional literature encourages this vital change in
outlook, first, because the writers involved are clearly not writing for
grades or jobs, or with the prospect of fame. They may have some
mundane, practical aims when they take up a pen, yet higher priorities
quickly loom: the pleasure of self-inquiry, the desire to validate their
lives through vivid accounts. The more spiritual incentives to write
become strong enough that the writers sacrifice time for rest or chores
in utter dedication to print. Obviously I am ignoring the many private
writings by women that are little more than banal reportage, devoid of
the verbal embellishment and the sharp illumination of self and world
that for me characterize "literature," especially if the label is not restricted to a fixed canon. The writing by women to which I am applying
it here provides inspiring proof that the effort to record experience,
whether on the Nebraska frontier or in a modern dormitory, can have a
humanistic function beyond vocational rewards. More precisely, it
demonstrates to students that ordinary people can use writing to learn
about themselves and the universe in which they dwell, to explore
their identity and their society, to conceptualize what it means to be a
particular person in a particular place at a particular moment. If writing is perceived merely as an ordeal to endure for the sake of escaping
a teacher's punishment, its quality can amount to only so much; if it is
perceived as a method of raising and perhaps answering questions
crucial to the whole enterprise of living, it stands a significantly
greater chance of being done well. By supplying evidence that writing
can operate for anyone as a powerfully relevant heuristic—sustaining

life as well as clarifying it—the literature I am advocating might have more capacity to prod students than anthology pieces culled from the *New Yorker* have.

One of the most instructive and poignant comments about writing that I have ever come across appears in a book entitled *Mollie: The Journal of Mollie Dorsey Sanford in Nebraska and Colorado Territories, 1857–1866*. Frustrated by the limited job opportunities open to her in the Nebraska City of 1859, Mollie indicates what she prefers to sewing, the labor that occupies her at present: ". . . I am sure I shall never pose as an author or writer. But I do often wish that I might be something more than a mere machine" (98). Ironically, she conceives a literary career as the marketing of doggerel verse, unfortunate examples of which are threaded through her volume. The contemporary reader can observe that she did become a writer, albeit in another sense. The very journal in which she registers her dismay turned out to be an impressive chronicle of her travels west, along with her internal rearrangements of thought. Her descriptions of a trek by wagon train, an attempted rape, encounters with Indians, the sordid chaos of Denver, and other real-life dramas prove compelling. However, the psychological dimension of her story earns the closer regard of a literature-and-composition class, for it reveals a woman grappling with difficult issues in a most unmachinelike manner. Throughout the nine years the journal covers, Mollie struggles in it to resolve the schism she feels between her duty to her parents and her longing for distant adventure, between her respect for religious scruples and her irrepressible spirit, between her concept of a heroine as a domestic, quietly virtuous woman and her concept of a heroine as the center of grand exploits. In short, she uses writing to interrogate the self, refusing to accept the role of a machine that blindly adheres to prescribed rituals. As I have noted, too many students view writing as mechanical drudgery, compositions as products to be churned out according to a teacher's program. The dissociation of writing from machinehood that Mollie avows and practices, her affirmation of writing as an informative human activity, can initiate in them a fertile reversal of opinion.

A second advantage of women's nontraditional literature is that it can help students recognize the importance of developing their own voices as writers, help them understand the concept of a writer's voice in the first place. Several authorities on the teaching of writing have decried the tendency of students to flaunt in their essays language that is pretentious, vague, and willfully dull.[2] Perhaps such indulgence stems from the belief that Teacher craves formal diction; perhaps it echoes years of vocabulary drills. No matter what the cause, the result is a barrier to readability and to the writer's chance to discover truths about the imperfect human he or she is. Besides acquiring the motivation to write, students at the beginning of a literature-and-composition course have to grow alert to the self-image a writer's style projects, so that they can choose words that will express their real personality. They need to find out the kind of person they sound like in their writing before they can thoroughly employ writing to explore who they are. Now, any mode of discourse, however formal, can permit the student to achieve self-discovery in a sense, and most literature-and-composition courses must eventually make students adept at impersonal prose. But to instill that initial sensitivity to voice and to its connection with the potential of writing for assisting self-discovery, autobiographical readings and papers seem highly appropriate. The personal tone of Mollie and other nontraditional women writers renders them excellent models for study and imitation.

Dramatic shifts of voice in *The Maimie Papers*, for example, reveal equally dramatic changes in the author, therefore telling much about the relation of style to self. The book is a collection of letters written during the period 1910–22 to the Boston philanthropist Fanny Quincy Howe by a poverty-stricken former prostitute, whom the editors give the pseudonym "Maimie." In the first letter, Maimie's insecurity threatens to overwhelm her desire to communicate with someone who might sympathize with her:

> I have heard of you and sort of kept in touch with you through our friend Mr. Welsh. He told me of how ill you were, and I was genuinely and sincerely sorry; and when I learned you were well, I wanted to write but did not because of the same feeling that I had, right along, that you thought me particularly silly and very rude. All that feeling of resentment that I nursed against those who were kindest to me has all gone, and I am now deeply grateful to them and to you, too, for insisting on being friendly to such a "chump" (that is the only word I know, in the English language, that exactly expresses what I am). In the past week, you have been in my mind very often—and I wanted to write but that same obstinate feeling comes to me, and I ask myself all sorts of questions as to why you would want to hear from me. I am writing now, anyway—   (Rosen and Davidson 1)

By contrast, the tone of Maimie's last extant letter resonates with the basic confidence she has gained through her search for economic independence, her deepening capacity to form human relationships, her lasting bond with Fanny, and her ability to derive knowledge of herself from her writing:

> We are in a hotel, but it is one of those that have full arrangements for cooking and housekeeping. Bennie had selected this place be-

fore I came. It is desirable, inasmuch as it is new and spotlessly clean, but it is patronized almost entirely by big, fat Jewish ladies and their thin nervous husbands. However, I use the downstairs attractions very sparingly, so avoid contact. I have not met anyone here, so take it that they do not find me any more worthwhile than I find them. (416)

Yes, we can brand her a snob. But a more important point for the class to consider is how the juxtaposition of the two letters illustrates both a difference in language and a difference in the writer's attitude toward herself. Students then can see how their experiments with the language of autobiographical writing can help them arrive at an edifying personal voice.

An oral testimony can spur enlightenment about voice in another way. Because it would constitute a transcription of a person's spoken commentary—perhaps edited, perhaps not—it would enable students to investigate the relation between voice in speech and voice in writing. Ought they to be absolutely identical? If not, what adjustments might have to occur in the crossover to print? What modes of discourse would demand what modulations of the spoken voice? In what writing situations would this particular woman's oral testimony encounter acceptance or rejection? Although I have not taken a survey, I would guess that many literature-and-composition courses neglect taking time to sensitize students to the differences and similarities of the spoken and the written word. Oral testimonies could be a highly effective tool in the process.

A third advantage of women's nontraditional literature is that it invariably leads students to consider the process by which human beings come to discern patterns in their lives. It points out to them how a sense of narrative develops and functions in the existence of ordinary people, not just in the approach of Dickens and his critics to *Bleak House*. By seeing how a diarist or correspondent or autobiographer becomes aware of recurrent themes or events in the act of writing and by discovering for themselves, as readers of the works, motifs that the original writer may have overlooked, students realize the centrality of narrative in human thought and the ability of their own minds to construct it. Tracing the stages of Mollie's conflicts or the steps in Maimie's quest for dignity may, in fact, better prepare them to cope with the intricacies of a Dickensian plot and to grasp the evolving structures of their own essays.

Editorial intervention in the shaping of women's narratives ought not to be swept aside. On the contrary, recognition of it can again help students decide what characterizes a person's story. *The Maimie Papers* bears the marks of a textual editor who deleted sections to make the book short enough for commercial distribution. One assignment I give in connection with it asks students to write a letter to the editor, defending her inclusion of a particular passage and recommending the excision of another. They are therefore obligated to decide which strands in Maimie's writing are major and which simply marginal. Not everyone, of course, entertains the same vision of coherence in analyzing the text, but the disparity makes for lively in-class debates.

Finally, women's nontraditional literature seems advantageous to me for the very reason English teachers might hate it or dread it: the challenge it poses to the alleged sanctity of the traditional canon and of the traditional applications of the term "literature." Its presence in a literature classroom suggests that the canon and the whole concept of literature ought to embrace more works than they have and that works previously enshrined need defense. Worse, it suggests that the omissions have resulted at least partly from sexism, in the form of a failure to understand or appreciate the only kinds of writing that many women have been able to produce within the narrow sphere assigned them by a patriarchal society.[3] That many present-day academics abhor such implications can hardly be surprising. It can seem monstrously fatiguing to assume the burdens they seem to demand: looking for works not presented in graduate school, justifying as literature the works one does select for a course, attaching some communicable definition to the word in the first place or letting the class view it as problematic, remaining attentive to the role of politics in life and art and decisions about the two. However, a plunge into metaphysical angst is not inevitable. My experience tells me that the teacher who advocates women's nontraditional literature and adopts a disputatious stance toward entrenched beliefs about literature can feel liberated, for new areas of scholarship open up, new dimensions of literary criticism arise, new connections between one's discipline and social history come forth. The excitement that can accompany these developments must not itself drift away from a firm sense of responsibility. After all, to confer the prestige of art on a journal merely because a woman wrote it, or to denigrate a play merely because the critical fraternity has revered it, merely shows intellectual slack. But so does the automatic acceptance of customary notions about literature, and the frequency of the second act threatens more to drain vitality, sooner or later, from the teaching of English.

In this essay, however, I have been more concerned with the impact of literature-and-composition classes on students. I mentioned earlier that women's nontraditional literature can demystify reading and writing for them. The most prominent feature of the process is indeed the skepticism it encourages toward the standards of literary evaluation—articulated or not—that the course has normally upheld.

Some first-year students, dependent on rules and authorities, express chagrin when they discover they will not receive sermons on the classics. Most others, though, relish the chance to probe the various definitions literature can have and the various links the forming of the canon has had with the nonacademic world they inhabit. They feel empowered in their new awareness that the judgments of past critics are fallible, that the study of literature can help them grapple with their society's and perhaps their own biases, that they can play an active part in the shaping of a literary heritage. In fact, they realize to their delight that they may contribute to the corpus of worthwhile literature by rescuing a grandmother's diary from an attic, setting down the oral testimony of a neighbor, even writing one of their own papers for the class. These changes in perception should not let loose an anarchy of personal tastes. Once more, a sense of responsibility is important. Students who spurn public arguments about criteria and fix on private, intuitive ideals of literature demonstrate nothing more than egocentricity and lose their opportunity to enhance the reputation of their chosen works. Actually, skepticism toward conventional wisdom about literature demands increased mental exertion, for students must then carefully discriminate among the writings of the past and argue about the principles they follow, whereas before they could sit back as passive recipients of an officially certified culture.

I conclude with at least one conspicuous omission of my own. Although I have briefly indicated what some of the characteristics of literature are for me, I have neglected to provide an extensive analysis of the concept, together with an elaborate defense of my own understanding of it. Not because I wanted to dodge the issue—even if it is complex. Nor because the explanation would take more pages than this book might contain—even if it would. My sole excuse is that I do want to convey the impression that the subject is problematic and hence should be dealt with as such in a literature-and-composition course, whatever its reading materials. Certainly I have a number of ideas about literature and the canon, which I throw out to students in our discussions of women's nontraditional literature—not necessarily for them to swallow, just to chew. Frankly, we have never yet managed to ingest all of our ideas and regurgitate an indestructible aesthetic theory. Still, when they walk out the door at the end of the semester, I am left believing that they are more literate because of their exposure to women's private writings, if more full of doubt.

Perhaps my friend would declare such results contradictory. And perhaps, in the long run, he and other teachers of English will come to appreciate this resource only through their own experiments with it. Fine with me. But the weapon of irony must be lowered, at least somewhat, for a true investigation to begin.

Notes

1. When I refer to students, obviously I have in mind both men and women. Just as obviously, I might have focused on how the literature has a particular relevance to the lives of female students. That subject, however, would make for a whole other article, and I wanted to stress here that both sexes can benefit from the material.

2. William E. Coles, Jr., offers a roundup of labels hurled at typical student prose (19).

3. I use the word "partly" because the teacher of this literature could and should look at other factors like racism and class prejudice.

A Lost Diary Found

The Art of the Everyday

Dure Jo Gillikin

The first semester I taught the course on women's nontraditional literature, my major focus was the diary, with minor emphasis on oral
history. The chief texts were *Revelations*, edited by Moffat and Painter,
which contains excerpts from the diaries of many women, the famous
and the obscure; *The Journal of Mollie Dorsey Sanford*, an account of
her homesteading adventures west of the Missouri from 1857 to 1866;
May Sarton's *Journal of a Solitude*, a complete work by a well-known
writer, but free of artificiality; and *Heart Songs: The Intimate Diaries
of Young Girls*, edited by Laurel Holliday. Shorter readings included
Alice Walker's "In Search of Our Mothers' Gardens," Lillian Schlissel's
"Women's Diaries on the Western Frontier," and Elizabeth Hampsten's "This Is Christmas Eve and I Am in Tintah." For written assignments, the students read and analyzed the complete diary of one of the
women in *Revelations*; kept a diary during the semester, including any
material they chose, and wrote an analysis of it; and examined an
unpublished diary or did an oral history.

Two in-class presentations brought the diary to life. During one
class session, a former composition student talked about the diary she
had been keeping for seventeen years, ever since the death of her
husband. The published diary and the mandatory keeping of a diary
for the course brought valuable insights, but none so real, so present,
as did this diary in progress, kept willingly for survival, clarity, and
companionship. The students' questions showed progress in their perceptions of what a diary is, its forms, contents, and purposes. This
experience also provided vital connecting links between the published
diaries, the ones my students were keeping, and the hands-on experience of locating and analyzing an unpublished diary in Staten Island,
Brooklyn, or Manhattan.

The second class presentation that generated enthusiasm for research occurred while the students were engaged with the unpublished diaries, their own as well as the few found ones. I had accidentally discovered an unpublished diary by an unknown person in the cupboard at the head of my bed. Too good to be true—an unpublished diary I did not know I had. Bought from an antique dealer in East Haddam, Connecticut, by a friend of mine, the diary had got lost in the after-vacation shuffle. But there it was, just when I needed it most. By that time, the students were asking me how to approach the diaries. In-process and unpublished diaries elicit a kind of awe and, at the same time, stimulate questions about the value of such writings as literature, as history, as sociology. Bringing the East Haddam diary to class for a practical demonstration heightened our involvement and appreciation. An additional advantage was that no textbook posed the questions or hinted at the answers. The students had to tailor their questions themselves; they had to identify the diarist, understand her time and place. Finding the answers necessitates exploration and all its concomitant thrills. There are too many worn paths in criticism and biography that discourage or dull the would-be traveler. Undoubtedly the critics who brought Kate Chopin or Jean Rhys to the public's attention this century experienced the rewarding thrill of discovery. For my students and for me, however, these diaries provided our first experience of opening roads into new territory.

In writing or any other enterprise, however, worn paths do offer initial access to a new entity; and since a diary is a form of literature, it is only natural to ask literary questions about it, questions as basic as who is the writer? how do I find out? (questions rarely asked in literature classes unless the time period is medieval). Why do diarists rarely identify themselves or the other people in the diaries other than by first name or initial? What content (deeds, thoughts), what word choice indicate identity? character? gender? Can the person from whom you obtained the diary offer any information? Once you know the name, is this individual in *Who's Who* or, more appropriately, *Who Was Who*? What are the relations of the other people in the diary to the diarist? To one another? When and why are they together? What do they do together? What revelations about character are given? Then there are the multitudinous questions about plot—the crises, resolutions, significance. Often more puzzling and sometimes impossible to answer are the questions about setting. Discussions of setting in literature classes have become routine, but trying to piece together the names of towns and rivers and restaurants from the entries in a diary is not only necessary, it is enticing. The student researching an unpublished diary is discovering a new world and in writing about it shares that discovery. After identifying the place, the researcher can check the obituary columns of the local newspapers for more information on the diarist, her family, friends, and accomplishments, perhaps even a photograph.

In college, professors usually assign books by known authors. It is altogether different to search for a text and to be responsible for identifying the author and evaluating style and content. Such a reading and analysis of the diary hones literary judgment as students consider the story, how it is told, and, most importantly, how the diarist un-self-consciously creates herself and her world. Out of necessity, students develop research capabilities quickly, and they show a willingness and a pleasure that are rarely evident when they write the usual term paper. Analyzing diaries helps them gain a fresh perspective on all literature, serves a purpose beyond a course grade, beyond mastery of a story, poem, or novel. It can, and often does, uncover new knowledge, new literary forms, new pleasures and purposes in reading.

The published book comes in either hardback or paperback, is printed, has a professional artist's cover, and costs us something. We buy books in stores or borrow them from libraries or friends. Unpublished diaries, though, we have to search for in historical places, antique stores, attics, basements, libraries, museums. Writers of books earn money for their writing, win prizes, attain fame. Diarists hide their books, denigrate them, write them on paper of any size, shape, or description; they lose them, forget about them, use them for their own purposes, not for somebody else's—unless, of course, like Marie Bashkirtseff or Anaïs Nin, they are sure that their musings and meetings with others are worthy of public attention (though it is one thing for Bashkirtseff, an unknown, to hope for fame through the diary and another for Nin, a published novelist and hobnobber with the literary lions). But let me emphasize that the diaries I am writing about here are those written with no aim toward posterity. They are the everyday diaries of people who did not expect them to be pulled or pushed into the light of day.

There are, I'll wager, more forms for private diaries than there are for novels. When individuals write for themselves, without desire or hope of reaching the public's eye, they feel none of the published writer's pressures—no fear of failing to create an exciting plot or live an exciting life, no straining to find the perfect word, no forcing to make a unified story; and the forms, words, structures, and plots they use often startle with their newness.

Some diarists write in bits and pieces as they steal or take time from their lives to write something down. Such brevity is more than the soul of wit, it is the vast world made manageable as it is daily converted into fragments that contain the whole. Others live their lives in their diaries, not in the world. Brevity, for them, flies out the window. For diaries as for traditional literature there are tried and true forms. Dimestores, bookstores, department stores, and crafts fairs sell diaries—lined or unlined, leatherbound or clothbound, at varying prices—for those who plan to keep parts of their lives on paper, not trusting to memory, unreliable and unpredictable as it is.

The East Haddam diary that I took to class for discussion is one of those diaries. Its once black leather has now faded to snuff brown, its back broken, the cloth and ridges of its constituent pamphlets clearly visible through a cheesecloth covering. In gold, on its cover, is the title given to it by the Samuel Ward Manufacturing Company, Boston, Massachusetts, copyrighted 1892–1913. The first line of the title is *A Line a Day*, in big, simulated handwritten flourishes (little egos as well as big egos keep diaries); the second line, *Five Year Diary*, commits the diarist to a definite block of time. Anonymity and time—these are two of the chief prerequisites for diary writing. Underneath this line is a gold illustration that looks like a fancier form of the fleur-de-lis or perhaps wheat sheafs from Demeter. This diary, unlike any book sold at Brentano's or even Womanbooks, has a lock, its gold plating now tarnished and its key gone. The lock is not locked, but the strong leather thong that connected front with back has obviously been severed either by knife or by impatient hands unwilling to test the lock. As an object, then, this diary was of some value to its owner, increasing pride of ownership as well as the worthiness of the contents.

Inside the diary, Samuel Ward and Company, in a preface, have instructed the diarist on how to proceed. In it, they speak directly to the diarist, knowing her full well, or so they suppose.

> You have neither the time, nor the inclination, possibly, to keep a full diary. Suppose, however, out of the multitude of matters that crowd each day, you jot down in a line or two those most worthy of remembrance.

To ensure that the diarist does not exceed her instructions, they allot each entry only 2½ inches, with ⅛ of an inch thrown in for good measure. Matters, not meditations; what you did, not what you thought about what you did—that is the tyranny of this format. Each page of the diary has room for five days from five different years, making it easier for the diarist and the reader to detect patterns. After telling what kind of diary to keep, they tell the diarist why: "Such a book will be of the greatest value in after years." Their next statement succinctly summarizes what all such diaries do: "What a record of events, incidents, joys, sorrows, successes, failures, things accomplished, things attempted." And the diarist, following their advice, does enter the events; however, she rarely places a value judgment on them. She has no need to, for the values are inherent; for example, when her close friend falls ill, becomes hospitalized, and dies and she notes these events in her daily entries, she does not express her fear, grief, or helplessness. The statements of fact carry these feelings.

In literary terms, the diarist's entry for each day forms a narrative, within which are smaller narratives that may be new or may build on previous entries. The plots and subplots start out and reach a peak and subside while new ones start and old ones end. Others start and go nowhere. Inevitably, the whole diary forms an open-ended narrative of the diarist's life for that five-year period. It is one thing to look at a work of literature like *Antigone* and note that it has a beginning, middle, and end and quite another to look at the record of that person's life kept in this sparsely objective, record-keeping fashion and to see that person's life grow and take shape as you read. Individuals do construct their lives.

To catch the calms and tempests of a life, to see the stories it tells as they develop or disappear, to see the patterns and images it evokes and sometimes repeats, to note the entrances and exits of characters— that is what the diary does, most impressively in its sparsest form, the record-keeping diary.

Such diaries, though inherently autobiographical, are not the carefully thought-out, engineered narratives of the published life story. No hint of how-this-event-made-me-who-I-am hovers over the day-to-day entries. Instead, the reader lives that life word by word as it is written by the diarist. Diaries can be the most direct route to another person's essence. This organic form makes the diary more valuable, more authentic, because it demonstrates the pervasiveness of narratives in all lives. With diaries, too, especially ones like the East Haddam diary, the reader often does not know who the diarist is and must do research to establish actual identity. More important, a diary provides the essence of who as it relates to the what of a life.

Identifying the East Haddam diarist was no simple problem; in fact, I had incorrectly assumed that the blue address label pasted in the front of the diary would be sufficient. However, as I read, I realized that Pennsylvania, the state on the address label, did not match the state—Connecticut—so frequently mentioned in the diary. After reading several months' entries, I had enough information about the writer to return to East Haddam. There, when I related these data to the antique dealer who had sold the diary, he said Anne Rogers Minor might be the diarist. But when I told him the last date of the diary was 21 December 1946, he was certain Minor had died long before that. *Who Was Who* (1950) saved the day because it listed her death date as 24 October 1947. The conclusive identifying reference is the entry dated 30 September 1945, when she was settling her affairs since death was approaching.

Sunday. Cloudy. Cooler. Irene and I worked all morning on studio. Getting out *Father's Minor* pictures to show Mr. Douglass of The Lyman Allen Museum & in straightening up mine for him to see. Had dinner upstairs. & worked more after nap. Set clocks back. (my italics)

The key identifying phrase is underlined. Because of haste or age, it is likely that she inadvertently placed the possessive ending on "Father" instead of on "Minor." "Father Minor's pictures" does make sense, especially when this diary entry is juxtaposed with part of an article on Anne Rogers Minor that appeared in the DAR's *National Magazine*:

> she exemplifies to a refreshing degree the beautiful school of older painters to which her father-in-law, the noted Robert C. Minor, belonged and whose pupil she was, living in his home after her marriage and absorbing the atmosphere of his studio, which is now her own. Mrs. Minor has had pictures in many noted exhibitions, and has held exhibitions of her own.   ("Notable Daughter" 42)

As student and daughter-in-law, Mrs. Minor was the logical choice for caretaker of Robert Minor's paintings. The East Haddam diary contains many references to her own paintings and to three 1942 exhibitions in which she placed them, two in Connecticut and one in Norfolk, Virginia—the last was devoted solely to a showing of forty-six of her pictures. The same DAR article also describes her paintings:

> As an artist Mrs. Minor has a wonderful power of putting on canvas the inner spirit of the scenes among which she has lived and worked. The rugged New England coasts, sunny spring and autumn woods, broad pastures and picturesque fishing boats and wharves are her many themes, all depicted with a technical skill and deep love of nature in all its moods which fairly makes of her canvas a living thing, full of sun and wind and clouds and waves. (42)

Woodland Pool, Gray Day, and *Autumn Flowers*—titles of her paintings mentioned in the diary—seem to substantiate further the diarist's identity.

Although Anne Rogers Minor thought of herself primarily as an artist, she was also noted for her work in the DAR. From 1920 to 1923, she was president general, the highest office in the DAR. Throughout the diary, there are numerous references to her activities on the national, state, and local levels. Although nineteen years had passed since her term as president general, she attended the Chicago national congress in 1942. In her diary on 27 April, she noted that she was writing a speech for that meeting. At the congress, she nominated someone for president general, attended the national chairman's breakfast, and gave greetings at the opening and the benediction at the close. On a local level, she often mentions her attendance at the Lucretia Shaw chapter; on one occasion, she attended dressed in a Martha Washington gown and wig.

This article and the date in *Who Was Who* corroborate a third piece of internal evidence. Both cite her as director of the Connecticut State Farm for Women. The diary entry dated 8 July 1942 reads: "Got official appointment from Governor as Director of State Farm." Apparently, she served in this capacity for many years and took her duties seriously, as several entries verify.

Another diary entry, dated 2 March 1942, further matches information given in these two sources. Both list her as a trustee of American International College, and this diary entry reads: "Betty and I drove to Springfield to Am. Int. College Trustees meeting. . . ."

That Anne Rogers Minor had something of a national reputation, assuredly connected with her DAR work, is indicated by these entries from her diary on the occasion of her eightieth birthday. On 7 April 1944, she writes:

> *Friday.*   Pleasant. My birthday. 80 years old. Oh my: I do not feel that old. Miss Betty so much. She always came in my room and said, "I am glad you were born." Dear Betty: 49 cards came this morning from all over the country.

And in the entry dated 8 April 1944 she notes, "Many more birthday cards came, over 200 of them."

These matching pieces of external and internal evidence convince me that the diary in my possession need no longer be called the East Haddam diary; it is Anne Rogers Minor's diary.

In this diary, we have the events of a life—selected, yes, but with no aim to tell a well-rounded story. The events range from three painting exhibitions to a nap after lunch, from opening and closing the meeting of a national organization to a pleasure drive around her own home town, from directing the Connecticut State Farm for Women to savoring the September scallops harvested in the water only a few yards from her house—daily events abut significant events, ongoing events and deadend events. There is no weighting of these episodes. Any emphasis placed on them comes from the readers of the diary: the primary reader (the diarist herself), the owner of the diary (me), or the wider audience that the publication of this diary will create. This jotting-down-of-events diary engages readers, making them participatory authors as some avant-garde novelists deliberately encourage today.

No longer solely spectator, the reader helps to create the story by adding in the details based on experience and on readings in literature, history, psychology, and sociology. Such a diary further demonstrates the oneness of events—their democracy, if you will—as it details the dailiness of life. Drinking eight glasses of water each day is an ordinary event, and yet, without it, no life. Foundation of all that we do, these routine activities create the ambiences that sustain us as we move from them into the not-so-ordinary aspects of our lives.

This diary, like many others, contains a pattern of repeated elements in each entry, a few dictated by format and the rest primarily by diarist's design. For example, the month and the century are basic to any diary's printed format. Writing in the year and the day of the week, the diarist begins her responsibility and places herself in a specific time period. The first date of this diary is 1 January 1942, a Thursday in the United States' first full year of World War II. The diarist's references to the war show something about her as well as about the country. The scarcity of such entries illustrates the war's lack of impact, although she feels some discomforts—for example, the blackouts and the search for ration stamps, even when she is in Chicago attending the national DAR congress: "Then went to City Hall to sugar rationing place. They sent me to another place where I found that I was too late" (8 May 1942). The sighting of a convoy off Virginia Beach makes the war visibly present, as does fire in the sky: "I saw what I thought was a burning aroplane about 3 AM. as I looked out of window and saw what I thought was a plane on fire. Probably a flare dropped" (6 May 1943). In two entries she responds to the end of the war in Europe: "Heard over radio that Germany had surrendered but it was not to be officially announced until tomorrow" (7 May 1945) and "Heard President Truman announced V. Day also later Mr. Churchill" (8 May 1945). This vital news, however, is sandwiched between her daily weather report—"Pleasant in AM. Growing cloudy. Rain."—and this entry—"Wrote. Nap. Polly, Eunice went for errands to [illegible] & [illegible] P. O. to mail letters & to [illegible] for groceries. Then to Niantic for groceries and fish." Can there be a better example of the everyday side by side with the newsworthy? Writing, napping, food, mail—these daily activities are her sustenance, the concerns of a woman probably writing her memoirs, always conserving her energy with a brief sleep, communicating with the outside world, detailing the way food comes to her through her considerate and loving friends. And, in between, the details broadcasting peace. The longest entries describing the war's close are these two: "Word of Japan's acceptance of surrender terms. President Truman gave word that Japs had surrendered at 7 PM. Whistles blowing, horns & a few fire crackers but very quiet here. I went to sleep" (14 Aug. 1945); "President had declared a two days holiday—no mail & most stores closed" (15 Aug. 1945). The other details in these entries describe the weather and name the people with her.

Such is the art of the everyday. Lean yet incisive details that capture the core of the war and of an aged American woman. Rendered clearly and calmly, these facts create her character—the imperturbability of age and experience that lets her observe, then sleep peacefully. It would be interesting to match these World War II entries with the ones from World War I, when she was in her prime. As an official of the DAR, she was able to participate in international peace solutions. The DAR article mentioned her contribution to this effort:

> When the United States Government was seeking a place for the meeting of the plenary sessions of the great Conference on the Limitation of Armament, Mrs. Minor offered Memorial Continental Hall for this purpose, which offer was accepted at once with grateful thanks by Secretary Hughes. (42)

But in the 1942–46 diary, none of this surfaces. She is a woman out of the fray, savoring the sunshine of her last years.

A world at war for the second time in the twentieth century thus provides the largest background for her life at this period. The smaller but much closer backdrop is the day's weather, that ubiquitous, uncontrollable aspect of each day of her life. It is the basic component of her entries, and she almost always includes it. The weather commands her attention. It is her daily element, her way of touching the pulse at the heart of existence. These reports further show her keen eye and her deft verbal touch that create miniature landscapes in words.

After the weather report in each day's entry comes the heart of the diary—people met, food eaten, places visited, health checked, things done. The details, though brief and objective, are nevertheless the snippets of plot that trigger memory, keeping it permanent and tangible. This major portion of the entry forms many narratives, several of which continue in other entries, providing the traditional "What then?" suspense that gathers momentum until there are enough events to satisfy the reader's quest for a more complete sense of who the diarist was and what she did. The entries add up to one large narrative that covers a five-year period from 1 January 1942 to 21 December 1946. Chiefly, it tells the story of a woman—painter, DAR member, and philanthropist—who is seventy-seven in the first entry and eighty-two in the last, written a little less than a year from her death on 24 October 1947. This larger narrative breaks down into two parts: 1942, her last fully active year; and 1943–46, notable for its account of the sad necessities of aging—physical decay, the putting away of the things of this world, and arrangements for burial.

Her career as a painter peaked in 1942 when she placed pictures in three exhibitions: the New Haven Pottery and Clay Club Show; the Connecticut Academy Exhibition on 28 March; and an exhibition, devoted to forty-six of her paintings, that opened in Norfolk on 12 April. As if this were not enough, in September she went on a seven-day painting trip to Gloucester with her friend Amy.

To demonstrate the pattern of her entries, illustrate their character, and show how small narratives build into larger ones, I now list fourteen entries in the order of their occurrence. I have omitted three, the ones for 3, 5, and 11 April, because they do not refer directly to the exhibition.

March 30

Mond.   Ground covered in snow that had gathered in night. Worked all day with William packing pictures. Read in eve.

March 31

Tues.   Cloudy. Moderate. Wrote and helped pack rest of pictures. Kay came in and stayed for highballs.

April 1

Wed.   Cloudy and sunshine. Wrote all morning. Express man came and took pictures for exhibition. 13 of them. Drove to N. H. to get my pictures not exhibited. L. & B. going with me. Went to S. to see about getting reservations for Norfolk.

April 2

Thurs.   Clear, warm. Did laundry work & writing in AM. Laid down a while & then B & I drove to New Milford to get my ticket and reservations for Norfolk. Read in evening.

April 4

Sat.   Cloudy. Warm. Wrote and mended all AM. Had Mary Conroy for hair in afternoon. Took nap and read for rest of day. Had telegram from Amy saying pictures had arrived.

April 6

Mon.   Clear, beautiful, hot. Packing to go to Norfolk. Min & Betty drove me to New Milford to 3:46 train ar. NY 6:06. Put bags in pkg. room & went up to Mollie's then for dinner Chas. came & M. [illegible] took me to train. Met a young girl who was put in my car. Douglas Brooks.

April 7

Tues.   My birthday. I cannot realize I am 78 years old. Ar in Norfolk on time. Amy met me. We did errands and then came home. Amy had had all pictures unpacked. Took nap and wrote.

April 8

Wed.   Cloudy. Clearing. Warm. Worked all am marking prices on pictures. After lunch put screw eyes on small pictures. Took nap.

April 9

Thursday.   Wrote and worked on pictures all am. [illegible] came and we put pictures in truck and Amy & I went over in her car and got them up in gallery.

April 10

Friday.   Rain and cloudy. Amy & I started at 9:30 to go to Museum to hang pictures. Arthur White came & did most of hanging. We went out & got a sandwich and Coca Cola. Home at 4:30.

April 12

Sun.   Clear, cold, beautiful. To Church with Frank. To opening of Exhibition in afternoon. Mrs. Swan called up at lunchtime and asked Amy about buying a picture for Museum. About 100 came to see show.

April 13

Monday.   Clear. Cool. Beautiful. Home all morning. Amy and I met Mrs. Swan at the Art Museum to talk about a picture for the permanent collection of the Museum.

April 14

Tues.   Clear. Calm. Beautiful. Amy & I off for Williamsburg at 9:30. Took lunch. Went through Yorktown and drove about Williamsburg. I stopped at Museum on way home. Ar 4 PM.

April 15

Wed.   Pleasant in AM. Warm showers in PM. Ar. from Norfolk at 6:40. Took bags to G. C. Station. Biltmore for breakfast. Lord & Taylors where I bought 2 hats. To Gallerys then to Mollie's for lunch. Mrs. Bingham there. 3:46 train for N. Milford. B & Min met me. Stewart & K here for dinner.

Of course, the narrative—the Norfolk exhibition—does not begin on 30 March 1942, nor does it entirely conclude on 12 April 1942, when the exhibition opens. It could include the days of painting, selecting the pictures for the exhibition, framing and naming them, not to mention that moment when the diarist chose to become a painter. The narratives in each day's entry, of necessity, are minimalistic. Just as pointillist painters use small dots to shape boats, trees, and people into a landscape, so the diarist selects bits of plot from each day and by accretion creates the sum and substance of her life.

The entry dated 30 March, for example, contains three threads of narrative. First is the plot of that day's weather, one step in the process as winter changes to spring. Alone, the words form a static narrative, but read successively they take on movement just as a series of still pictures flipped by hand forms a movie. The weather, we might say, is nature's plot. And the diarist is ever the faithful recorder of its progress.

The second thread of plot—the narrative unit about her Norfolk exhibition—builds from entry to entry to form a more complete narrative, which in turn is a step in the larger narrative of the diarist's year as a painter.

The third thread records her habit of reading in the evening. This part of her existence is not the daily fixture that the weather report is, though there are enough entries in the diary to indicate that she read herself to sleep each night. She never develops this thread of narrative by recording any reaction to what she read. The reading functions not to show her as critic but to ease her into sleep. Only rarely does she name the book she is reading: once she mentions that she was reading some science, and on another occasion she notes: "Read of 12 years with Mrs. Eddy by Tomlinson."

The entries on the Norfolk exhibition have other bits of plots that begin and end (her relations with Min and Betty, who take her to and from the train; with Mollie, whose hospitality she enjoys whenever she passes through New York City; with the stranger on the train; and with Amy who helps her with the physical and bargaining details of her art). These are the bare bones of plot, yet personality surfaces when one reads the facts successively. What personalizes the diarist is her emphasis on the weather and her willingness to help pack the pictures, although she obviously needs other people's help to do anything. Other identifying features are her habits of writing, taking a nap, and concluding the day by reading. In celebration of her exhibition, no doubt, she stops at Lord and Taylor to buy two hats. That she has good friends shows her ability to create loyalty and her willingness to be helpful in the most mundane of tasks. She is precise in stating times of day, arrival and departure times, names of places—New Milford, Norfolk, Grand Central Station, the Biltmore. The Norfolk exhibition was a notable event in her life, yet she is never self-congratulatory—she simply states the facts. Here, as in the rest of the diary, it is the amount of space given in the entries and the frequency of reference that convey her sense of a topic's importance.

Such then was one part of the year 1942. The diary contains many more narratives about her painting and about her activities in the DAR and other philanthropic activities. But they evidently were her last hurrah, for at the end of the year she falls ill with a cold and never again makes so many trips or does so much.

The rest of the diary, 1943–46, narrates the last years of a woman who is old, suffering from ill health, and making plans for her fast-approaching death (a word she never mentions). No sentimentality here—she simply writes her will, buys her cemetery plot, gets her papers in order, and sells off her property. In this way, the diary is like May Sarton's journals or Florida Scott Maxwell's *The Measure of My Days*. All three are the diary accounts of women in old age. Minor's diary is different, however, in that it presents the sparsest of facts, does no philosophizing; ultimately Minor is unaware that her life is a narrative as she jots it down. It just unfolds facts, which speak eloquently and courageously of a life soon to be ended. Problems with her teeth, arthritis, and anemia (perhaps leukemia) afflict her during this period, necessitating constant nursing, rest, hospitalization, heat treatments, "liver shots."

The art of the everyday—its simplicity, its compression, its clarity—is apparent in the entry dated 8 August 1943:

> Up early. Got dressed & to NL to dentist to have tooth extracted at 9 AM. It came out in three pieces & he had to cut gum to get it all out. Took stitches & I have to go Thurs. to have it taken out.

Her apt selection of detail implies all the horror of going to the dentist, made even more terrible by aging, which requires having teeth pulled or the eventual plate worked on. Understatement necessarily plays a large part in the art of the everyday. And humor, denoting courage, also figures into the diarist's character. In the entry for 11 March 1945, she says much in little: 'B., L. & H. went to church. I having no teeth stayed home & painted." She never states her religious beliefs; she only says she goes to church, letting the word imply all. Similarly, she never comments on her techniques as a painter; she just says when and where she paints.

In July 1946, the entries in the diary become intermittent, and with all the deftness of a professional writer, Minor pulls together the themes of aging, dying, and achievement. Here we see the briefest of facts, expressing the habits of a lifetime and the sloughing off of that life.

July 8
Mon.   Pleasant. Cooled in night. Irene went to work. Work at desk. Dr. came & found I had not been getting liver enough. I stayed upstairs all day. Miss S. came to see about selling my house.

July 9
Tues.   Cloudy. Cool. Work at desk. Nurse came. I worked on cemetery account. Didn't go down today.

July 10

Wed. Cloudy. Very hot. W. & E. here to work, & took clothes home to wash.

July 11

Thurs. Cloudy. A little cooler.

July 12

Friday. Cloudy but pleasant. Nurse came at 10 oclock. C. P. came with two little daughters to call. Early dinner and nap. Then Polly drove me to Beauty Parlor to get hair done. B. & M. came in eve and M. brought me Field Glass.

July 13

Sat. Pleasant. Hot. Work at desk. Winnie came, brought cloth and bill $4.75. I paid her.

After this the entries are more scattered, the handwriting weaker. Still, they are typical of her as she continues to live her life the way she has always lived it—calmly, with friends and family around her; actively, writing and painting, working at her desk. For six days in October, she has strength enough only to fill in the days of the week; for many days, there are no entries at all. True to her life's interests, the longest entry after October is for Armistice Day, 11 November 1946. Typically, she spends it with friends, eating and driving around. Then nothing until 20 December, when she notes: "Friday. Irene went to Waterford and got her hair done." The last entry of all: "Sat. First snow in night, turning to rain. Home and painted all day." And so the diary ends, uniting three major themes of her record—the weather, her home, and her art.

Record-keeping diaries, notably this one by Anne Rogers Minor, epitomize the art of the everyday. With little more than two and a half inches per entry, the narratives are excessively brief, and Minor's character develops through incident, not through reflection or analysis. The descriptive details, reduced to a word or a phrase, assume the value of precious gems, for they must imply totality; for example, the two words—"Clear. Warm."—sum up the weather for Monday, 14 September 1942. Yet they are enough to bring that day into the reader's reality. The diarist's intellect and sensitivity melt down each day's happenings and then recast them into a few words that must carry a magnitude of meaning, meaning derived from implication and memory. From these smallest of details come narratives; from these small bits of plots, augmented by day, comes a life. Of necessity, then, the diary's pace is slow, allowing time to stop and look at each day and to savor it before going on to the next. Leisurely and subtly, plots and characters unfold. Plots start out, arrive, and conclude within the framework of the life narrative. But they are not the result of a biographer's or novelist's manipulation; they are organic, not cultivated. The settings, the events, the people are real; and the reader can supplement the information by interviewing survivors and by reading articles in newspapers or magazines.

Finally, the record-keeping diary satisfies because it demonstrates that life does indeed imitate art, that each life, on some level, has the structure and the meaning that art contrives.

"What to make of a diminished thing," Frost asked. "Much," devotees of record-keeping diaries respond: "the world in a grain of sand"; the "flower in the crannied wall" that if we can but understand, "root and all, and all in all," we should know all that there is to know.

Hearing Voices

Oral History as an Aid to Reading

Judith Stitzel

Reading and listening are skills; they are also arts. They can be taught, and they must be honored. Reading and listening, no less than writing and speaking, are activities. When they are passive, the intellectual and imaginative losses are great. But how do you teach reading and listening to students who think they already know how—who do know how if we narrow the definition enough? Teaching oral history, in addition to granting access to the stories of people who may write and read infrequently, can help students to read—if by reading we mean not merely decoding but making meaning.

Students cowed by writing and also in need of interpretative skills can learn those skills as they learn oral history. Students need to understand what they do when they read; they must be self-reflective about the activity, aware that it is a collaborative act, a creative act, a responsible interaction. Such awareness is difficult if they consider what they are reading to have been always a finished product, spewed forth whole from a writer's mind or gut, or if, alternatively, they see the work as somehow authorless or disembodied and consequently feel no obligation to it. A corrective to both these extremes is to see the work as a response or a series of responses often made and modified over a period of time. Some students find this view hard to achieve when an essay is already in print. A writer's drafts, of course, can enable them to achieve it, but so can oral history, with its emphasis on process as well as product.

Collecting and interpreting oral history can also help students recognize that who they are and what they know (and don't know) may affect their reading. In "What's So Special about Women?" Sherna Gluck, without setting down any hard-and-fast rules, indicates the extent to which an oral history can be enhanced when the interviewee realizes that the interviewer is "one of them," whether the "them" is defined by religion, race, or gender. Gluck points out that an "outsider" conducting an interview has an obligation to prepare "as best she can so that she can understand the attitude, vocabulary, and body language of the group or subgroup with which the interviewee identifies" (7). Furthermore, behind this call to responsible preparation is an acknowledgment that (at least in a sex-stereotyped society) gender is an unavoidable determinant of meaning.

While Gluck's insight stemmed from her experience collecting interviews, a similar recognition comes through interpreting them. I realized this when I had students analyze completed interviews that, though recognized for their value as local history, had not been prepared with any special attention to their potential usefulness for women's history. I asked two students to consider where in the tapes they would have proceeded differently or probed further, where they felt the male interviewer had stopped short or undervalued a particular observation. The students were appropriately tentative in their criticism of the more experienced interviewer, but even their introductory work in women's studies had given them enough confidence in themselves and pride in the women to whom they were listening to make the following observations:

> One of the things that I noticed in listening to the tape was that Ella liked very much to talk of her family. But . . . she talked mostly of her father or grandfather, never of her mother or sisters or brothers. Also, . . . she used the pronouns "we" and "they" and rarely if ever did she include herself in the story. I wonder if this had something to do with her upbringing or if it was the way in which the question was phrased? I would have probed further into the relationships between Ella and her mother and between the siblings.

> I found that the ideas I thought important in this tape, as far as women are concerned, David had also touched on, such as women's roles in the home. Of course, I would have further questioned Ella at the point that I thought would have brought out more important information about women in Helvetia [the community being explored]. . . . I believe that I would have further explored the relationships that women had with other women. In these tapes, I did not notice anything of women friends other than in social organizations. I very strongly believe that a woman's relationships with other women are an important part of her life and also give us clues as to the women themselves.

> I'd wonder how women felt about other women. Did they idolize some of them, hate others, or accept people as they are? . . . I would have asked further questions pertaining to the women themselves, not so much about the society they lived in; i.e. their

feelings, their hobbies, the places they went and how they felt about themselves.

Because the listener could realize at what points she might have handled the interview differently, how she would have participated differently in creating the final text, what she might have asked, she did not regard the interview as the final word. Although recent work in reader-response theory has sensitized many teachers to the interactive nature of reading, surprisingly little attention has been given (except by feminist critics) to gender as a major determinant of meaning. But in both the interpretation and the conducting of oral histories, the importance of gender is unmistakable, and allowing students to experience it makes them aware of their responsibilities as readers and healthily skeptical of any claims to universal truth made on behalf of a single work.

Confronting completed texts, whether by professional writers or by fellow students, or even confronting their own first drafts, students do not always realize that material might have been omitted or presented otherwise. Without this realization it is impossible to arrive at any notion of style in writing or reading. Working with oral testimony gives insight into literary devices that might otherwise strike a naive reader as unnatural and alien. Concepts that might remain abstract when understood only in terms of the printed page (e.g. tone, pace, ambivalence) become audible, concrete, and therefore accessible for discussion even among students who would find similar stylistic or rhetorical discussions of literary texts beyond their scope or interest.

Even students who seem comfortable talking about symbols and symbolism often treat the concept mechanically, as if symbols, instead of being organic parts of literary wholes, were grafted onto works after they were finished, the clever excrescences of overactive minds. I was reminded how unnecessary this tendency was when I listened to a student interview an aunt whose house, once convenient to a sleepy county road, was now adjacent to the interstate. An intermittent hum of traffic was audible throughout the interview as the aunt and her niece talked about differences between "then" and "now," and I recognized in a new way how far the potency of the symbolic is its rootedness in the literal. When we judge someone as too literal-minded, unable to appreciate the imaginative or the fanciful, we often assume that the cause is lack of imagination when it might be insufficient attention to the material, to the actual, to the detail.

Voice, another concept used frequently in teaching writing and reading, can also be made more accessible through oral history. Since reading means, in part, activating the voice on the printed page (listening), what better way to concretize the concept than through listening to and trying to "read" actual human voices? Hearing a tape, for instance, the student can recognize the origin of written dialogue in heard voices, as when an interviewee, jogged by an auditory memory, moves un-self-consciously from narration to dialogue—as when an eighty-four-year-old woman remembering her busy mother's neglect of her as a five-year-old suddenly re-creates the harried voice of four-score years ago shooing her out to play. Likewise, listening carefully when a speaker's flow seems magically released by a pertinent question heightens a student's awareness of how ideas develop and tales get told and can make a listener aware that there are allusive as well as logical—metaphorical as well as literal—connections in what she herself may say, write, or read. In the following excerpt from an interview with Eleanor Summerville we can follow the speaker, an eighty-four-year-old woman, from generalization—"I had a good relationship with both my grandmothers"—to discovery.

> Interviewer: Tell me about, like a day with your grandmother and then tell me about a day at home, with your parents. What would be the major differences between them?
>
> Response: I had a good relationship with both of my grandmothers. In fact, I was closer to both of them than I was my parents. . . .
>   My grandmother always lived on a farm and she knew all about farms, and vegetables and trees and plants   and she, she used to take me.   I didn't notice it then, but as I look back, I notice I was always the one she took with her when she went out on the farm. When my grandmother would go out to the fields, to pick her vegetables and fruit, she went out everyday, and she would take me with her and that was just wonderful and she not only took me with her but she talked to me and I was just a little kid   about five or six.   And this that I remember, when we first moved to the farm she would take me with her and she would talk to me. She would explain. I wanted to know about things. I asked, I know I must have asked a lot of questions and she would explain it to me, you know, [here the speaker's voice slows down—becomes meditative] about the different plants and this is poison and this is and she'd pick   she liked wild greens, and she picked herbs, wild herbs, like they used for medicine back then   and she always picked them and diced them and fixed them and put them in jars and used them for different things, for colds and coughs, and poultices for this and that [laughter]. She had remedies for everything. And these wild greens, in the spring they would come before the others. She used to plant the mustard and spinach and kale in the garden, but the wild greens would come earlier, and she would go out in the fields and pick these wild greens, you know, to eat and they were good and I still go pick them   And I like them. If I'm out, and my sister said, "People will wonder what you are doing out huntin' stuff like that" [laughter]. I said I don't care what they think. So Mrs. S across the street, I told her, I said I'm pickin greens. I pick wild greens. I like them and she said I'd like to taste

them and I said ok, next time I cook them, I'll, so I gave her a dish of them and she liked them, and she wanted me to show her the kinds and I said, you have to be careful at first, you know, until you know them, you know you could get poisoned. And I remember now that's why I know—that people do not give children credit for knowing as much as they do because I was so young and the things that I learned then are more vivid in my mind than anything else.

A student listening to this reminiscence will hear the transitions and the modulations, the pauses and the laughter that I can only label or refer to—and that is, of course, the unique value I am claiming for oral history. There is simply no mistaking those profound engagements with the speaker's past that illuminate her present sense of self. The caressing account of the grandmother's patient explanations, the singling out of the grandchild for attention, the willingness of the grandmother to talk to her, to answer her insistent questions—these memories become parts of a parable about the wisdom of children and the independence and self-confidence that come from being cared for, cared about, affirmed.

The interviewer is unobtrusive during this tale, but her presence is essential, her receptivity active rather than passive. Many of us have had the glorious experience of being in the presence of someone who evokes our best and most articulate self. Sometimes this happens naturally and the harmony comes unbidden, the catalyst not even fully aware of the atmosphere she or he is creating; but aware or not, she brings to the situation readiness and receptivity. The preparation that makes more likely those questions that tap the speaker's energy is comparable to the preparation that has (or has not) preceded the reading of an unfamiliar work. And the relatively abstract notion that a reader has a responsibility to a text can become concrete for the students whose experiences with oral history have made them sensitive to their dual roles as listeners and shapers, as audience. Such students will come to texts with questions that inform their reading. Likewise, they will recognize and respect a text that refuses to answer their questions but poses its own. They will recognize that accessibility is not a quality inherent in a work but rather a name for the place where readers and work meet each other. Finally, because they are aware of the continuities and discontinuities—the circumstances of gender, class and race—that can bind or separate reader and author, interviewer and subject, they will recognize that the attributes of a good reader as well as of a good historian are moral as well as intellectual, that self-knowledge, patience, and care should attend our reading of printed texts and of each other's lives. To enlarge our understanding, reading or oral history must involve a dynamic alternation between connecting oneself to and differentiating oneself from an other. Like oral history, reading should be and can be an encounter.

Women's Shorter Autobiographical Writings

Expression, Identity, and Form

Susan Waugh

Shorter autobiographical writings have their origins in essays written for periodicals and also in the freshman English composition course, which has included proponents of personal writing for some years. At least two textbooks on autobiographical writing have become basic texts for the freshman writing course. Most teachers of writing seem ready enough to acknowledge that beginning students benefit from writing about themselves. Not only does autobiographical writing allow students to write about subjects that they know well and that interest them, but in telling their own stories they are most likely to find their own authentic voices. Many teachers of writing argue, however, that such personal writing is most appropriate for the beginning weeks of a writing course and that eventually students should be "weaned" from this pleasant and easy sort of composition and assigned "objective" topics that utilize the classical rhetorical modes. Many teachers who have used the autobiographical approach will recognize this argument; they may also remember their own bewilderment and disappointment at the deterioration of many students' writing as the topics became more "objective." I have no advice for fellow writing teachers, since I continue to follow this rewarding and heartbreaking sequence in my own composition course, having found nothing better.

The excitement of autobiographical writing, the frustrations of teaching writing courses, and my interest in women and their writing resulted in my creating a one-credit autobiographical writing workshop for women. I taught several classes of twenty-two students over several semesters. With few exceptions the students were over twenty-five and had never before taken a college writing course; their writing ability seemed unrelated to their previous education. The course proved so important to the women that each group insisted on additional class meetings.

The women brought a great deal of energy and hope to the first meeting: there was nervousness and fear, normal on the first day of any writing class, but also an eagerness I have never sensed from other writing groups. Some of the women had been "intending to write," and this class seemed a promising beginning. Others wanted to think and write about their own pasts or to prepare family histories or collections of vignettes for their children. Some were experiencing personal crises that compelled them to analyze and to express. While some sought to consider how their personal and family histories related to American history, others longed to re-create and preserve intensely private memories.[1]

In my ignorance, I had ordered for the class an excellent paperback collection of women's autobiographical extracts, *Growing Up Female in America: Ten Lives*, edited by Eve Merriam, which I thought would both interest and inspire them. Although I continued to order the book as a supplement to the class, no group ever discussed more than one of the short selections; beginning with the second class, we did little but listen to their own writings read aloud and discuss them in the group. Once the ice was broken—more quickly than in the feistiest creative writing class I have ever taught—only politeness gave restraint to the writers' demanding to read to the group. The atmosphere was unreservedly open, warm, and accepting; the class felt like a group almost immediately. Was this because it was homogeneous, composed almost entirely of traditional women socialized to be skilled at human relations? Their age may have made a difference, too; they exhibited none of the reluctance to write or the maddening passivity and dependency that Florence Howe has described so accurately among some eighteen-year-old college women.

Fortunately, I had not wished to dictate forms or methods to these students but had structured the writing assignments according to topics, so that at each class meeting each writer had been working on the same "problem." The source of the topics was a paperback now regrettably out of print, *Telling Your Story: A Guide to Who You Are and Who You Can Be*, by Sam Keen and Anne Valley Fox. Anything but a conventional book about writing, it contains many useful exercises in jogging the memory, analyzing the past and present, and even imagining the future. I asked each student to write a piece for each of five meetings after the first: (1) the past—a portrait, an incident, a fragment, an extended analysis, or a theme followed over a period of years; (2) the present; (3) the future; (4) a fantasy; and (5) a final piece of her choice. Most writers produced more than the assigned number of pieces, but they found it helpful to use the book and the class discussion to anticipate the difficulties of the next assignment and then to enjoy the astonishing variety of responses from the group.

We never discussed form, but we addressed the difficulties of self-knowledge, the trickiness of memory, problems of truth, the difficulty of creating a complete portrait of a person in words, the selection of detail, the freeing of imaginative and creative powers, and other matters of interest to literary critics, writers, psychologists, historians, and philosophers. While talking about the portrayal of past, present, and future we discussed the entire range of issues explored in the critical literature about autobiography. We spoke entirely of content and how to discover or expand it, never about method—a sobering thought for the composition teacher. The women created their own forms, quite without self-consciousness.

We may see the variety of forms the women created in their responses to the problem of writing about the past. Few attempted to represent the totality of the past in any sense. Some chose to narrate an event of great significance; others chose incidents that could in some way represent the whole by the part. An example of compression of past, present, and future is the conclusion of an essay entitled "Going Home," an anticipation of a visit to the author's birthplace in Minnesota to celebrate her mother's eighty-third birthday:

> One of the reasons I love this home so much is that few things have changed over the years and the things that have changed have come about so gradually that it seems always a part of the past. . . . Even my old room has changed so little and on Saturday night of this week, when all the guests have departed, I will again lie awake on my old bed listening to the sounds of the night. Suddenly, from an opened window a soft light will fall on the wall to my left and swiftly make its way across the room lightly touching objects in its path. It is a light from a lone car coming down from the hill behind the house. I am fascinated by the dancing shadows on the wallpaper. For a split second in time, it is 1933 and I am eight years old again.

The incident is likely to resonate in the experience of any reader, further increasing its power: who can fail to remember her or his childhood bedroom and how it felt?

Some approaches were more analytical. In a piece entitled "Visits," another writer extracts the basic patterns of parents' visits to grown children over three generations; here follows a penetrating confrontation with changes in her own mother—and in herself:

> Mother was as verbal and witty as ever but her once pontifical opinions were sometimes a little quivery and her usual acerbic

comments that I used to find intimidating had lost a lot of their sting. Late Sunday afternoon she confided to me that she was lonely in Florida, that much of the ways of living in their area are superficial and it is difficult to make real friends. And there were the brief half-humorous remarks over the weekend that thinly veiled a dread of old age and its infirmities.

The portraits in particular contained subtleties of thought and of expression. Consider the quality of description, the subdued persona of the narrator, the sophisticated and precise word choice, and the restrained emotion of this final glimpse of "Cousin Melva," whose adored son had been killed in an automobile accident:

> Melva kissed my brother and me, she patted my mother and grandmother on the arm, she held the door open for us and watched from the threshold as we headed toward the car. She called a faint "Be careful now" after us, and in that instant I turned, I wanted to say something kind to Cousin Melva, to help her forget, but her gaze had already gone from us; she was looking the other way, across the fields, where, in the soft spring sunlight, amid bright yellow flowers and the songs of birds, there romped a little red-haired boy, his sweet laughter already drowning out the sounds of our goodbyes.

"Cousin Melva" is typical of these autobiographical writings in placing little emphasis on narrative. The author describes a particular visit on a particular afternoon, but she does so primarily to depict her own gradual understanding of the depth of Cousin Melva's loss. The narrator's presence is understated but continuous; although the ostensible subject is another person, the piece is very much "about" the author, her sensibility and consciousness, her initiation into adult pain, human sympathy, and life's tragic dimension.

Some of the autobiographical writings, including "Cousin Melva," use fictional techniques. The distinctions between autobiography and fiction were not part of any class discussion in any group. All the techniques that the writers used were their own inventions and grew directly out of their content, out of the realities they were trying to represent. Making the content assume a coherent, comprehensible, and pleasing shape appeared to arise naturally out of the desire to tell the story. The story, too, was never paramount, as is often the case with plot-obsessed student fiction. The people, the ideas, the emotions—these elements, not plots, were the substance and motive of these nonfiction stories.

Expression of feeling was an important part of autobiographical writing for many of the women. Although many human beings have difficulty recognizing their own feelings, especially negative or otherwise unacceptable feelings, women as a group face a particular set of internal constraints. Many of the women in my class were traditional wives and mothers accustomed to focusing on others, not on themselves, and to repressing any thoughts or feelings that would rock the boat. Some looked inward with explosive results:

> My anger comes out in different ways. Writing about my life is one way I deal with it. After it runs around my head, it comes out through my typing, I let go of it. My anger could be felt in the tips of my fingers, the fingers have feelings of super strength. Could I kill with them? Squeeze a neck until no air is left? It is a burst of power that I feel when savagely I cut an orange or grapefruit to stuff it down the disposal. Wait a minute, this orange did not do anything. Remember accidents when I am angry with me and it causes me to cut furiously, slicing part of my finger.

As the groups responded with sympathy and acceptance to such writings, more women found the courage to express strong feelings and to read them aloud. Some of these pieces were rambling, others focused and controlled. Few of them would have been written, I think, had not the groups themselves created a community of listeners. Although about particular selves, the expressive pieces were in some sense creations of groups of women urging each other on their separate internal journeys.

Issues of identity were integral to class discussions and to the writings. Autobiographical writings are natural vehicles for the exploration of identity. One remembers Boswell in his *London Journal* trying on various personae for size, or Montaigne's asserting:

> In modeling this figure on myself, I have had to fashion and compose myself so often to bring myself out, that the model itself has to some extent grown firm and taken shape. Painting myself for others, I have painted myself with colors clearer than my original ones. I have no more made my book than my book has made me. (281)

Especially since women have been brought up traditionally to lead contingent lives, to expect others to define and direct their lives and purposes, and to experience identity as something formless and beyond their control, autobiography is an ideal arena for thinking about "fashioning and composing" the self one chooses and creates.

One woman treated this matter with great inventiveness and humor, presenting her present self by writing descriptions of herself from the points of view of her husband, her mother, each of her three children, her sister, and a friend. Each short piece utilized a special vocabulary and style and created a portrait of its narrator as well as its subject. As a group, the pieces constituted a complete portrait of the subject from the outside, if not from the inside. This writer's class considered the piece especially suited to depicting a person deeply interdependent with other people, largely defined by others, yet asserting a definite, chosen, and cherished self at the center.

Humor was surprisingly common among autobiographical writings concerned with identity. Many writers brought lightness to analyses of their sexuality. In a culture that encourages women to consider sexual attractiveness coterminous with self-worth, women benefit from writing about their relations with their faces and bodies. In a piece called "Hand-Me-Down Fantasy," one writer in her thirties remembered her mother's dissatisfaction with her body and an elaborate game she played with her daughters in which they would agree "in fantasy" to exchange bodies, but not heads, with the next woman who came around the corner. She concluded the very amusing essay by asserting her comfort with her own body and her own self:

> It would be wonderful to see what the world feels like just once from the top of a pair of nice long skinny legs, but I couldn't stand losing my identity. Even if my build is more Japanese than Svelte model, I'd hate to give up my hard-earned truck-driving muscles for a body not as strong and sturdy although more glamorous. The known body of me is comfortable and tells my story, the story of my living. I'd hate to lose even the smallest scar of my life: my bout with chicken pox, a broken toe from hockey, my leg scars from a lawnmower accident, an ice pick gouge in my hand, my stretch marks, my surgery scars, and these rubbery breasts that have nursed my children. My body is the map of my life . . . the proof that I've lived, worked, and loved. So the end result of my hand-me-down fantasy is to always feel better, even protective of what I am. Thanks, Mom.

Although raised in a culture inimical to their feelings of self-worth, many women have managed to form strong identities and to maintain self-esteem; their triumphs can be articulated and celebrated in autobiographical writing.

Women may also use autobiographical writing as part of a spiritual quest for identity or as a means to self-transformation. Mary Daly emphasizes that self-growth requires a continuing and purposeful effort to "recall the endless series of oppressive, violating, insulting, assaulting acts against herself. As she moves on the enspiriting journey she experiences a lessening of confusion, guilt and despair . . .

[that] if not converted into energy of creativity prepossesses her" (348). Most of the women had no acquaintance with political feminism, and I as the instructor made no effort to explain any feminist ideas or even to give the titles of books. With the support of a group of women, however, many writers did explore how being female had affected their childhoods and shaped their adult lives. Female socialization was a common subject of the autobiographical writings, as it is of many formal, published autobiographies by American women who have had public careers. Many of these pieces utilized contrast, explaining such topics as differences in the treatment of daughters and sons within the family, the most and least popular female high school classmates as teenagers and at the twentieth reunion, contrasts between a mother and an aunt as influential role models, and differences in relations with first and later husbands. Mothers were especially popular subjects. Some of the essays were more abstract and meditative. One entitled "I Am a Child of the Light" was in no sense a narrative; rather, it expressed the author's current spiritual state and relation to God, with much of the abstract and time-transcending flavor of the last books of St. Augustine's *Confessions*.

Personal identity was only one concern of these autobiographical writings, however. Many of the pieces produced in the "future" and "fantasy" assignments also dealt with the meaning of human life, collectively and individually. Consider this dreamlike but chilling glimpse of its author's imagined passage into death:

> I keep examining myself for new signs of deadness. . . . After awhile I look forward to leaving my body behind. After all, the putrefaction is becoming obvious. The sore on my leg expands and oozes. . . . My father, at about age thirty, stands with two of his friends at some distance from me. They all wear army uniforms. My father is so handsome and vital, his face unlined. . . . They walk toward me with their arms thrown about each others shoulders singing "As We Go Marching through Georgia" in raucous voices. I am a child jumping up and down, clapping my hands with joy. When I look beside me, there is my father as he is today, gray-haired, wrinkled, no longer young. He watches me, a bemused smile on his face. I am astounded, crushed, tricked. "Oh, Daddy," I cry, "Why did it have to happen to us?"

Far from being mired in details of the past and present, these women were eager to consider the meanings they had created in their own lives and their relations with memory, time, death, and eternity.

Adult women obviously have many experiences to write about and the motivation, talent, skill, and wisdom to write autobiographical essays of professional quality. They are able to produce this writing not because of instruction in form but because of their own courageous examinations of their lives and the confirming presence of other women in the group. These women made me reconsider my past thinking about women's lives, about autobiography as it is read and written, and about teaching writing. First, women understand their own lives, thoughts, and emotions more clearly than many of us think. I approached the first group with the prejudice that self-conscious thought by women about their lives is impossible without feminism; I was quickly disabused. I expected the same confusion and lack of self-knowledge that one sees so frequently in young students and in many adult women; women who sign up for classes in autobiographical writing cannot be a totally distinct species, and this was reassuring to me. Finally, though the lives of conventional wives and mothers are considered dull—I myself confess to this belief—I never was bored in the class or in reading what the women had written. Whatever the external circumstances of their lives and however little they are within their control, women's inner lives can be as rich and as consciously shaped as their autobiographical writings. It is hard for me to believe that a group of feminists whose lives and concerns are more like my own—or a group of men[2]—could produce more compelling autobiographical essays.

Accordingly, I read Suzanne Juhasz's "'Some Deep Old Desk or Capacious Hold-All': Form and Women's Autobiography" with astonishment. On the basis of her work teaching writing to younger women, she argues that the apparent formlessness and inclusion of less significant details in her students' work is a product of the multidimensionality and dispersion of women's lives. She argues further that "It is because the nature of meaning itself in women's lives is right now such an unclear and open issue that, finally, the diary model for women's autobiography seems most appropriate and helpful" (668). My experience of writing and reading women's shorter autobiographical writings has been different. Without instructions from me and without knowledge of many formal autobiographies or of any secondary literature on autobiography, the women produced coherent and polished work. Even those who had lived for many years the fragmented lives of traditional women were not prisoners of a common subject, style, or form. The form of the life does not inevitably dictate the form of the autobiography. Not only did the women choose coherent, chronological, focused, logical, and consciously shaped forms over rambling, diarylike, or diffuse ones, they were also highly experimental. Without being conscious of form, they invented new forms, and they demonstrated creativity in writing about their lives as well as courage and seriousness in thinking about their identities.

The shorter autobiographical essay, in fact, seems an ideal place for the creation of new autobiographical forms. Exciting and expressive shorter forms are waiting to be born in the lives and minds of women. Not only can women's autobiographical writing provide occasions and means for constructive thought about women's lives, it can provide literature for the enjoyment and enlightment of all. It can ensure that women's stories will not be lost to themselves or to others. It can communicate to the world the substance and feel of women's lives. It can provide various role models and possibilities of identity for women, along with many possibilities for autobiographical content and form.

These adult women affirmed both my respect for women and my conviction that autobiographical writing is valuable for the process that produces it and the wisdom and beauty of the written product. Autobiography allows both writer and reader to think about their lives descriptively and analytically; it also encourages and reinforces the idea that one may consciously choose and shape one's identity and one's future. Autobiography is a legitimate art form. The skillful writer of autobiographical essays should be regarded as a creator of artistic truth, a conveyor of historical truth, and a storyteller for people and family and nation as well as for sex and self. There should be special college writing classes in autobiography—as there are in other exalted forms—for both sex-segregated and mixed groups. Such classes may have much to teach composition and creative writing teachers about how well students can write when content—including ideas and emotions as well as facts—is emphasized more than modes, structures, or forms.

Autobiographical writing is especially important for women, however. Providing the occasion for groups of women to write it has taught me new reverence for the lives of "average women" and their abilities to understand and write about their lives. Writing and reading about the lives of "ordinary" people can be occasions for learning and teaching, for imagining a better world, for respect and love. Autobiographical writings can also be forges in which new identities and new literary forms are shaped.

Notes

1. For the historically minded, useful books include Trimmer and Kettler, *American Oblique*; Watts and Davis, *Generations*; and Ryan, *Womanhood in America*.

2. The idea of an autobiography course for men was very exciting to my department chair, who is also interested in writing and autobiography, although he feared that men would have more trouble than women being comfortable and open in such a group. Ironically, he was not able to offer the course because the administrator concerned could not "see the point" of an autobiography course for men. Sexism cuts both ways.

Preparing a Collection of Regional Autobiographical Materials for Use in the Composition Classroom

Susan S. Kissel

For the past two years, under the auspices of two institutional community research and services grants from Northern Kentucky University, I and my colleague Margery Rouse have been collecting and publishing regional autobiographical materials. The first volume was prepared for use by students in composition classes at our university; other volumes may follow. This essay describes our vision of the collection, the process we followed in gathering and assembling these materials, and their uses in the classroom.

Freshman composition generally produces frustration and dissatisfaction in faculty and students alike. Despite a virtual avalanche of new rhetorics each year, no text ever seems to fit the particular needs of the students. While the composition committee at our university continues to recommend several texts to satisfy a variety of teaching approaches, it seeks, at the same time, to develop materials that will have particular appeal to our students and their needs. Regional materials, we felt, could have that appeal.

Because no university archives contained regional materials, we began by asking students to research their own families and friends to help locate a community writing tradition. The results were varied and interesting: the 1895 diary of a twenty-two-year-old family companion; a neighbor's collection of anecdotes about her children, recorded in secret over a thirty-year period and duplicated, bound, and presented recently to family members; a turn-of-the-century journal of a grandmother the student had never known; a sister's unpublished collection of poems; an uncle's reminiscences of his depression-era move from the city to the country; several students' own diaries and short stories; courtship letters from a past cultural tradition; and many others. Clearly, the area has produced and continues to produce much writing, as students are often surprised to learn. Writing papers about their discoveries, conducting interviews, and consulting newspaper accounts and published works to establish a historical context, students found reason for their effort and pleasure in considering a writer's form, style, voice, audience, and subject. They found themselves on the cutting edge of a community project, locating a writing tradition within their own families and neighborhoods. In several instances, they obtained permission to include these materials in our regional autobiographical writing collection. In a small way, we had begun.

At the same time, we had gone into the community to encourage residents to help us with our task. We gave talks, sent out letters to individuals whose names others had suggested, and wrote a few articles for community publications about our project. Our message was always the same—that these materials have a special value and a special life; that they can give us a sense of the past, a sense of ourselves; that they can help us understand the relation between fiction and fact, between speaking and writing; that through them we can find and restore to readers a lost heritage of the lives of ordinary men and women in this country; that they need to be preserved to provide members of the community with an essential awareness of its development; and that they should be a part of the university curriculum for student learning.

From the outset, we were surprised by the number of individuals who had accumulated private treasures of family papers, who valued these writings but felt that no one else would, and who had stored them in trunks and desks to protect them, even while the relentless process of decay continued. Among the collections community residents allowed us to copy were one hundred letters tracing a family's westward movement from Virginia to Kentucky and on to Missouri; an eleven-volume verse diary of a former Confederate soldier; and a letter recounting the often-heard tale of a woman's feats of heroism during an Indian raid on her Ohio River frontier home in the late 1700s. As the process of sharing continued and as it became more and more obvious to us and to others at the university that there were numerous uncollected firsthand accounts in the area, a university archive was developed to allow someone to work full-time publicizing the importance of community literature and working for its preservation. The archive is the most important accomplishment of this project so far, and it will have far-reaching and long-lasting consequences for the entire community.

We also soon found, of course, that we had sufficient material to accomplish our original goal—the publication of an initial collection of local autobiographical writings that we hoped would stimulate continued community interest in the significance and preservation of regional materials, as well as a greater understanding of writing. In choosing which materials to include, we used the criterion of variety. First, we wanted to offer community members and students as much variety in human experience as possible by including materials from different time periods, beginning with the late 1700s and continuing through the early twentieth century, by offering a balance of women and men in our selection of writers, and by choosing writers of varying ages and occupations, from merchant to housekeeper-companion and farmer.

Second, we wanted to offer several different kinds of writing. We selected letters, of course, making sure that some were part of an ongoing correspondence and others were occasioned by a special event or a special need. Some were retrospective, spanning many years and many incidents, while others offered primarily the news of the day. We also tried to include several kinds of journals and diaries: one selection was an 1895 diary with day-to-day entries; the next was a quite different verse diary covering many years and many volumes, from 1896 to 1927; while another selection, a journal, offered a memoir account of the most important events in the writer's history. We felt that it was important to stimulate students to think about writing in terms of varied audiences, circumstances, purposes, and forms. We wanted them to consider the differences between journals and diaries, between retrospective and chronological accounts, and between authorial tone and technique of expression from one piece of writing to another, even in selections by the same author writing for a different audience or for a different purpose. While these rhetorical matters are all important to instruction in composition, they are also relevant to the analysis of imaginative works of literature. Nontraditional literary materials can illustrate and validate writing in both its practical and its expressive functions.

Other editing decisions remained before we were able to make a final decision about the material for the volume. Unable to print most of the journals and letter collections in their entirety, we needed to select the material we felt most relevant to the region, most interesting in its subject matter, most representative of an author's individual voice and concerns, or most expressive of an entire work. All of these were matters of individual choice and editorial judgment. There was always, too, the temptation to edit out unfavorable statements and incidents. We knew that sentimental passages from the male writers— for instance, effusive love poems and lofty tributes to the beauty and purity of young girls, mothers, and women—would be rejected immediately by contemporary readers as silly, unseemly, or sexist. At other times, the obviously racist or otherwise prejudiced and unkind remarks of both male and female writers would threaten the respect and sympathy contemporary readers might come to feel for them. And what of those boring, repetitive, inconsequential diary and journal entries? Were they to be included as well? In each case, we decided to present the author and the work as representatively as possible, retaining trivial, sentimental, and even offensive passages along with the more moving, eloquent, and interesting portions of particular works. Although our desire as editors and readers alike is often to glorify and simplify the past, to remove the unpleasant and undignified in our predecessors and our heritage, we felt, finally, that it was important to resist that temptation. Since regional writings often reveal the complexity of both the writer and the age, we decided to retain that complexity wherever we could. Further, we had to decide whether to correct the writers' "errors" in spelling, punctuation, and grammar. Once more, we decided to retain the actual spelling, colloquialisms, and punctuation the writers had used as much as possible, making clear in an introduction that spelling and punctuation were not standardized throughout much of the nineteenth century. For the sake of readability, we did adapt to contemporary expectations of sentence structure, inserting periods instead of commas between sentences to let readers follow the flow of a writer's thought more easily; we retained other unusual punctuation, however, as helpful in contrasting the past and present functions of commas, dashes, and colons. In making these decisions, we needed the consent of those who had given us permission to use the material, and we obtained signed release forms allowing us to present the selected passages in their original form.

With selection and transcription at last behind us, we were ready to assemble the final collection, complete with an area map and photographs of a few authors and pages of the original manuscripts. At the outset we had planned to mimeograph the selections, staple them together as booklets, and sell them at cost to students and interested community residents through the university bookstore. As the quantity of material increased and our project became more ambitious, however, we secured grant money through the university to print a paperback volume, *The Story of the Pewter Basin and Other Occasional Writings: Collected in Southern Ohio and Northern Kentucky.* This book has been used by over six hundred students in twenty-four sections of English composition and has, of course, been available to interested members of the local community; a notice of the volume's publication has appeared in the university alumnae magazine, *Com-*

muniqué, and we will continue to give talks and presentations using materials from the collection throughout the community during the coming year.

We have, it seems, accomplished our goal, yet the project remains to be evaluated. The community will measure its success in terms of the renewed interest it brings in locating, preserving, and publishing such autobiographical materials. In the composition sections, the volume's success will rest on its usefulness in helping students respond more fully and write more sensitively. Already composition instructors have scheduled several sessions to share ideas about ways to use this supplemental text of regional autobiographical writings most effectively in the classroom. I feel convinced, as a result of the student work I have seen thus far, we will find that nontraditional, noncanonical regional authors are able to enlighten students and engage them in the writing process more successfully than the most sophisticated and entertaining contemporary essayists represented in the traditional rhetorics.

An important reason for the effectiveness of such materials is the absence of error-proof, edited final pages. Most of these materials, handwritten with words and phrases freely crossed out, have obvious errors in spelling, punctuation, and grammar. Writers apologize for their lack of skill and acknowledge their composing difficulties throughout, as when Martha Jane Haydon writes from Randolph County, Missouri, to her sisters in Boone County, Kentucky, in January of 1875:

> I must bring my scribling to a close as I fear I have already tired you with my unconected letter. this leaves us in our usual health hoping it may find you all enjoying the same blessing write soon from your affectionate sister.

She adds this postscript: "excuse mistakes and bad spelling as I am writing on my lap." This is writing as students themselves have experienced it; the process of writing is clearly evident here.

Moreover, students can identify with the regional perspectives and concerns of these materials. Place-names, persons, and events are often familiar, giving students the pleasure of recognition and the sense of inclusion that unites them with unknown writers. Often both author and reader have walked the same streets, viewed the same mountains, or farmed the same lands. They share a sense of place, a familiarity that can lead to surprise when the reader discovers changes that have taken place in customs, attitudes, terrain, or living conditions through the passage of time. My students, for instance, are amazed to discover Charles Green Land's description of Cincinnati, Ohio, in his 1844 journal kept on a boat journey west from Lexington, Kentucky, to Missouri. In his entries he characterizes Cincinnati as having "a larger proportion of foreigners . . . than any place I have seen"; as already possessing a downtown ice-cream parlor "with the best ice cream I ever tasted"; and as having in Fourth Street (today a crowded street in the downtown shopping district) "a most beautiful street, being shaded with trees of many varieties and lined with magnificent dwellings" (12, 15). Such descriptions give students a new historical perspective and a sense of the past's significance in relation to their own experiences.

Further, these materials stimulate student imagination and response, providing an excellent basis for both out-of-class research and in-class discussion and writing. One student who brought in her grandmother's early-twentieth-century journal followed her readings by interviewing her father and other relatives and investigating family records and picture collections to reconstruct through her own writing the life of a woman she never knew. Other materials may provide topics for an entire class to speculate about. For example, Frances Moss Botts writes in the mid-1800s,

> Prepare I go to yield my breath.
> Upon the rugged rocks below
> My mangled form shall lie.
> Come cruel parents come and see
> The victim of your cruelty.

Students use the evidence found in the rest of this poem, in her other poems, and in their own experiences to speculate on Frances Botts's unhappy adolescence. And when the account is, on the contrary, clear and complete, students are able to discuss the actions of those involved and the values men and women of an earlier time have expressed through their choices. The following narrative in our collection, for instance, concerns a pioneer woman named Susanna Geoble who not only saw her husband and step-brother die in an Indian raid on a 1790s frontier Ohio River settlement but rushed out amid the fighting to carry in the bodies of both men. Her actions and words have provided my students with a stimulating subject for written and oral response, as in the following example:

> "Come help to take revenge. Poke up the fire"—she getting a suitable kettle and hanging it on a hook of the long iron crain spanning its back wall from end to end over the kindling chunks and coals in the broad fire place for "running" bullets (so Susanna without her mother's permission, though in her mother's sight went into her mother's two sets of table dishes herself and husband Pryor brought with their other needs and furniture when begin-

ning housekeeping). When the pewter was melted they two "run" the bullets. Then she poured the bullets into a sack and told Stephen to hurry off to the Fort [Washington] with them to shoot the Indians with. Stephen was afraid, and strove against her and his mother's looks, and signals though helpless to resist Susanna lest she might lose him, her last living son. But Susanna dragged him to a back window, opened, and lifted and pushed him outside and telling him to run to the Fort with the sack of bullets. Indian bullets were whizzing about the boy's head on his way to the Fort. And when he arrived at the Fort, and got inside the Fortification, he was so overpowered with fright and fatigue that he fell on his sack of bullets holding up unconscious before saying a word. (7–8)

Students must first work out the difficult punctuation of the passage to grasp its meaning; having done so, they find many issues to write about and discuss: the conflicts between the mother's values and those of her daughter; the assumptions about men and women underlying Susanna's actions; and Susanna's personality traits as revealed through her behavior. They respond, too, with their own reactions to her choice and explore outside sources presenting the Indian side of the skirmishes or the role of Fort Washington in the Ohio River valley.

Nontraditional materials such as these force readers into active, involved roles. At times the reader becomes an eavesdropper on intimate confessions meant originally for the silent page alone. At other times the student plays aunt, sister, brother, husband, or close friend confided to in the pages of a letter or journal. In such roles, students can experience the surprise and drama of daily events as they unfold and present unexpected challenges to the writer; students also learn to read what is unspoken but implicit in a writer's words and tone and to share in the emotional intensity of a close personal relation from another period of time.

By playing roles, students experience as readers what James Britton has called the "expressive mode" of writing. In *Writing and Learning across the Curriculum*, the "expressive mode" is described as one

> *in which it is taken for granted* that the writer himself is of interest to the reader; he feels free to jump from facts to speculation to personal anecdote to emotional outburst and none of it will be taken down and used against him—it is all part of being a person *vis à vis* another person. It is the means by which the new is tentatively explored, thoughts may be half-uttered, attitudes half-expressed, the rest being left to be picked up by a listener or reader who is willing to take the unexpressed on trust. (Martin et al. 23)

The authors of *Writing and Learning across the Curriculum* further believe that, for students themselves, writing in the expressive mode is essential to the development of voice and thought needed for effective writing in other modes; they argue that the expressive mode,

> being the form of writing nearest to speech, is crucial for trying out and coming to terms with new ideas. Because it is the kind of writing in which we most fully reveal ourselves to our reader in a trusting relationship. . . . Expressive writing we think is the seed bed from which more specialized and differentiated kinds of writing can grow—towards the greater explicitness of the transactional or the more conscious shaping of the poetic. (26)

In reading nontraditional materials such as letters, diaries, and journals, students must take on the trust and concern of established relations; listening to other voices seems to help them acquire their own. I can only surmise that when students have felt the importance of expressive writing through their involvement as listeners and responders, they feel both more free and more engaged in expressing themselves.

Regional materials have the power to open students to the drama and mystery of writing: how it touches them and why; what they remember and why; how personality is conveyed through word choice and placement, as well as through punctuation; by the differences between public and private versions of life; by the subtleties of truth and falsehood; by the shaping force of authorial intention; by the contradictory emotions of love and hate that can, at the same time, inspire the writer; by the formal distinctions and interrelations among collections of letters, diaries, memoirs, and journals; by the influence of a close, personal audience rather than an unknown, distant one; and by many other considerations of importance to the composition class.

Questions such as these give rise to a number of possible classroom writing activities. Students can experiment with trying to punctuate one of these pieces—resolving conflicts in choice by considering the author's personality and how it might have been reflected in the selection of dashes, exclamation points, semicolons, or commas had the writer been familiar with their present-day uses. They can treat a letter as a sentence-combining exercise, considering afterward the stylistic, expressive changes that have resulted from their efforts. Students may also respond as the recipient of a letter, writing in reply—questioning, suggesting, consoling, assisting, or arguing with the author as dictated by the role they have assumed throughout their reading. They can present their own version of the writer's life, citing evidence from interviews with living relatives, historical research, or simply a close reading of the writer's extant works. And, of course, they can rewrite a letter, poem, or journal entry with the intention of removing the author's mask or filling in an author's silence to correct the distortions and omissions they believe they have found there. These assignments are just a few that my students have enjoyed pursuing—assignments through which they improve their own skills as writers and gain, at the same time, a greater understanding of writing.

Writing is important—that is the message that nontraditional materials keep repeating to composition students; the instructor need never say it. The letters, diaries, and memoirs suggest again and again that for countless individuals, past and present, the written word has offered friendship when there has been no one to listen, value in the midst of the mundane, an ongoing affirmation in a life filled with accomplishment, or dignity and vindication when life has become intolerable. Through these written accounts, periods of history come alive, and little-known writers, strangely enough, acquire an authenticity, personality, and immediacy that, for students, the contemporary journalist seldom possesses. The magic and mystery of these accounts, however halting, hesitant, or intermittent their prose, encourage students to keep their own daily records and affirm their own lives through words. They also have the power to stimulate the kinds of reading and research, thought and questioning, that are most valuable as sources of student writing because they are spontaneous and sincere. The special life that nontraditional materials hold and give promises to provide an answer, which I, for one, have been looking for, to the problem of student-teacher discontentment in the composition classroom.

Literature in Performance in the Place Where the Partridge Drums

Susan Ward with Joan Olsen Donovan

The St. Regis Mohawk Reservation, also called Akwesasne or the Place Where the Partridge Drums, is located along the St. Lawrence River. Two thirds of its territory lies within Canadian borders, one third within the borders of upstate New York. Many of its people work in the industries of Massena, New York, or Cornwall, Ontario; some of them maintain small farms on the reservation. The majority are Christian, but a considerable group follows the traditional Longhouse religion of the Iroquois. Most of the people describe themselves as progressive, but the Longhouse group tries to live as closely to the old Indian way of life as possible. Some of the reservation inhabitants are United States citizens, some are Canadian citizens, and some claim allegiance only to the Mohawk nation, of which they are tribal members. Three different sets of chiefs try to govern the reservation. Split by religious and political differences, differences in lifestyle, and the boundaries of two countries, the Akwesasne Mohawks nonetheless struggle to maintain their integrity as a people.

In the spring of 1980, we began a weekly forty-mile trek to the reservation to teach a course entitled Oral Interpretation of Literature. Funded by a federal grant from the United States Office of Indian Education directly to the tribe, our course enrolled six students ranging in age from mid-twenties to late fifties, all seeking to complete Bachelor of Arts degrees. On obtaining their degrees, some hoped to obtain better jobs, others to feel more secure in the ones they had, one or two to teach eventually in the Mohawk school or to work in Mohawk education-related projects on or near the reservation. Although we did not intend to teach a course based solely on Native American materials, we found that our students brought up such materials again and again as we put together scripts for classroom use. Not surprisingly, works by and about Native American women rated high among group members.

We began tentatively. At the conclusion of our first session, one of us stood up and said she would read a poem by a Native American woman. She added that she knew she was not Native American and that the reading might seem incongruous or even disrespectful, and she suggested we might discuss this aspect later. She read "Indian Love Letter" by Soge Track. At the conclusion of the reading, no one said anything.

The following week when students were each to choose a piece to read before the group, Minerva, a person of some influence as well as personality, stood up. "I am going to read a poem by Pauline Johnson, a Mohawk poet from Six Nations," she said. "I was impressed that one of our teachers who is not Indian would search out American Indian literature, so I did some searching of my own." Clutching a book tightly with both hands because poetry makes her nervous, Minerva began to read in an unpracticed and shaky voice.

From this point, interest among both teachers and students grew. One of us wrote to all the presses that publish materials on Native Americans and took the donated copies to the reservation as they arrived. The reservation librarians, at the students' request, searched the library shelves and began to make use of interlibrary loan. One student researched Native American history and did a presentation based on the speeches of an Iroquois leader of the Revolutionary War. Another based a reading on a legend of the founding of the Iroquois League of the Five Nations. Someone else read historical and contemporary newspaper clippings about the reservation and its inhabitants. Others began to discover contemporary Native American poets, dramatists, and fiction writers.

Because we liked both the students and the material and because we grew not to mind the forty-mile trek to the reservation, we taught the course again. When we did, we taught Oral Interpretation of Native American Literature, a course that grew out of our experience and out of the interest and help of those first six students. An aim of the course was the compilation of a performance script based on students' research of tribal materials; that script was performed for a senior citizens' group at Akwesasne in May 1983. The following is an outline of the research and structure that brought our new course into being.

The most efficient way to begin is to research materials and place them on reserve for students before the course begins. A general overview of Native American history, an overview of the history of the tribes within a given cultural area, an investigation into the history and culture of the specific tribe or tribes on the reservation, and a history of the reservation itself should be included in the materials placed on reserve. The *Handbook of North American Indians*, published by the Smithsonian, is a good place to start. Bibliographies in recent books on American Indian literature provide good follow-up material.

Students should be encouraged to talk to the reservation's people. Such conversations, particularly with older people, can lead to the uncovering of diaries, letters, personal clipping files, artifacts, and stories that might be scripted. Students and teachers must make an early decision, should they wish to work with such personal materials, about whether to record conversations. If they decide to do so, they should investigate the techniques of interviewing and the legal implications of working with oral histories.

Script materials culled from such sources are as limitless as the imagination. Students can edit historical accounts and juxtapose them in various ways to form interesting scripts. Tales of Native American heroes and heroines, told from biographical and autobiographical slants, work well. The texts of laws (one student gave a presentation on the many legal definitions of "Indian"), treaties (the Jay Treaty of 1794, which gave Indians the right to bring duty-free goods across the United States–Canadian border, is particularly pertinent at Akwesasne), and speeches (one student read from the moving last speech of Joseph Brant, who led a band of Iroquois from New York State into Canada to establish the Six Nations Reserve in Ontario) are good materials. Newspaper clippings from white establishment papers (one student gave a fascinating presentation on the image of Indian "criminals" in the pages of a local paper) or Native American papers (*Akwesasne Notes* is a good source for Native American response to national and local incidents involving Native Americans) or both (e.g., a comparison of views from both sides on one or a series of issues) make interesting scripts. Tribal legends and ceremonies can also be script material, if this use does not break a tribal taboo. Letters, diaries, and oral histories, once they have been transcribed, can form the bases of presentations. And Native American fiction, poetry, and drama are, of course, easily adaptable for performance.

Some materials of specific interest to the people of the Akwesasne Reservation may further illustrate the process of recognizing potential scripts in the results of historical research. The Akwesasne people are for the most part members of the Mohawk tribe, traditionally the oldest of the five tribes of the Iroquois League of Five Nations. The following materials make good scripts: collections of Mohawk legends and, by extension, of legends of the Seneca, Oneida, Cayuga, and Onondaga peoples (the other four tribal members of the league); some accounts of ancient Iroquois religious beliefs and ancient religious ceremonies; the great epic of the Iroquois, the account of the founding of the Confederacy of the Five Nations by Deganawidah and Hiawatha; and the text of the Law of the Great Peace, available in a few different versions. Beginning in 1799, the Indian prophet Handsome Lake had a series of visions that led him to codify and preach what came to be called the Longhouse religion; this story and the tenets of the code itself are also suitable for presentation. The stories of Iroquois figures—from Kateri Tekawitha, the Mohawk saint, to Red Jacket, the Revolutionary War leader, to Joseph Brant, who founded the Six Nations Reserve in Brantford, Ontario—are good subjects. Speeches by famous Iroquois leaders are a particularly rich source, since the Iroquois were and continue to be well known among Indian people as skilled orators. The history of the Akwesasne settlement (it was founded about 1759 by a band of Mohawks from Caughnauwaga led by a Christian missionary) introduces the note of Indian-Christian contact, which also might be worked into script material; early Christian hymnals and prayer books printed in Mohawk are preserved in the Akwesasne Community Museum. Many of the Akwesasne Mohawks attended the Carlisle Indian School in Pennsylvania in the early 1900s; some of their stories have been collected and an oral-history project might expand on them. A constant issue on the reservation has been the citizenship of its inhabitants; *Akwesasne Notes* gives a good account of the struggles that have arisen because of the international border that divides the reservation. The Mohawk Language Consortium has begun a project under a Title VII grant to collect traditional Mohawk legends as recorded by Arthur Parker and to publish them in bilingual editions illustrated by native artists; these books can form the basis for interesting presentations.

Turning primary materials into scripts, learning interview techniques, working with oral histories, designing and teaching courses in oral interpretation of literature—all could properly be the subjects of other articles. But to give some idea of the course as it will probably unfold, we should point out that it becomes the students' job to research the materials collected, to put together performance scripts, and to begin their presentations with brief accounts of the background of their pieces. Some students will uncover and research materials of their own. And cultural history, as well as the skills of oral interpretation, will become a subject of the course.

What matters most to students in a course like this is precisely their awakening interest in discovering bits and pieces of their own cultural past. They become excited at the recognition that the materials they are scripting and performing are relevant to them as Native

Americans in ways that no literature of the white establishment could ever be. They gain satisfaction from selecting and arranging materials into scripts that will enable them to share their discoveries with others.

What matters most to teachers of a course like this are the experiences of the students: their best experiences form their teachers' best memories. Ours include Julie's discovering the work of Leslie Silko and Anna Lee Walters and acting out an excerpt from *Hanta Yo!*, Beatrice's reading from the speeches of Joseph Brant, Karen's illustrated presentation of "The Box Tortoise's Shell," Helen's serving as Mohawk translator and pronunciation expert for the group, Rosemary's recital of the legend of Deganawidah, and Minerva's overcoming her fear of poetry because Pauline Johnson was a poet from Six Nations and a member of her own people.

Telling One's Story

Women's Journals Then and Now

Elouise M. Bell

Telling One's Story: Women's Journals Then and Now. That was the title given in posters and newspaper articles announcing the beginning of a class in women's nontraditional writings that I taught winter semester 1979 at Brigham Young University. In the course title lay also my thesis, the rationale for the class: that everyone had a story to tell, that each story was worth telling, and that every normal woman or man had the necessary skills to tell the story in one form or another.

I began with a simple assertion: the published history of humankind's long struggle in mortality (whether written as actual history or as prose fiction) was woefully deficient on the distaff side. We knew what the kings and generals had done; we had our human family's story as told by leaders of government and business, religion and industry. More than half that story, however, remains untold, because so few women's writings have ever seen print. It is important to recognize the distinction: Women have almost always written, but they have only rarely published. In this new class, we were going to see what we could discover by reading women's stories, heretofore so much neglected.

I did not specify what we were trying to discover. Telling people what to look for often means telling them what to see. I was more interested in learning what the students would find without being told. We may have to rework some of our definitions of literature so that many previously ignored, noncanonical genres can enter the circle. But another way to approach the problem is inductive: to read widely among the personal genres, to see what conclusions we reach about what is enlightening and interesting, and to establish criteria on that basis.

I proposed to have my students read widely (if not deeply) in the

167

personal writings of women. I spent little time with them talking about critical theory but a lot of time on the subject of how to read carefully—and how to listen, a skill that comes first and is crucial because many personal writings of women are, in actuality, women's talking, whether to other women in letters or to themselves or to some future reader through journals. Historically, many published works of men have been rhetorical, that is, intended to persuade. Many personal writings of women have had no such objectives; rather, they have had goals much more complex and interwoven, goals more closely related to the aims of ordinary conversation. Thus the need to listen as well as to read.

There were two sections of Women's Journals, and the differences proved illuminating. Originally, I had hoped to have in the class, along with the regular university students, a number of older adult women, reentry or nontraditional students, to provide balance and diversity. But when the class was scheduled for 8 a.m., I realized that few family women could be on campus at that hour. So I asked for a second section of the course, to be taught in the evening. As a result, we had a morning class that met three times a week, composed of ten women, average age about twenty, and an evening class that met once a week, also composed of ten women, average age about fifty.

On the first day of class, each woman introduced herself by telling the group a short experience or story that would help us know her better. This activity took almost two hours but was well worth the time. First of all, the storytelling drew the group closer together and created a warm, productive ambience (especially in the evening class). Second, since each woman obviously knew the details of her own story and was asked merely to tell it, not to write it (a request that frightens too many these days), everyone began the class with a positive experience. But most important, the stories provided us with a body of raw material from which to draw in discussions the rest of the semester. They also gave us material, right at the start, that we could look at and think about. We could begin right away, without waiting for people to complete reading assignments.

I asked the group what kind of questions might arise in regard to the individual stories. Here are some of the suggestions:

- Why did the teller choose that story, above all the others she might have told? Why is the story important to her? What is its central meaning to her? Does a listener necessarily perceive the same central meaning?

- What is left out of the story? Why is that material left out? Does its omission make any difference? If we needed, where could we obtain the omitted details? If we could get the omitted material, would that give us the "correct" or "true" version of the story?

- What kinds of information would we need to understand the story better? (What contextual or background material would be necessary?)

- What other stories is this one like? Does it fit into a category or pattern of stories—is it a courtship tale, a journey account, a "lost child" or "lost object" story? If so, what elements does it share with other such stories, and how does it differ?

- Is this the first time the teller has told the story? What difference does that make? Will the story be the same if told ten years from now?

- Was the story interesting? Why? Why is it that one story about a young girl losing her eighth-grade graduation watch can be more interesting than another person's account of living through a severe earthquake?

Textbooks for the course were chosen merely to give a sample of women's personal writings. We used *Not by Bread Alone: The Journal of Martha Spence Heywood*, *Letters of a Woman Homesteader* by Elinor Stewart, and a 1979 issue of *Book Forum* devoted to diaries, journals, and letters, which contained a number of excellent articles on the genre.

One objective in teaching the class was to let students see the variety of material available, though they had never heard of it in the traditional high school or college curriculum. To this end, I would often bring in for discussion a large book bag full of autobiographies, diaries and journals, or letter collections. I would briefly summarize each book, explaining its scope and often reading parts of it aloud. Other students who had read the book on their own would comment and make comparisons to works we were reading as a class. Students were encouraged to borrow freely from my book bag. And as the class continued, I found students bringing books of their own to show to their classmates. In essence, we were putting together an annotated bibliography of materials to supplement the required texts.

An important part of the course was an introduction to the library of our university, which has special Women's Historical Archives. The curator of the Archives was most cooperative; he met with the class, gave a background lecture on our holdings, and then led the group through a tour of the stacks and storage rooms where the papers of many Utah women lay waiting for someone to read them. The curator continued to be helpful on an individual basis as students came to him for assistance with their term projects.

I intended these projects to be the main learning experience of the course. This activity, more than anything else they did or I said, convinced the women that every person does have a story to tell and that it is important for us to hear and to save each other's stories.

In the course of the semester, we clarified what we meant by "everyone has a story to tell." We decided we did not mean the cliché, "Everyone's life contains at least one book." Perhaps if perceived by a Balzac, each life might yield the material for a novel, but the novel is really in the eye of the beholder. It is a distinctive art form born in the brain of the creator and only tangentially related to any exterior facts. This point is important because if you are interested in personal history, journals, and other private writings, sooner or later you will encounter people who say things like: "I've always thought my grandfather's diary would make a great book. Can you help me find a publisher?" Indeed, after a short Associated Press article on this particular course was run in a number of newspapers across the country, I received dozens upon dozens of letters saying just that. Others wanted to sell me great-grandmother's letters or have me write a book from their own oral history.

In the class, we made a distinction: personal writings were important and interesting for their insights into the human condition, insights that they yielded up in their own way, not the way of the novel or of the formalized short story. It became clear, at least to me, that whatever criteria we were eventually to use in evaluating personal writings could not be the criteria of traditional literary narrative. The aims, the methods, and the results of personal writing were different. To judge both by a common yardstick would be unjust to both genres.

Lacking a critical theory for personal writings, traditional academics have valued letters and journals for either or both of two reasons: if they were stylistically interesting on their own, having the virtues of, say, the personal essay; or if they shed light on the lives of famous people (usually men) who were important in some public capacity.

The latter value led to what we could call the "notable women" approach in personal writings. Personal papers were important to the degree that the woman who wrote them was important. The assumption here is that our primary interest is in the great people of a society or culture. But let us question that assumption. Let's suppose we are interested in women generally, or the human heart in its typical manifestation. Is our best course of action then to study the notables? I asked students: "If you wanted to know what life in Utah was really like, if you really wanted to understand this culture, you wouldn't take an airplane and fly from mountain peak to mountain peak, from Timpanogos to Mt. Nebo, from King's Peak to Bryce Canyon. Your best course would be to go down into the valleys where life is lived, to see from that vantage point how men and women spend their days."

We must first grant that personal writings are not dormant novels, unwritten short stories, abortive novellas, before we can clearly see what they are, aesthetically, and how we can evaluate them. My students, having little training in formal literary criticism, were easily persuaded not to expect a novel-in-waiting among Aunt Minnie's memoirs. And they were most pleased with what they did find as they worked on their projects.

A number of students chose to record oral histories, writing up a section of the oral history with editor's notes for the term paper. None was trained in techniques of oral history, though we did spend some time in class laying out the basics of oral-history methods; one or two had to gather material by sending lists of questions and a blank tape to a distant grandmother or great-aunt. All who did oral history had one experience in common: their subjects began by saying, "Oh, you don't want to hear me ramble on," or by objecting, "Oh, I don't have anything to say," and all ended by filling up tape after tape with lively details from all epochs of their lives. Thus the students learned first-hand that people do want and need to tell their stories and need to have someone listen. Each student who did an oral history had plans to go back after the course was over and do more with the subject or to do the same with another subject she had in mind.

Dealing with aged relatives or townspeople and searching for missing records had another result. Virtually every student developed a sense of urgency. Who knew how much longer Great-Aunt Ellen would be around? We developed a group vision (or nightmare) of countless diaries, journals, and letter collections mouldering away each year in attics, garages, barns, and back closets, of reams of material being thrown out with each spring housecleaning. A true anecdote we learned of during the semester intensified this picture. A woman of eighty-five had custody of some thirty-six years' worth of day-by-day journals written by her mother, an early Iowa pioneer and farmer. The journals were not merely health-and-weather jottings but considered, thoughtful entries. The aging daughter—her mother was dead, of course—was going through volume by volume, copying out important birth and death dates, and then methodically burning the journals, because she believed such books were private.

Some students elected to edit personal papers, selecting just a few documents in order to have a task of manageable size. The personal benefits seemed almost out of proportion to the projects. One young woman chose to edit a collection of letters between her mother and father, written at the end of World War II when the latter was stationed in Guam and the former was working in Salt Lake City. The resultant document was a good, well-edited piece of work, but the high point, for the student, was that she and her parents by necessity, had had to sit down together for several hours each night and discuss the context of the letters. As the student described it, the family shared more real communication during those five or six days than they had in her lifetime. She reported that her parents were shaken but joyous at the new level of intimacy and sharing of feelings occasioned by their daughter's research.

Another young woman, whose parents had served several years on a church mission, undertook an imaginative project. The husband's father was a church leader of high position, and it fell to the young wife to write weekly letters to her in-laws, reporting their activities and achievements as well as those of the six small children. The wife also wrote weekly letters to her own parents. The student decided to examine and edit two sets of letters covering the same time span, one from her mother to the in-laws, the other from her mother to the maternal grandparents. The two sets touched on the same events, activities, and problems, but the letters were, as the student suspected they might be, very different. In her project, she edited the letters and wrote a commentary accounting for the differences in tone, style, emphasis, and other qualities.

A project that I found of high interest was a four-generation interview. The student (age 18) worked out with me a set of questions on work, education, sex roles, and leisure activities. Then, in company with her mother (age 44) and her grandmother (age 68), she visited her great-grandmother (age 91). She led her mother, grandmother, and great-grandmother through a combination of oral history and panel discussion, as it were, and even in this relatively short project, one could trace the development of patterns, see where attitudes had changed and why, and raise interesting questions for future interviews.

One student of nineteen had eight or ten female cousins all roughly her own age (not unusual among Mormons). Since journal keeping has been urged on the Mormon populace as a religious responsibility, nearly all the cousins kept personal journals. My student requested that her cousins send her representative pages from their journals so that she might analyze them for subject matter, main concerns, journal-keeping techniques, and so forth. She reported that at the annual family reunion her term project was the center of attraction and that the family had decided they might make a habit of periodically sharing journal entries as a way of staying in closer touch.

The final project I will mention was the most ambitious. Diana T.

had never known her great-grandmother, Rebecca G. The only artifact of the woman was a half sheet of paper containing a blessing she had received as a young girl around the turn of the century. For some reason, young Diana became fascinated with this unknown ancestor and set out to reconstruct as much of her history as possible.

She began by tracking down living relatives who still remembered Rebecca and recording oral interviews with several dozen of them. She visited the places her ancestor was known to have lived and searched microfilm records at county courthouses and church offices. She read copies of old newspapers, learning, for instance, what the weather was like the day her grandmother was born, what textbooks were used in the grade schools in that region at that time, and what fashions were current during her great-grandmother's courting days. Bit by bit, as though working on a thousand-piece puzzle, she put together her perception of her ancestor's story. The project Diana did for our class was thirty or forty pages long, but she has since added to it until it is now a record of more than one hundred pages that she is submitting as a senior honors project.

Let me now discuss the evening section of this course, a group of ten women considerably older than the regular students. Only one or two were registered for credit; the others were auditing. Their status as auditors in no way diminished their interest in the class; in fact, I would say their personal involvement was even greater than that of the younger students. For most of them, it was the only course they were taking, and their energy level when they came together was high. They differed from the daytime students in more than age: their experience with life was wider, their formal writing skills rustier, their attitudes about writing journals more ambivalent. But most interesting to me was what we may call their hidden agenda—hidden even from themselves. In reality, the class functioned as a modest consciousness-raising group. In other words, what was of greatest interest to these women was that they had a story to tell; the vital lessons learned in the class were that others considered their stories worth telling and that they could do a good job of telling their stories.

It had not been my intention, of course, to design a consciousness-raising group for this evening class. Their schedule was the same as that of the daytime section. They read the same text, wrote the same assignments, followed the same discussion topics. But time and again the pattern emerged: they wanted to tell their stories and hear one another's. I do not mean to suggest that the class degenerated to the level of swapping reminiscences. But more even than the journals of others, these women were interested in their own journals. And writing those journals led them, more than it did the younger women, to self-examination and self-searching. This process brought them to key questions: Who is the implied reader of a journal? How honest ought one to be in one's journals? (This was the most hotly debated issue.) How private are journals? Just what are the ethics of reading another person's journals? (Maybe the aging daughter was justified in burning her mother's records.)

It was soon clear that most of these women had not had the opportunity to talk about themselves, their needs, their inner life, for a long time. Few seemed to have had in-depth discussions with women before coming to the class. The class was in some senses a new direction for them. They spoke of continuing on with the meetings after the semester was over. They exchanged addresses and phone numbers. One woman in her early forties, an attractive and talented mother of a large and busy family, wife of an affluent professional man in the community, said in so many words that the class had changed her life and that she didn't know how she was going to get along without it. All these comments, I believe, support the underlying thesis: people need to tell their stories. Personal writings may be one way of doing that. The overall human need must be understood first, because it implies several corollaries about the need to write one's story down. For instance, if one has, on some kind of regular basis, an opportunity to tell one's story orally to family, friends, neighbors, is one then less apt to write it, either in letters or in journals? Everyone who reads letters and journals becomes quickly aware of loneliness as a motive for writing. Do women in particular write journals primarily if and when we are lonely, estranged, cut off? If so, that implies a great deal about how we must read them. Another question: to what degree might it be therapeutic for older people to write or tell their stories in some formal way? Does one face death any more easily if one has ordered and told one's story satisfactorily?

I would like to conclude this review of my experiences teaching women's journals by explaining briefly how principles used in this class carried over to another, seemingly unrelated course. About a year later I was assigned to teach a junior-level expository writing course, a class I had not taught for some years. Included in the coursework is a library paper, usually a semester-long thorn in the sides of both teacher and taught. On this occasion, however, I told the students that they were to do a research paper on a topic from their family history. They were to weave together personal history and the strands of wider research to show the context, background, or relevance. I did not know how the idea would work, but I figured anything would be better than the much-dreaded standard library paper.

The results were gratifying. Early comments indicated that the students liked the assignment: "I've always hated term papers, but now I find myself anxious to make time to work on this one." "I've got my father and my grandfather involved in this, and we're having a great time." "I figured I must be doing something wrong because I was having so much fun writing this."

What kinds of papers did they write? One young woman had in her family a legend about great-great-grandfather who ran away and signed on a whaling ship as cabin boy. She wrote a paper tracing as much as she could find of his adventures, buttressed by research on life aboard a nineteenth-century whaler. Another had ancestors who fled from Ireland to Scotland and thence to America. Why had they left? What would cause them to uproot? What were the economic conditions of that particular decade in Ireland? He traced his family's migrations with a focus on the economics of such shifts. Another had an ancestor who had been part of the experiment in communal living known as the United Order. She examined the ideals that established the United Order and the realities that ultimately destroyed it.

One young woman wondered about her grandmother, who had been left a very young widow in a nearby mining town, now reduced to a ghost town. The town had many young widows because of frequent mine disasters. How did these women care for and raise their large broods, when the mines paid no pensions and no insurance and the state no aid to dependent children? From books on local history, from wide reading in old newspapers, and from family histories, the student put together a solid paper. Another student lived not far from a locally famous "Dream Mine," a mine that a local bishop had seen in a dream and was certain would bring him and the church astounding wealth. The visionary spent a long lifetime working and waiting for his dream mine to pay off. The story involved much controversy, a clash with church authorities, an excommunication, three generations of local history. The student, again using old newspaper accounts, church records, family letters, personal journals, and oral history, wrote a good paper on the ill-fated dream mine.

Perhaps the most interesting paper came from a student in his mid-twenties whose father had been for twenty-one months a prisoner of war in Korea. The young man had grown up knowing his father had been a POW, but for some reason the family had never discussed the experience, although the veteran occasionally gave speeches about it to local groups. The son resolved that the research assignment would be an opportunity to learn his father's story. When he telephoned to ask whether his father would cooperate in the work, there was a long pause at the other end of the line. Finally, gaining control of his voice with effort, the father said, "I'll tell you anything you want to know." It was the son's surmise that his father had been waiting all those years to be asked to tell his son that particular story. The student read books about the POW situation during the Korean conflict, reviewed a good many newspaper accounts, consulted other veterans' memoirs, and spent many hours talking with his father. His paper was outstanding, and I asked him to read it to the class. It was not easy for him to do so with perfect control, and a number of us listening were similarly moved, though the paper was written objectively and without sensationalism. There was no question that this was far more than a routine class assignment, for him and for us.

It may have been coincidental, but this was the only class I've had in twenty years of teaching in which *no* student failed to turn in the research paper on time. This group of writers was not particularly gifted, and the papers varied widely in quality, but they were unusual in degree of interest and personal involvement. Each student had a story he or she felt was worth telling.

What of the future? Women's Journals as a class will probably be taught only sporadically at Brigham Young University, but much from the class can be incorporated into my classes and those of my colleagues. First, colleagues can be encouraged to be aware of the personal writings of women and how these can be used in regularly scheduled classes—Victorian Literature, for instance, or Modern Poetry (so many of the fine modern poets, especially the women, keep wonderful journals or day-books), Western American Literature, or Introduction to Literature. Second, we have in the department a regularly scheduled class called Writing Personal History. The carry-overs here are obvious. Finally, I have been asked to give a seminar to the composition teachers about the experiment in the expository writing class, so that we can consider it as one option for the many composition courses we teach.

In theory and in application, many questions remain about nontraditional—or, more correctly, noncanonical—writings. We may be decades in working out good answers to those questions. But that task need not deter us from now making imaginative, invigorating use of the materials we have at present, or from continuing the search for more materials and for better ways to use them.

APPENDIXES

Writing Exercises

Writing Assignments Using Letters

1. Punctuate a letter. Resolve conflicts in choice by considering the author's personality and how it might have been reflected in the selection of dashes, exclamation points, semicolons, or commas had the writer been familiar with their present-day uses.

2. Treat a letter as a sentence-combining exercise, considering afterward the stylistic, expressive changes that have resulted from your efforts.

3. Respond as the recipient of a letter, writing in reply—questioning, suggesting, consoling, assisting, or arguing with the author as you have been persuaded to do by the role you have assumed throughout your reading.

4. Present the "true" version of the writer's life, citing evidence from interviews with living relatives, historical research, or simply a close reading of the text of the writer's extant works.

5. Rewrite a letter with the intention of removing the author's mask or filling in an author's silence to correct the distortions and omissions.

6. Rewrite a letter from the viewpoint of another person mentioned in the letter.

7. Rewrite a letter retaining the same information but altering emphasis to give another impression.

8. Rewrite a letter to send it to a different person.

9. Identify the writer of the letter—gender, race, class, educational background, historical period, etc.—through a close reading of the text.

10. Write a letter to the editor of a collection of letters, such as *The*

Maimie Papers, arguing that a specific letter should be omitted. Write another letter from the editor arguing that it should be included.

Writing Assignments Using Diaries

1. Using a record-keeping diary such as the three in *Women's Diaries of the Westward Journey*, edited by Lillian Schlissel, write the story up in (a) the briefest form and (b) a longer form with additions based on what one knows from experience and from reading.

2. Write a paper based on historical allusions in the diary, such as the relation between white plantation owners and black workers in the South in the late nineteenth century.

3. Write about the diarist's life in terms of his or her profession or family role.

4. Keep a diary for two weeks in which only incidents are noted. Then analyze the entries to see what narratives develop, what characters enter, and how the events reveal character.

5. Use the diary as survival kit. Possible assignments:
   a. Write a diary entry on your names. What difference have they made? Do you like your names? Do other people? How did you get your names? Do your names match who you feel you are?
   b. Write a diary entry about where you live. How has where you live made you who you are?
   c. Write a diary entry about how you look. Do you like the way you look? Do other people? What adjustments have you made? How has your physical appearance affected who you are?
   d. Write a diary entry about your inner self. Do other people recognize this inner self? Are you two people? If so, how do you reconcile them?

Steps in Teaching a Writing Course Using Oral Testimonies

1. Introduction to what oral testimony is and why one studies it, using the oral-history issue of *Frontiers*.

2. Separately and then in groups, work on a list of questions for a general interview and a list for a more focused interview (concentrating, for example, on a topic like work, immigration, growing up, marriage, or the family).

3. Practice interviewing a member of the class; each person asks two questions; the second question should be a follow-up question,

based on the interviewee's response, probing further than the first one. An outside person can be invited in to be interviewed.

4. Paired interviews with a third person functioning as observer and commentator.
5. Talk about summarizing, transcribing, editing, and writing up an oral testimony. For instance, examine two different published oral testimonies in *Southern Exposure*, and discuss how they are differently organized (one is set in a more historical context; the other contains more of the interviewer's voice and analysis). Compare the writing up of an oral testimony to a traditional essay with an introduction, body with quotations, and conclusion.
6. Read and discuss essays, stories, and poems related to oral testimony. See films that use an oral-testimony approach: the theme of mothers and daughters is a good way to connect literature and oral testimony.
7. Listen to excerpts of the students' taped interviews.
8. Share the written oral testimonies in groups. Read a few aloud to the entire class.

The Diary of Amelia Buss

[Most of the information concerning the Amelia Buss diary is contained in the Preface and Postlude, written in 1965 by Sara Overholt, Amelia Buss's grandniece. The original diary is located in the Special Collection of the Colorado State University Library, Fort Collins, Colorado, and is published with its permission.

The diary published in this volume is two steps removed from the original holograph. As Sara Overholt writes in her preface, she typed her copy from a typed copy Arthur Bates, Amelia Buss's grandnephew, sent her. His typed copy came from the original, which, at that time, was in his possession. We have followed Sara Overholt's typed transcript.

All of us—Arthur Bates, Sara Overholt, and the editors of this volume—have been faithful to Amelia Buss's spelling, punctuation, and sentence structure. Nothing has been altered.

The editors are indebted to Susan Armitage of Washington State University for bringing this diary to their attention.]

Preface

This is a copy of the diary kept by Amelia Butts Buss (Mrs. George Buss) in 1866–67, of her journey west and their first year in Fort Collins, Colorado. Varah or Vatie as she was called, was their 8 year old daughter. The a in Vatie is pronounced like the a in May.

Amelia mentions her four sisters, Ann (Hannah), Lydia (my grandmother), Grace (Arthur Bates' grandmother), and Sarah. She does not mention a brother Otis.

Arthur Bates of Florida, kindly loaned me a typed copy of this diary, but the original diary he keeps in a safe deposit box in the bank. Apparently the blank diary was given to Amelia when she left her home in Boonville, N.Y., and she returned it to her sisters after she had finished it. Arthur Bates' grandmother had it, then his mother had it, and then his mother passed it on to him.

They traveled by train to St. Joseph, Missouri, then boarded a river steamer and went up stream to Nebraska City, Nebraska. From there they traveled 31 days by covered wagon, to Fort Collins, Colorado.

In one place she writes, "Today another waggon joined us and now there is five in all". At another time she writes, "I am all the woman there is in this big train".

While they had no serious trouble with the Indians on their journey or the first year in their home in the west, they did have some interesting experiences with them.

Apparently her husband had been to Fort Collins, bought this log cabin some one else had built, put in crops of corn and potatoes, and then went back east to get Amelia and Vatie.

Arthur Bates writes that the spelling and punctuation are exactly as she wrote it and I have copied it the same way.

Sara Overholt

Utica   Aug. 15th 66

Arrived here safe & while I am waiting for the train west I pen this— we found it best to wait till four P.M. We all had a warm dinner & Vatie said tell aunt Grace what a good dinner we had but I think she did not eat one dollars worth. she is now amusing her self playing the piano but we are soon to go *west*.

Missigan   Aug. 16th

Last night we crossed the suspension bridge at Niagra but it being in the evening we could not see much of it. This morning we saw lake Champlion & we crossed over at Detroit on a ferry. We were 15 minutes going over. Vatie & myself stood out to see all we could. the water was a lite green color.

Aug. 17th

Have had a pleasant time saw lake Missigan just at night got into Chichago in the evening took a sleeping car & found it nice as any parlor had a good nights rest & felt very much rested took our own breakfast & staid in the same car till noon.

St. Joe   Aug. 18th

We came on board the steam boat Denver this afternoon and it has been very warm but now the sun is down & its delightfully cool the moon is shining all is quiet. We all went up on the hurry cain deck & I could not keep thinking of all of my friends & wishing they could all be there for a short time. Mailed a letter home today.

Missury river   Aug. 19th

This is the sabbath day but it don't seem like it. there is quite a number of passingers on board & the cabin & state rooms are so warm they are on deck & there is no comfortable place to be a lone & we are obliged to hear all kinds of talk none of them seem religious. Today Vatie is 8 years old.

Aug. 20th

We arrived today at 11 A.M. o'clock in Nebraskey City. there is some fine building here and business seems to be very lively. I am now in my room up three flite of stairs & I have a good view of the place from the other side of the house. the Missoury is in plain sight. Many of the buildings are of brick. I like it here.

Neb City   Aug. 21st

I have a hard cold and am just about sick & some home sick. The sight of so many dirty returning emigrants has had much to do with the later sickness. Then I have been a stranger in a strange place. I am anxious to once more be in my own home.

Neb City Seymour House   Aug. 22nd

It is just one week since we left home and it seems to me a month insted. I woke up this morning and it was raining hard. I fear we shall not get away unless it stops. it is chilly and with my cold I feel it very much. Vatie is not feeling well I fear she will be sick. Mailed a letter to Ann today.

Aug. 23rd

four miles out of the city we left there yesterday & came here to wait for a Mr. King that is going to Montana. last night we slept in our waggon or rather staid. I felt to much afraid to sleep although we were close by a house still we wer in the road & it was very new to me but nothing disturbed us. we had the same kind protector there.

Aug. 24th

We are still in this place Vatie is real sick with diareah I feel very anxious about her it is well we had to wait for she could not have stood the ride. I have been washing some of my things & I found it very tiresome bending so low. Vatie is some better tonight. I am very tired but most well.

Aug. 25th

We left Nebraska at 7 this morning & now I am writing while the men hitch up the teems. we did not have any wood & we took a cold dinner but hunger is a good sauce & mine relished if it was nothing but bread & butter raw tomatoes & cold tea Vatie is quite like herself but sick of the waggon the first half day.

Aug. 26th

35 miles out This is the sabbath but nothing here makes it seem so we would have staid over but the company go so we would be left a lone & now while I write I think of the B___ sabbath school as they are now assembled for worship & praise my heart is there if I am not. it has been *cold* & have worn a *thick* shawl all the forenoon.

Aug. 27th

55 miles out. this is a warm pleasant day. we have had a long morning stoped by a miserable looking log hut just high enough for a man to stand up in I hear *locus* now for the first time in my life Vatie is not well yet but drives the *horses* some she enjoys that. I am not in love with any of this country no wood & not much water.

Walnut Creek   Aug. 28th

We are waiting for a cattle train to get over the bridge this is quite a pleasant place there is a few trees here—last night we had not been in park but a few moments when four *Indians* came there they wanted something to eat & then they were going to lay down by our waggon & Geo. told them we did not want them there.

Aug. 29th

This has been a very windy day the dust blew very much but the most of the time it blew at our side & took the dust away at noon we had four more *Indians* to see us they wanted dinner & matches. one of them was a squaw. one of the men wanted Vatie for his *squaw* he bid us good by when he left us this is a terible night & I feel tired & sick of such *fusings* I fail to see any thing *desirable* in such travling it is hurry up in the morning & get a hasty breakfast & have a cold lunch for dinner & at night get supper & bake bread & not get through till 9. Am I ungrateful if I *do* complain some *times*

Aug. 30th

An other day is gon & we are one the nearer to our home. it has been pleasant but this afternoon a part of the time we faced the wind & the *dust* from the other teams was terible. This morning we met a train comeing from Californy there was 7 waggons & some 50 horses. the children looked dirty & ragged but seemed to enjoy them selves they wer running a long a mong the teems. this afternoon met a big ox train some 3 hundred & such a cloud of dust I never was in before we are parked tonight beside the Platt river & now we shall have plenty of water. G. is out watching the stock till 12 then he will be releived. it thunders & raines a little Vatie & I are a lone

Aug. 31st

There has not been anything of importance taken place today. but it has been the same dull tiresome travling & it was so late I could not make any bread for an other day.   today an other waggon joined us now there is five in all.   it has been a nice day to travel but windy tonight

Sept. 1st 66

Saturday night. we are within 5 miles of Fort Kearny got here at noon. Geo. went up to the post office but there was no letters for us I felt very much *disappointed.* We are waiting for more men   Last night it rained very hard but we did not get wet. it has been a little muddy today & is quite cool tonight

Sept. 2nd

This has been the sabbath & we have not traveled & I have wished many times we were on the move for the day would have been more quiate we have been obliged to hear all sorts of talk & swearing it was cold and rained this morning but has been very warm this afternoon & plenty of *misquetoes* to night as usual.

Sept. 3rd

Monday we started again at noon for our onward march. I made two batches of bread & roasted coffee this fore noon. Mailed a letter to Lydia at Kearny Village 2 miles above the Fort. did not get any letter today   It thunders & lightens very hard   G. is on guard again to-night   it makes my head ache to ride so much

Sept. 4th

It rained very hard last night and was very cold this morning. I wore my shawl and gloves all the forenoon   it was very warm this afternoon and *mudy*   I never saw such lightning as we had last night nor such a glorious *sun set*   The Platt was a mile wide there & there is some of the handsomest *islands* in this river I ever saw

Sept. 5th

This has been a cold day I have worn my shawl & had a army blanket over me.   in the afternoon it rained. We went out without any break-fast road till 10 than stoped till 3 that is our *captains* way but we do not like it. it was almost dark when we parked & it rained. G. got supper and we took it in the waggon

Sept. 6th

This was a cool forenoon. I laid down & snoosed some till 9 when we stopped for our breakfast & dinner in one meal   this morning we passed 4 ox trains going west in less than two miles   business is lively but how *new* to me. We met the stage going east this afternoon & a little child was looking out   his *face* was all sun burnt but he will get browner before 300 miles are gone over.

Sept. 7th

We have not been but 10 miles this day one of the men broke down & the train had to wait the rest of the day. I get along very well when we are moving on as fast as we can but now nothing to do & no company   I feel very lonesome & all most home sick   yesterday G. met some of his 21st men & it seemed pleasant for him to meet old friends but all are strangers to me.

Sept. 8th

We left camp a little after day light & passed through *Cottonwood*. I was disappointed in not getting a letter. I feel almost forgotten by my friends the wind has blown a gail the dirt flew like snow & was very disagreable to face. we took our dinner in the waggon on account of the storms. The blufs on our left are a grand sight but there is nothing on them but grass that is faded.

Sept. 9th

This is the sabbath we are traveling   it is much quieter for me but very different from former sabbaths the wind blew all night a perfect gale & made me long for the morning but the wind & sand are terible to endure today. it seemed to me my eyes would be put out when I was getting our dinner my bread was well pepered with *grit*. I am all the woman there is in this big train

We met a government train & also a mule train there was 200 waggons in all of them we did not park until nearly dark & it blew a gail & rained. I cooked my meat & tea with Emerson & we eat it in the wagon. it was G. turn to go on guard but his rheumatism would not admit of it   he offered Emerson one dollar to go in his place   he went but refused any pay.

Sept. 10th

This is a cold rainy morning but it don't affect me now that we don't have but two meals a day it cleared up before we parked for our first meal which was a bout 9 A.M. I had a nice time making bread & washing my dishes & a few towels It has been warm this afternoon & I sat out with G. we met a Californian train I thought the women and children were fortunate in going east   we came close to the Platt this afternoon & it was a beatiful sight so many *Islands* some large & many small ones we say we follow the Platt & so we do but some times we are several miles a way & do not see it in all day. Vatie has been singing some of our old sabbath hymns & it seemd good to hear—once more amid so much cursing.

Sept. 11th

This has been a pleasant day. we have very cool nights and mornings there has nothing new taken place this day but has been the same dul roteen of travling meeting returning trains. we saw some 200 this day but there is but little satisfaction in seeing dirty ragged men & hearing them crack there big whips over the poor oxens back till great ridges raise up. there has been *cacktus* or prickly *pear* all a long the road today the buds on them are good to eat & some make pies of them they are a bout the size of a butternut & have a pleasant sour tast. I have just been startled by the sound of a pistol & a call for help. it proved to be men trying to steel horses they got a way without being injured or getting any of our horses & mules.

Sept. 12

This has been a very warm day last night the horse thieves tried hard to get some of our stock the guard fired on them & they left. we reached Juelsburg just at night & are parked a short distance from the town it is a small place there is not more than a dozen houses & three stores & a billerd saloon they are all new it was burnt by the Indians two years ago it is just a bout the *division* between Nebraska & Colerado the town is in the former place. we met a train of Rocky mountain people there going east there was several familys a long & small children. we are now 400 miles out. I wrote a letter to Grace tonight.

Sept. 13th

Another fine day this morning we went past Ft. Seagrave 4 miles from Juelsburg it is much larger than the later place the buildings are all government property. I never saw so much grain as there was in sacks outdoors covered with canvass. besides two long barnes full some of the buildings are built of wood & some of them are doby or sod plastered on the out side

Sept. 14th

The wind comenced blowing a bout 8 oclock this morning & it was so strong I could not go near the fire the flames spread out so far there was danger of getting on fire G. fixed the meat for breakfast We have had hard sandy roads for 2 or 3 days we are now travling where there is no trees but it is not so dreary to me as it was in Nebraska there we could see so far & nothing but sky and grass. here most of the way it is a narrow strip of land with the river & its beautiful islands some of them are quite large others don't look larger than a foot stool there is no trees on them. some have willows others tall grass & all of them of a rich green here the bluffs all add much to the scenery

Sept. 15

This morning we met a train of 18 waggons they were drawn by six mules to a waggon they was loaded with shingles & wood which come from the mountains & was going to Juelsburg & last year the latter brought $125.00 a cord only think of such a price for one cord of pine wood it was a nice train the mules were all fat the waggons & harnesses new. I fride some cakes for our dinner than went to the river & done some washing. We have had hard roads today one place of half a mile the sand was sodded & it was a nice road but the first house we came to a man came out & took one dollar for every waggon. he will soon have to build an other house to hold his money at that rate

Sept. 16th

Godfrey's station Sabbath evening we have been travling to day & I hope it is the last sunday we shall be out. it has been a quiet day considering all things this morning the teems had to double to get up a sand hill but us Vatie and I walked up the wind has been cold & not very comfortable to rid this is my 32nd birthday we past by just at night the graves of eleven men that were killed by the indians 2 or three years a go. we are now following the south fork of the Platt river we have been cheered all the way by the sight of the telegraph *poles* & most every day the stage. met a big train of returning people going to the *states* this afternoon.

Sept. 17th

Two miles from Ft. Morgon we have camped here for the night the wind is cold & it makes me long for a better shelter. there is some pleasure in such a trip but the hardships and inconveniences are so great they more than double the former I have not as yet seen any thing so very charming but have seen a *rattle snake* today with 7 rattles on his tail that made him as many years old Emerson killed him G. killed one some days ago with two & a button I am not feeling well to night & a good deal blue as G. intends to leave the train in the morning & go a shorter route if he can get a pass I am so a fraid of indians I can not bear to go.

Sept. 18th

23 miles west of Ft. Morgan we left the train at 7 oclock this morning & have been travling a lone & nothing has harmed us but I have suffered very much from fear. we have not passed but two houses since we left the train & the road has been a very lonely one. many places we could not see far on account of the high bluffs. one especially called *Fremont's* orchard they were very high & but a narrow strip of land between them and the river. there is now some dozen cotton wood trees standing in the place & it is an awful place in case of an atackt from indians or anyone. the road has been near or what is called the river road but sometimes it goes over the bluffs then it is sandy & hard. I saw some prarie dogs & ground owles this afternoon they and rattle *snakes* all live in the same holes together This is a terible night to me we are out all a lone & it raines. G. is guarding his horses close by the waggon we met a big ox train & a Californy one this morning the later had several familys a long they will have some 3000 miles by the time they reach the states by waggon

Sept. 19th

It commenced to rain last night just after we camped & it was a very wet night G. was out all night guarding the horses. we started on our journey at 10 A.M. it kept raining all the time but our horses wer very cold & we could not make a fire every thing was so wet & we wer 10 miles from a house. we had not gon far when the rain turned to snow & it kept it up nearly all day. when we got to the first house the stables wer so poor we drove on 12 miles further & it was a cold tedious ride for us all. we had not had but very little to eat & that was cold so we bought our supper & had our team put in the barn and fed hay but slept in one wagon & had to pay $3.00 for it they offered us the bar room but there was no floor in it & it leaked at that we thought our wagon a better place if it was some wet I saw 2 prairie *wolves* this morning & a Jack rabit they are a curious little animal we met just one wagon this day. I have not suffered any fear today the storm has taken my mind from that. it is 29 days since we have been in a house and it is not much better than none.

Sept. 20th

We rested very well last night it froze quite hard we saw the mountains this morning for the first time they were covered with snow & to me it was a grand sight we road 7 miles then we stoped to a house & I went in & made some buiscuit & got our breakfast & had to pay 50¢ for the privilege. we crossed the Platt a bout noon had no trouble but the water came in our wagon some it was a great releif to me to be safely over but I could not look out it made me so dizy we forded the Cashlassonder in the afternoon & found the water deeper in that than in the Platt but not so wide. we are now within 7 miles of our home but it is sundown & the teem is tired we are on Mr. Whitney's farm & close to his house. had a cold biscuit & nothing more for our supper a bout 9 oclock

Sept. 21st

This morning Mr. Whitney came out & invited us in to breakfast I found Mrs.W. a very pleasant woman we had a nice meal they gave us two large squashes & two nice pumkins & Vatie two little kittens. we left there feeling very kindly toard them we arrived at our place a bout 11 oclock A.M. & found everythin looking very bad one window every light was broken out & the lower sash broken & spoiled in the other the family got their things out in two hours. I did not get out of the wagon till they left the house & when I went in such a sight it sickened me but every thing but the windows looked as I imagined it would before & I was not in Mrs. Jones hoped hapily disapointed but here I am & now must clean & work & all ways be over run with bugs & dirt. A neighbor brought some *cabbage* & gave to us.

Sept. 22nd

We all camped down on the floor & slept some. we wer up early this morning on packing. some of my dishes were broken. we have all worked hard G. has been repairing the *windows*. Vatie has been a good deal of help but she has made me feel bad many times by asking for such things as I could not give her. I find it very hard to go to work after my journey. I need rest but there is none in this world for me.

Sept. 23rd

This is the sabbath & our first one I have not kept it as strictly as I aught but necesity has forced me to work some G. went to the office this noon & came back with no letter but two of our Evangelist it don me good to get them but I was sadly disapointed in not yet getting any news from *home*. I have looked at my albums but none of them speak to me & it only agrivates me.

Sept. 26th

I have written a letter to Sarah today to let them know of our safe arrival at this place. Francis Grant is here helping G. cut some hay as not a spear of it was cut. much of it has been fed off & the frost has injured it but the horses must have something in stormy weather every thing is in a sad condition the *corn* all *distroyed* by *cattle*. not a stalk left.

Sept. 27th

I have been washing today & am very tired but had something very aggreeable before I got through in the shape of a letter from sister L. & it don me so *much* good to hear from home once more I was not long in finding out its contence and aggreeably surprised to find aunt Marys & Agustas picture in the letter if they did not speak to me I can look at them

Sept. 30th

An other & we are all well Lieut Manderville called here this morning & he brought me sister Anns first letter I feared I should not get it how good to hear a gain so soon. Just at night Mrs. Sherwood called on me she said "I really pity you in comeing here" it was a comfort to feel I had the sympathy of even a stranger.

Oct. 6th

My work has kept me from writing & I have been to low spirited to make any effort till today G. has been gon all day to the mountains & I have been very lonely. Just at night Herbert Gleason & a friend of his came to spend the night with us & G. got me a letter from sister Grace her first one I did not get.

Oct. 7th

Our company left a bout 11 A.M. & I wrote a long letter home & spent a portion of my time in reading a *sermon* in fathers book it was good but some how I could not get in the spirit of worship & felt a longing to sit down with the good people of B. & join with them in praise & prayer.

Oct. 8th

I have been washing today G. went to the mountains after logs to log up the cellar & it will be a great relief to me when it is finished the house is not safe as it is. I some times wish it had gon in to the cellar before he ever saw it when G. came home tonight he brought a quarter of beef & had lost the letter I wrote yesterday my patience was tried but that was all the good it don

Oct. 9th

I have been baking bread boiling meat & ironing while I was at the latter an Indian came in & wanted a drink of water he had a poney & a long rope on him he had one end of it in his hand all of the time although the door was shut he looked all round the room & a good deel at me then he left & I was not sorry my letter was found by a man & he said he mailed it

Oct. 14th

Sabbath day I have enjoyed this one better than any since I left home I have been very much interested in my Bible dictionary & shall derive much knowledge from it in the future   George is 37 years old this day & we thought we would have a treat for dinner   it was dride apple *sauce* on our bread & ginger cake for *desert.*

Oct. 15th

It rained a little last night for the first time since I came here & this morning the ground was white with snow the *gabel* ends of our house are not battened & the snow blew in so much I thought I would stop the holes up & took cold in my teeth & they ache very much. G. has taken one of our goods boxes today & made me a small cubbord for my dishes but there is no door to it.

Oct. 19th

I have had the teeth ache every day this week till this & now they are very soar. Mrs. Arthur came & spent the afternoon I found her social but some how I felt more home sick after she went a way then I did before she came. she *laughed* at me for being homesick & said I had better go round & see my neighbors how they lived & I would come home satisfide. It is no comfort to me to be told I have things as good as any one around me & I wish I could feel contented. I can not tell anyone how I feel I some times fear my health will fail if I do not soon feel better. I feel the want of sympathy very much.

Oct. 21st

Sabbath day I have been writing to sisters Ann & Grace. I received letters from them last friday night & how it carried me back to them & how it made me long for an interview with them. They may think my letters are gloomy but I put the best side out. if I had told them just how I felt they too would have been *sad*.

Oct. 23rd

I have don a two weeks washing today & am very tired did not get through early enough to clean the floor. my hands are cracked and chaped yesterday G. went to the mountains Vatie & myself are very lonly when he is gon all day & I shall be glad when he gets all of his logs down.

Oct. 24th

I have cleaned my floor & ironed my clothes. a bout noon two squaws came I went to the door just as they came up. I thought I would not have them come in & said to them what do you want. they smiled & said "see". I steped back & they came in & stood round half an hour. It was amusing to see them & hear there low talk & a relief to have them go away. I did not ask them to come again.

Oct. 27th

I have been helping G. in the cellar for the two last days. I have not had any time or any thing to write G. has gone over on Tompson creek after potatoes some 15 miles from here this afternoon a great red Indian came in he was a Sioux I was very fraid of him & Vatie looked as though she would sink he opened the door & came in & put out his hand & said as all of them do *how*. I shook hands with him and said *how* in return. then he began to look a round the room & said *in* I did not know what he ment & told him so. he then took up my best butcher knife & that was what he wanted I said I can't spare that but he ask me twice more for it but of course did not get it. he looked at Vatie & said *papoose* I told him yes she was my papoose he laughed & shook his head & said *no* I insisted that she was & every time he said no. then he steped close to me & pated me under my chin I began to think our time had come. he then saw Vatie's doll in the cradle & said papoose & took it up & felt of it all over then laid it down & went off & we wer glad to see his back I asure you

Oct. 28th

An other lords day & all is well. I felt as though I could not stay at home from church & told G. I wished he would read while I don my necessary work for I had an other homesick fit. he laughted at me but took the Evangelist & read it a loud. the day is nearly gon & I am one the nearer my home. G. did not get home last night till 8 oclock he bought 20 bushels of potatoes for 75 cts per bushel & they were large nice looking but prove to be soggy. We had a bout 15 that was raised on our place the man had dug the most of them & sold them before we got here G. had to dig the rest him self. his farming this year has been 400 dollars out of pocket he says & every thing has gon to rack & ruin

Oct. 29th

This morning G. went to the mountains after wood. when it was 10
AM I saw a teem over on the Bluff runing a way I feared it was his &
while I watched them a man on a horse came after them it was half an
hour before they got near enough to tell who it was & it proved to be
our teem & Mr. Sherwood had caught them they had taken the advantage when G. fired his revolver at a Badger to come off & leave him. he
lost his game & had the pleasure of walking 6 miles before he met Mr.
S. who took his horse & went to meet him the lines wer broken & it
took him the rest of the day to finde them & get them mended up. this
is the beauty of living so far from wood

Oct. 30th

G. has been for wood again today & did not get home till 8 in the
evening & did not get more than half of a cord that he had to throw
several times over to get it down where his wagon was. I have been
washing & that & the anxiety I have felt a bout G. has a bout used me
up for today. I must have something all the time to disturbe.

Oct. 31st

I have had a feast today it consisted of news from home 3 letters from
my dear sisters Ann Lydia & Sarah. I sat down & answered Lydias &
while I was writing an Indian rode up with two Antelope on his poney.
G. called me out to see them they were pretty fellows & I pityed the
poney to carry them & his master on his back

Nov. 2nd

This has been a fine day just 6 weeks since we got here Vatie & I
called on Mrs. Sherwood this afternoon. had a pleasant time.

This evening G. made a little shelf & put up our *clock* & it made
this dismal room look a little more cheerful & home like & now I can
tell the time of day any where in the room

Nov. 7th

We are having beautiful weather but it is not like any fall I ever saw
there is no beautiful trees all covered with gay colored leaves A government train camped just below our house this afternoon & will spend
the night there there is nothing of interest except G. shot two rabbits
this morning & we had them for dinner Vatie said poor fellows they
were so happy this morning

Nov. 8th

We did not allow our selves to sleep very sound last night fearing some
of the train would take some thing. but nothing was disturbed with us.
but some one took four *mules* & one horse from them. they had 6 to a
wagon & they started out all but 2 men they went in search of the lost

ones but could not get any track of them G. has been to the office this evening & got a letter from Grace she sent Vatie some flowers & some of Willies feathers & it all most made her homesick. I have baked *five pumkin pies* today they are the first ones I have made since I left B.- it had been three months & I had all most forgoten how. the milk was given to us by Mrs. *Ranger Jones*

Nov. 11th

Sabbath day & a lonely one it seems a great pity to be kep at home when one wantes to go to church so bad. some one has set the prarie on fire & the smoke is plentiful this afternoon. we are not in any danger as it is a cross the stream. G. went to the Post last night & some one took his nice large Buffalow robe that he paid $18.00 for last winter. but he sais the beauty of it is he knowes who stole it. they hitched their horses to his wagon. he went out of the store, & he knew the horses & supposed they knew his teem & would not disturb it or any thing & went back a few moments to find the buffalow taken & they wer not out of sight

Nov. 13th

G. went to the mountains yesterday after wood it began to snow after he left home & kep it up all day. he did not get home till after dark. he called on the ones that took his Buffalow robe they were quite surprised but gave it up however. There is a traveler here tonight. G. has been putting stop casings to the windows today it is cold

Nov. 18th

Sabbath after sabbath roles around each one bringing us all nearer to that never ending one of rest. & now at the close of this day as I behold the beauty of the sky I think what it must be "in heaven a bove where all is love" I am such a great sinner I am not worthy to even see the glories of this world or the wonderful things God has made

Nov. 20th

G. had four men to help him on his log stable & they wer here to dinner. I got roast beef boiled potatoes & a *current dumplin* with sauce to eat on it bread and butter cole slaw & tea. they all seemed to relish their meal. they got through at half past 2 PM & soon after two Indians & a squaw paid us a visit they staid till after six then they called for *supper* & *lodgin* G. told them we had nothing for them & they had better go to *tepe* that is lodge in their own language. they left imediately but not as soon as I wished for I don't like my floor made a spitoon. Oh if I had the wings of a bird I would this moon light night fly a way from this place & the red man I suffer very much from fear & there is no hope for any thing good very soon

Nov. 24th

I have been a visiting this afternoon down to Mrs. Arthurs it was *nine weeks* yesterday since we landed here & this is the first visit I have made Mrs. A. don all she could to make it aggreeable but after all there was not much *satisfaction* in it. Vatie went with me & we walked down but Geo came after us. we had an invertation to a party when we had been here 8 weeks but did not go to it.

Nov. 25th

Sabbath evening   how I longed to meet with those people in B. tonight that have met for prayer. I have so many things to *anoy* me. I can not *"patiently* endure my every trial" & I hope my christian friends at home will remember me that I am shut a way from all their religious privilages. G. has read one of Spurgeons sermons this evening. we usualy *sing*

Nov. 27th

I have been doing some very hard washing & am very tired Geo was away & I had to bring my water & the wind blew so strong it would take out a good deal from the pail. I was so tired I could hardly eat my supper & that did not relish. a little *butter* on my *bread* would have been a *feast* to me. & a good easy chair a great *luxury*. but soon I shall camp down on the *floor* & try to rest my tired bones

Nov. 29th

This has been Thanksgiving day. we invited F. Grant to spend it with us but he did not get here till evening. I felt quite unwell but got him some supper & made two beds on the floor. This morning G. found a rabbit in the cellar and he killed him & some day we will eat him. Vatie went down in the bend of the river & got some old *rose* buds to fill her vase. she wanted to trim up because it was Thanksgiving & the red buds did ad to the looks of our dingy room while she was gone she found a place where some corn had been split by a train that camped there. she went back & picked up over a quart. I want very much to go to church & their meet with my friends at home & thus ended my first thanksgiving in the *west*.

Nov. 30th

This has been a fine day   F. Grant & G. have been putting up his log house it is a mile from here. I wonder if I shall ever see Ella comeing over here. if she don't come I hope some good woman will I have been a bout sick today & so has Vatie. the tent cover I washed monday was to much for me & I have not been well since nor able to do my other washing this week

Dec. 2nd

This is the sabbath & a cold windy day G. went yesterday after wood & comeing home lost his horses nose bags & this morning he took an early ride to finde them he had to go some six miles before he found them. it was a long day but I had the more time for reading. in the evening G. read one of Spurgeons sermons

Dec. 6th

I had a letter from Lydia today just after we had been to dinner F. Grant came here I got him some dinner then he & G. went to look after his oxen they got home after dark but had not found them. it makes a great deal of work when the whole prairie is a pasture & no fence a round it, & rivers to be forded. but that is the way every one else let their stock run

Dec. 7th

This has been such a funny day I must tell you all a bout it the sun rose brite & clear the weather was warm at 10 AM the wind comenced blowing & I never saw the snow fly any worse than the *dirt* did till noon then it began to snow & it kept it up till nearly 2 PM when it cleared off & the sun a gain shown & it was calm at sundown it began to snow a gain. all this weather we had in sunney Col. in one day where it is not so changeable as it is in Boonville. well all this is *nothing* if one can be *contented* & call it *good* but I am just ugly enough to remind the rest when they do not notice it. that all of the change-able weather is not in *B-* G. has been gone all day & it is now 9 PM & he has just got home

Dec. 9th

Vatie's sabbath lesson was very interesting to day & she often sais pa would you like to know what it is a bout it is easy & interesting but she don't feel the loss of the S. school as much as I wish she did but she has more taste for reading & as long as I can put good books & papers in her reach I think she will not forget all her early influences

Dec. 10th

Well I have something good to tell this time. G. has finished our *bed sted* to day & we are to sleep on it to night for 16 weeks I have had to put my bed down every night & take it up every morning & it has been a very hard thing to do. Then it adds so much to the looks of the room no costly furniture ever looked as well to me as my homely bed sted with a good bed on it. & on the outside sister Ann coveled I have looked at it ever so many times & it all ways remindes me of her. it nearly looks to good to mus. I have a tent cover a gainst the wall all a round it. & my mat in front is a gray *wolf* skin it will be soft & warm to our feet this winter

Dec. 14th

This has been an eventful day. I have been trying tallow. A pedlar came here & we sold him five dozen of eggs for as many dollars. took our pay in traid coffee soda & an apron for myself but the worst of it

was he called for a dish to dip the coffee & I lent my new print basin &
he carried it off. he was formily from Onondagna Co NY

Dec. 19th

G. was going down to Mr. Arthurs on business & he ask me to ride
down there for a call. Mrs. A. was getting supper & she urged us to
stay as she had some fresh *pork*. Vatie was anxious to stay & Mr. A.
began to unhitch the teem so we did not get a way till after 8 that is
the first time I have been out in the evening

Dec. 22nd

I have not had a letter in over two weeks till today I got one from A. &
one from L. there was good news from home but some how I have felt
very low spirited every since & that old homesick feeling comes back to
me. an other week is gon & O how cold the wind sounds tonight G. &
V. are a sleep & I am a lone

Dec. 23rd

This is the Lords day & no sabbath bell invites one to church. I some
times fear I shall become weaned from such sacred things. but now one
knowes the loss I feel now but those that have had the same experience
I have good books to read & they in a measure fill up this acheing void.
but I thirst for something more. I have written to L. today.

Dec. 25th

And this is merry Christmas to all. Santa-Claus did not pay us a visit
last night his "eight tinney reigndeer" wer to small for such a long
journey & he wisely staid a way. I have spent my time as usual only got
an extra good dinner. Chicken and cracker pie potatoes beef & coffee
with bread but not any butter. in the afternoon G. saddled Kate & let
Vatie have a ride she enjoied it very much & did not seem a fraid he
then came in & insisted on my going out & trying. I did not want to but
to please him & Vatie went. but my how afraid I was & I did not get
over it in two hours & thus ended my first attempt at horse back riding
& my first Christmas in the far west

Dec. 29th

Yesterday G. went to the mountains & he did not get home till to day
noon Vatie & I staid here last night all a lone with our kitten one of
them was bitten by an old cat 4 weeks a go & we kept him till now
thinking he would get over it but as the wound heeled it closed up the
water passage & it suffered so much G. had to kill him it was Vatie's
favorite kitten.

Dec. 31st

The last day of 1866 & cold & stormy it comenced snowing last
night. we have now 4 or 5 inches of snow for a winding sheet to the
dying year. it also remindes me of the flite of time & the certainty of

death. G. has been mending his boat & then he oiled them & while
he was doing it hit the dish & *nocked* it off the stove & made a grease
spot that will last *one year* I am afraid. I have been covering a box for
a chair or stool we now have two old camp chairs one board chair &
this new stool.   Vatie has got her lessons & amused her self by
spelling out words with the big letters Grace sent her.

Jan. 4th

Yesterday it began to snow a bout 2 P.M. & it did not stop till in the
evening. G. thought he would make a new table out of an old one &
comenced it yesterday but did not get it don till 3 P.M. today we took
our breakfast on the *stone harth* this morning & then fasted till the
table was finished our folks would think it only fit for a sink room now
but I have to put up with it if there is no leaves or paint on it.

Jan. 5th

This is a very cold day & the first leasure one G. has had since we came
here. he went down to Mr. Arthur's a horse back & Billey rather stray
out on the prairie so he just left him at the door & started for home but
was 3 hours comeing when he got here I put him in the stable & on
sadled him G. had a 4 mile walk home rather more of a good thing than
he wanted

Jan. 6th

This is the first sunday in the year staid at home as usual there has
not been any meeting for some time I saw a sled today pass by here
drawn by two *mules* the first one I have seen in the country. Just at
dusk two men came here & wanted to stay all night so we kept them &
there 2 horses & a pair oxen G. sold our oxen some time ago.

Jan. 9th

Mrs. Arthur & Mrs. Davis & her little boy came here when I was
getting dinner & staid all day. I poped some corn for them it was the
first they had seen in *4 years* & they enjoyed it very much. I had never
seen Mrs. D. before she is young & not much company for me. I feel the
need of good *society* very much.

Jan. 10th

G. has gon to the mountains this day to comence a job of drawing logs
to a mill five miles from the mountains on his wagon if the snow is not
to deep & he will not be home till saturday night I was very much
oposed to his doing it & said all could a gainst it but he must do
something to keep the wolf from the door and nothing else presents it
self at presant

Jan. 12th

Geo came home this evening & had been gon 3 days & two nights &
had not drawn but one small load to the mill the snow was to deep for

his wagon & he spent part of his time in making a *sled*. I felt so discouraged about it he had expended 13 dollars on his *wagon* besides a weeks work. I felt that I was not paid for my trouble   it is not pleasant to stay here day & night with no one but Vatie   the first night I had to take the lantern & go out after nine oclock & drive the cattle a way from our hay   I was a fraid to go but there was no other way for me   Vatie was a sleep & I was all a lone

Jan. 15th

Geo went to the mountains yesterday morning to be gon all the week. I did not feel very well & after he had gon gave vent to my feelings in a flood of tears. it may seem foolish to those that have neighbors & friends around them. I get a long very well through the day but the long evenings & night are *horible* I could not tell any one my feelings. the wind comenced to blow after the sun went down. I have looked out several times to see if our *hay* & *buildings* wer standing or if they had blown a way. it is half past 9 PM I have just been out & drove som 25 *horses* away from here. if this is not a life of privation & hardship I am mistaken in the meaning of that word

Jan. 19th

Saturday night has at last come & so has G. his weeks work has not been a paying one   I feel low spirited the most of the time. these are dark days such as I imagined & should see & shrank from undertaking, & when I feel it was not necessary I bear it with poor grace. the only way now is to trust in our heavenly father & he will open some way for us to supply our daily wants.

Jan. 20th

Sabbath morning we found it snowing hard when we got up. A big ox train passed by here in the storm   it has not stoped snowing this day & that reminds me of Boonville & of the church & sabbath school. they do not miss me there but how much I feel the need of there teachings here

Jan. 24th

We have a foot of snow & the weather is very cold. George went to the mountains this morning & left me to take care of two horses instead of one. our best one is sick & is not well enough to work & has not been for some time   Mr. Dunken stoped to warm   I had never seen him before & did not know who it was for some time

Jan. 26th

Geo cam home tonight without his overcoat he got hindred & so did not go to the cabin after it   he was very cold. the horses wer white with frost. I went out with the lantern & helped him. I have found it very cold doing the chores & chopping water holes   friday morning the air was full of frost & every bush & tree was cristalized & in the sunlight they were splendid.

Jan. 27th

Sabbath day   our usual quiate was somewhat disturbed today by callers in the morning   a young man called in in search of work   we had non for him   just as my supper was ready to take up two teems drove up   it was Mr. & Mrs. Straton   Mr. Meldrum was a lieut in the 21st Mrs. Stone & Mrs. Forbs the later lives 6 miles from us the others at the post or Ft. Collins (5 miles) they staid one hour & had been to dinner   we waited till they had gone about eating ours.

Jan. 31

I have been very busy getting Geo ready to go to Denver City   he went to the mountains monday morning & was gon two days & this morning early he started for D. I have been very busy all day regulating & have not had time to be lonesome but evening is now come & it is not so easy to keep cheerful   I shall spend the most of it reading in the Sunday School Times

Feb. 3rd

Sabbath day   it has been a very windy day & snow squalls in the mountains but Vatie & I enjoyed it nevertheless   I read a sermon to her out of the *SS Times*   it pleased her very much. At noon she wanted to say her SS lesson & sing as we used to in B. in a short time she came to me and said it did not seem like a S School because I did not pray so this evening we have had a little prayer meeting of only 2.

Feb. 5th

G. came home from D. this evening all safe but with a very bad cold   he brought back 1744 lbs of frait for Mason & Allen which amounted to $43.60 but the worst of it is he had to let it all go as the saying is for a ded horse.   but I am thankful for the opportunity of doing even that & sometimes I hope we shall be in better circumstances, if it wer not for *hope* what should I do

Feb. 9th

I took a bad cold last Thursday sitting by the fire the wind blew very hard all day & I did not go out of the house nor I could not keep warm in it & I have been about sick ever since   G. is getting better of his but has been about home all the week & this morning he finished our *privy* I have not been in to one since the 22nd of last August & I can't tell you how pleased I fell with it   if it is built of logs & has a dirt roof the seat is good & so is the *door*

Feb. 10th

Sabbath day and a warm pleasant one   staid at home as usual   just as I got our supper on the table a stranger called in   he said to rest but I think he smelt my victuals & made that an excuse. G. ask him to come to the table & he very willingly accepted & said while eating he wanted to get work & had no money. his meal rested him & he took his leaf as all beggars do (eat & run)

Feb. 11th

G. went to the mountains this morning to be gon all the week & I feel very lonely again I have been coloring some stockings with tea & baking bread & it is very nice Vatie is now eating a piece & she seems to relish it if there is no butter or any thing on it. hunger is all the *sauce* we have & that is an exelent kind for poor folks if they have a plenty of plain food as we have so far hunger will be satisfide.

Feb. 16th

There has not been any thing during the week worth noting down nothing but my daily cares in doors & out. my horse must be fed & groomed & her stable kept in order & my hens fed twice each day. I don't get but two meals a day when G. is a way he did not get home till nine PM brought a load of poles for fencing

Feb. 18th

I wrote a letter this fornoon to sister Lydia then I helped G. some & at 3 PM he started for the mountains & we are again a lone.

Feb. 19th

This morning there was a dense fog & I suppose there will be a frost in June to pay for it. I expected G. would not be home till saturday night but just at dusk he came home & Hubert Gleason with him & he brought a load of logs for fire wood. a *pedlar* called after the sun was down & wanted to stay all night I hated to tell him no but I would not keep him when I was a lone. soon after G. & H. came & I had supper to get for them & they don it justice as they had fasted since morning

Feb. 20th

This has been a cold disagreeable day & has snowed some. after dinner I had bread to mix & before I had finished it G. came in and ask if I would get dinner for two men that came a long & I don so. at night while I was waiting for G. to finish his chores a young man called & ask if we wanted to keep him over night for nothing he was dirty & very raged G. said no and he left.

Feb. 21st

This morning Hubert went a way & G. started for Denver a lone on business for him self & two other men he had checks for them to the amount of 15 hundred dollars & I feel very uncomfortable a bout him & very lonely now we are a lone a gain he has gon with two horses & I have the others to take care of & it is quite a task

Feb. 22nd

The wind has blown very strong from the west all day & I never saw the snow melt a way so fast the ground is covered with water Mrs. Stone has a dancing party this night & we had an invertation but should not have gone if G. had been at home he sais he has no five dollars to spare & I have no desire to go I could not honor my *saviour* at a *ball*

Feb. 23rd

We had a change in the weather last night. it snowed a little & blowed a good deel & I had to work one hour & a half to clear the snow out of the chamber it drove under the shingles & every thing was covered with it & not a very warm job on an empty stomach the wind blowes very cold tonight

Feb. 24th

I have not enjoyed this sabbath day very well I read in Spurgeons gems till my teeth ached so bad I laid down for one hour this evening I am feeling some better & Vatie has read a number of papers from the same book tonight. How long it seems since I have been to church or any meeting

Feb. 27th

This has been a warm nice day I have been ironing & the room was so warm I had the door open nearly all day. how different from 12 years ago sister Ann wedding day I have thought so much of her all day. Geo came home tonight from Denver all safe but I do not feel at all pleased in the way he has managed he was gon 7 days & Vatie & I staid a lone all of the time

March 1st

I declair I am afraid I shall get to be a very bad woman I have so many things to try one & so little patience to bear them last night two men staid here one of them was a sort of a pedlar I did not know it till he came to pay his bill. G. took a paper of *onion seed* & paid the trifling sum of *two dollars* it vexed me to think he don it but it don no good & now I have the house to clear of mud from top to bottom & my stove to cleans from tobaco *spit*

G. went a way this morning & will not be home tonight I have the 4 horses to care for & it was every thing but nice the mud & water ancle deep between the house & stable I had to change my clothes when I got through. aint this a fine account for one day

March 2nd

I got up this morning & found it snowing hard but the horses must be fed and watered for all that G. did not get home till late in the afternoon I have been cutting out a pair of buckskin pants for H W

Gleason they last a long time & are worn very much in these parts by white men as well as by Indians

March 10th

This has been a cold windy day   it snowed a little   I had hard work to keep warm & at last put a shawl around me when the wind blowes from the north west it is dificult to keep fire enough to warm so large a room   I have enjoyed the day however reading Spurgeons gems & explaining Vaties lesson   my Bible dictionary was a great help to us

March 14th

This has been a nice day but cold, it has been very cold for several days last Monday I don my washing but it was late & I did not hang out my white clothes & they have been in the tub till this morning I had to put several pails of boiling water to thaw them out   it has been such weather as I like to burn all of the dry wood I can instead of that our wood has been *scarce* & not very dry. today is the anniversary of sister L. marriage how much I have thought of one year a go. how different this day has been with me from that one. when I look back & think of all that has transpired in that time it seems many years insted of one. I presume L. thinks it both long & short when there are 12 more years added as there is to my married life one year will not look so long after all

March 15th

G. went to the mountains this morning after wood & will not get back till tomorrow. it is very cold a bout 8 PM Mr. Duncan came a long with a drove of cattle & wanted to stay over night his own home was 6 miles farther on & his cattle to tired to go any farther. I told him seeing him to be a neighbor he could stay I then got super for him and his man they had there own hay   Vatie & I slept up stairs on the floor & gave them our bed to sleep in

March 16th

G. got home about 3 PM & his eyes wer in a bad state   he was snow blind & could not see but a very little   Mr. Duncan left about 8 this morning   he offered to pay me for his 4 meals but I would not take any thing

March 17th

This is a very bright suney day & we have all the curtains down on account of G. eyes I cooked mothers corn for supper & how much I thought of her while eating it   it will be a long time before I have any more *suckertash*

March 18th

This morning Mr. Duncan called & presented me with 3 lbs of butter. he was determined to pay me & the butter was very acceptable as I had non

March 22nd

Today G. bought two cows & paid $100.00 for them they are very thin & I think will not be worth much this summer

March 25th

G. has been after hay today ours is all gon it is now selling for $17 a ton the snow still stays on the ground

March 26th

I have been washing & when I was cleaning my floor a soldier from Ft Sanders 80 miles north of us called & wanted some dinner I got him & he paid the going price for it one dollar & went on down to Lathram

March 28th

F. Grant was here to dinner & just before it was ready that soldier came a long on his way back he came in & wanted dinner but this time he had no money poor fellow he did not know how to use it well & paid it out for that which don him no good G. has been to Collins this afternoon but did not get any letter

April 1st

This is all fools day & G. got the start of me in the morning & then told me what day it is. it realy seems like spring to hear the birds sing so sweetly

April 4th

Mrs. Sherwood & Jessie came here for a call this afternoon & staid two hours but did not take off their things they came with a *sleigh* or rather a substitute for a sleigh

April 6th

The weather continues fine & the return of spring is drivinge the winter from my heart. yesterday 3 of the Engineers company called here & wanted a dinner of bread & milk. I got it for them & put on butter & a pumkin pie they seemed to enjoy their dinner especially the pie they paid me three dollars for their meals I would not object to getting them a dinner every day at that price

April 7th

This is a pleasant sabbath but the roads are very wet & mudy the snow goes off slowly by the sun. how much my thoughts have wandered to day & I have been in minde if not in person at *church* I think of those this day that sit a round our lords table & I rejoice that he is not confined to places but is even in the dark corners of the earth & can hear as well from a cabin as from a church

April 8th

Today I have been making Vaties doll a new suit & I have been well paid. she is so pleased & dolly looks so nice in her blue silk dress & saque & white waist.

April 9th

I have been washing & churning, had 5 lbs & 6 oun it did seem good to churn once more & after cleaning this big floor I felt very tired

April 10th

The ice broke up in the stream this morning & once more it rushes on free from its icy bonds & the wild gees & ducks are returning in to it this afternoon I was invited to Mrs. Sherwoods had a very pleasant visit G. came up to tea

April 12th

This evening we had our first shower & rained more than it has any time since I have been here

April 13th

G. has been setting out some young Cotton wood trees round the house & he has not done any thing that has looked so well & if they live will answer two purposes shade in summer & keep off the wind in the winter. it has been lowry all day & we have had a few showers still but very little water has fallen I have been cleaning & baking & dresst a chicken today

April 14th

Sabbath day & it has been very pleasant I read till I was very dull and sleepy & we all walked out on top of the bluff one mile in front of our house & the mountains seemed just as fare from there as they do from here we had been back a bout 15 minutes when a man brought us a letter from Sarah & our paper

April 16th

This afternoon Vatie had company for the first time Jessie Sherwood & her brother. Vatie & I sung "Theres something in heaven for chil to do", hoping she would try & learn it & I ask if she would not I ask her again to try on the cho. & when we got to it Vatie looked at her to let her know we wer ready & she began to cry & it was nearly an hour before she composed herself she is bashful & can not read much it made me feel bad & I shall not dare try it again

April 17th

This has been a nice day just at night we had a few sprinckles of rain & the seckond of the season

April 19th

Went down to Mrs. Arthurs this morning on the hay rack & staid all day walked home at night Mrs. A. gave me some letuce & pea seeds

April 20th

Have been to the mountains today it was a grand sight and a solem place to me the weather was fine & warm

April 21st

Sabbath day & the wind blowes very hard one pane of glass has come out of the window & broken it will take 30 cts to replace it

April 22nd

I have churned made potatoe yeast & a kettle of soap besides getting 3 meals & doing other work & am a bout tired out

April 23rd

I have been washing & it snowed & I put my white clothes a soak & hung the others up stairs for the first time

April 25th

This is the anniversary of our marriage 13 years have passed a way. the weather is pleasant G. has been plowing & I have ironed the clothes

April 26th

This forenoon it was raining but cleared up a bout noon & G.- plowed the rest of the day

April 27th

This is the last sunday in the month & a very dinday one it seems as if nothing could withstand it, the sun shines warm here but it snows in the mountains

April 30th

This has been a fine day I have been baking & ironing G. & Vatie went to Mr. Arthur's for hay & Mrs. A. sent me 2 nice cabbages & some radish seeds

May 1st

I helped G. wash his wheet this forenoon & it was quite a job we spread it on the waggon sheet to dry & then I had that to wash or rather rence out it is a very heavy thing when it is wet

May 4th

I have been very busy all of the week yesterday got the milk into the cellar & today have been papering some of our kitchen with news papers to stop out some of the bugs

May 5th

This has been a very winday day it was difficult to hear one a nother talk. Just at night I was feeding our horses some salt & one of them bit my thimble finger a little but it is very soar

May 7th

I have been papering the logs up stairs & it was very hot work & I am feeling very tired

May 8th

A pedlar came along to day & I sold him 6½ dozen eggs for 45 cts per dozen & bought Vatie some every day shoes & paid $2.75 for them

May 9th

Have been planting garden seeds. the river is very high the banks are full & the water is soaking in to our cellar

May 10th

We have 26 little chickens now Vatie has had company this afternoon & they brought her some flowers that grew on the prairie

May 12th

Sabbath day & winday how often they come a round Oh if I could go to church & sabbath school how much good it would do me

May 13th

Our trees are all *leeving* out but one & some day will make a nice grove every thing is looking green now

May 14th

I could not wash last week on account of my finger & to day have done a 2 weeks wash after we had tea a man came & wanted to stay all night & had him to wait upon & no reward but the peace one feels after doing what they can for the heroes of the *war* he had lost one eye in the *service*

May 15th

It has been snowing in the mountains all day & snowed part of the time down here

May 16th

I have nothing to write of importance. a big ox train went past here but on the other side of the river from us

May 18th

I have baked bread & cleaned my floor & put my things in order for the comeing sabbath & wish I could go to church in B. & to SS school

May 19th

This has been a stormy day snowing & raining by turns & we have had a good fire all day

May 21st

Mrs. Arthur came here this morning & staid till 3 PM G. had my horse this morning she took cold last fall when the teem ran a way & has had catarrh all winter & not been able to work but very little since then. besides this she & the other one (Vaties Kate) both met with an other misfortune caused by there run & a great loss to us. we are not getting suddenly *rich*

May 22nd

It rained some this morning. I drove the teem several times across the land while G. held the plow it had never been plowed before

May 23rd

I have been washing it began to rain a bout 8 AM & never stopped till night my white clothes are in the tub

May 24th

It was fair weather this morning & I dried my clothes we had a few sprinkles of rain this afternoon

May 25th

It has rained very hard all day & I could not do much elce but stand with my mop in hand to wipe up the water I had to move nearly every thing on the east side & suth end it drove through or between the logs it is now 10 PM & raining just as hard as ever

May 26th

It rained all night & till 9 AM when it turned to snow & has snowed as hard as I ever saw it in the winter. there is a foot of water in our cellar & we have got every thing out & piled in to our kitchen. we look as if we had got ready to move G. came in & ask me when I was going to start The river overflowes its banks now & every thing is a float there has been so much rain I have not been out of the house in two days. it is a rough time for our little chickens & every thing elce G. has the whole care of every thing

May 27th

The storm still rages some times it snowes & then it raines but does not beat in to the house I have been busy all day regulating G. put up some shelves in the south east corner & we hung up a blanket & that will be our milk room this summer

May 28th

Nothing but rain & no wood ahead & green pine to frishe a way in the stove

May 31st

Today the sun showed its face for the first time in 8 days

June 1st

Mrs. Sherwood called on us this afternoon to see how we got a long through the long storm

June 2nd

This has been a nice warm day G. could not find our cows to night. having the whole prairie for a pasture is not always conveinant

June 3rd

G. found the cows at 9 AM a cross the river a dog drove them over yesterday

June 4th

I have been washing & had two weeks washing just as I got my white clothes on the line then came up a gale of wind & lifted the midle post out of the ground & my clothes all came down in the dirt & there was not one spear of grass for them to fall on & by the time I got them off the line they wer as black as the ground its self. I then put them in the tub & rubed them on the board & then put them a soke till an other day by this time I felt very tired & I thought of those that had grass clothes yards

June 5th

I have been sweeping the chamber & every time I wish it wer the last time it is so hard to sweep both sides of it but in a weeks time it will need it again

June 6th

I have been ironing & chasing off cattle & had my patience severely tried in the latter. we had a fine shower in the afternoon the river is higher to day than it has been any time this spring

June 7th

Had a call from Dr Smith as he was passing by it has been showery all day & cold enough to snow

June 10th

I had just nicely got to washing when Mrs. Jones & her girl and Jessie S. came Mrs. J. only made a call the girls staid till after dinner. in the afternoon Mrs. Wygal called on me for the first time. I thought monday not a very good day to receive so many calles but I got through it after a while

June 13th

I have had so much other writing & there has not been any thing of importance I have neglected this

June 15th

This has been a rainy day Mrs. Sherwood sent me a nice peace of fresh beef this morning

June 22nd

I finished cleaning house to day & washed my windows Herb G. came to night

June 23rd

Henry Gleason came down a few moments this afternoon & Mr. & Mrs. Sherwood just at night. the river is very high

June 30th

This has not seemed like sunday there has been so many trains passing. every sunday in this month we have had 2 or 3 hours of hard wind filling our house with dust & dirt

July 1st

the days are very warm but the nights cool & nice to sleep in if we could feel that our crops was secure but in sted of that it is a constant care day & night

July 3rd

This morning 2 of my chickens wer blind & before nigh 10 more could not see. I have been weeding & setting out plants in the garden

July 4th

We staid at home & in the afternoon had a call from Mr. & Mrs. Arthur & Mr. & Mrs. Eaton I had never seen the last named before I liked them very well for the first time

July 5th

This afternoon I visited Mrs. Davis for the first time I went in western stile that is on horse back Vatie stayed with her father

July 6th

I went up to Collins this afternoon calling on some of the people & took tea with Mrs. Stratton. I went with Mr. & Mrs. Arthur. had a pleasant time

July 7th

This is a lovely sabbath how I would like to go to church we have sung our selves hoarse.

July 8th

I had so much work I did not wash & I got very tired after 5 PM Mr. & Mrs. Drake came here after tomatoe plants. they live *10 miles* a way I got tea for them they staid till after sun down then I had to milk for G. & wash my dishes

July 9th

I have been washing to day I went out to milk & one of the cows is a fraid of me. I have milked her several times but to night the wind blew very hard & she was a fraid of my dress it blew out just as I had comenced milking she kicked me over & hurt my leg so I could hardly get to the house & tore a big hole in my dress and drawers. she broke the skin & started blood

July 10th

My leg pained me all night & is as black as need be & is very soar & trouble some still I have been ironing & standing on it the most of the time to day

July 12th

We had beet greens for dinner out of our own garden. it is very warm

July 13th

I went down to Mrs. Arthurs this morning on *horse back* & staid all day she had company when I got there

July 14th

Another sabbath remindes me of the flite of time & of my loss in spiritual instruction the sky is clear the sun is warm but there is plenty of air we had peas for supper for the first time

July 31st

This is a long jump but I have had but one thing to write in all of this time. I have not picked *berrys* in the hot sun but have been pulling sunflowers out of the *wheat* every minute I could get for the last 14 days & now I must leave the rest of this to close up my year with

Sept. 21st 1867

One year this day I entered upon my new duties & when I look back over the past I have no wish to live another such a year. still in counting the mercies I fine they are many & I think I never felt more thankful than I have in the past year, but at the same time I have complained very much at my hard lot if I could feel duty called me here I could be reconsiled to give up all my former privalages & the society of friends. Now I have settled down with the belief that here I shall end my days & the sooner I make it home the better my prospects look brighter to day than they did one year a go. we have raised enough for our own use & some besides & very slowly we are gaining a little of this worlds goods.

This little book may seem full of trifling troubles to you, but at the same time they wer great to me, more than I knew how to bear. you may think me very foolish to complain so much & so it was & now farewell little book you shall not carry any more complaint to my friends at home.

Jan. 2nd 1868

I wish you all a happy new year we are all well but have colds.

Amelia

Postlude

Amelia Buss died in Fort Collins, Colorado on May 14, 1884, at the age of 50. Her husband George died in Fort Collins on April 7, 1908, at the age of 79. Their only child Varah, or Vatie as she was called as a child, married Jacob Armstrong in 1877 and they had four children. Although her husband Jacob died in 1917, at the age of 66, Varah lived to be 89 years old. She died on Nov. 23, 1945 at St. George Utah, and was buried at Logan, Utah.

For over 40 years Varah Armstrong was one of the best known florists in the west. She and her daughter Lucy set up the business early in the 1900's.

Besides the four children of Varah and Jacob Armstrong, their descendants number fourteen grandchildren, one of them is William P. Nye of Logan, Utah, over thirty-five great grandchildren, and at least one great great grandchild. Most all of them now live in Utah, California, or western Canada.

In writing down the daily events of her life during that year of 1866, we have a picture of what living conditions were like in the west at that time. The expressions she used, like, "put the clothes a soak", "been very busy regulating", "took our breakfast on the stone harth", and "I on saddled the horse", show the way people expressed themselves in those days.

Amelia was a very religious person, and being deprived of the fellowship of prayer meetings and church attendance was a real spiritual hardship for her.

When we think we have trials and hardships in this day and age, it is nothing compared to what our ancestors had to endure when settling this country, and we should be thankful and grateful for the legacy they left us.

Sara Overholt

Mattituck, N.Y.
August 1965.

The Letters of Delina Hopper

The Delina Hopper letters are located in the archives of the Western Reserve Historical Society, Cleveland, Ohio. They are listed under her husband's name:

> DANIEL D. HOPPER. Papers, 1853–1883 (1861–1865).
> ½ box. MS 3413
> Primarily personal letters addressed to Lieutenant Daniel D. Hopper, Company F, 10th Regiment, Ohio Volunteer Cavalry, from his wife, Delina (Woodrow) Hopper, and from other relatives residing in Youngstown Ohio.

Delina Hopper was born on 24 August 1835 in Champion, Ohio, and died on 17 November 1867 in Youngstown, Ohio. She and Daniel were married on 5 January 1859 and had four children, only one of whom lived to maturity: Charles Warren (b. 23 Dec. 1859, d. 15 Apr. 1861), Kate Luella (b. 13 Mar. 1861, d. 30 Apr. 1861), Luther Grant (b. 4 July 1863), Mary Elizabeth (b. 7 Mar. 1866, d. 8 Mar. 1866).

Daniel Hopper enlisted in the Union Army on 27 April 1861 and was mustered out as corporal on 29 August 1861. He reenlisted on 23 October 1862 and advanced in rank to captain by 1865, when he was mustered out on 24 July.

All the letters except the last, which was written by Dan's sister, were written by Delina to Dan. The first letter was written before they were married.

The original letters are in holograph. I have transcribed them just as she wrote them, keeping her punctuation, capitalization, and spelling.

I wish to thank Marge Grevatt of Cleveland, Ohio, for bringing these letters to my attention.

Leonore Hoffmann

Letter One

(1858)
Mesopotamia   July
(Sabbath Evening)

Dearest Dan
    Your letter was not received until Saturday night and I hasten to answer it the first opportunity.
    Dear Dan I am so sorry that I wrote to you as I did last week but you will forgive me I know you will when you come to think of it seriously. I felt so grieved and half angry with you and I always say more than I ought to and things I am sorry for afterwards but Dan I can't feel so towards you any more, you have given me your word of honor that it shall not be so again and I know you will keep it this time. I will have perfect confidence in you and oh! Dan you will never betray the trust will you? *Dear Dan* I am *so sorry* I have hurt your feelings so I did not know how true and generous a heart beat in that bosom, and for me only. Oh! Dan I understand you better than ever before and with the knowledge of your real feelings my heart is drawn towards you closer than ever. You seem to think that I cannot love as you do. Oh! Dan *no one* but the "Searcher of all hearts" knows how I *have* and *do* feel towards you. I love you Dan as a *woman* can *never* love but once. You are the *first* and will certainly be the *last*. There I have told you *all* have laid bare my *innermost* heart to you as I once thought I never should to any living man. Have I entrusted my *all* in this world to one who will ever keep *sacred* the trust. Dan I have heard that there are *very few* men that can be told what I have just told you that is they do not *value* a love that they are *sure* of is it so; or are you one of that precious few. I hope so and believe you are or I would not have told you.
    I do not know whether I can get home in three weeks from the time I left or not will try to I shall not stay longer than four anyhow I will probably write you again before I go home that is if I receive an answer to this one which will be soon will it not?
    Now dearest Dan do not think any more about this unpleasant affair we have both been to blame for it, let us forget and forgive the past, any thing but what we would wish to remember and try to do just right in the future. Dear Dan I hope you are well and doing well You do not know how much I think of you and pray for you while I am absent from you take good care of your precious self for my sake and think of Del once in a while as she loves to be remembered by Dan and have confidence in her that she will *never never* forget Dan unless he *makes himself* unworthy the name of man. then she would try to forget

him, but I have no doubts but that he will prove in time to be all that I could wish.

I am going to direct this letter to you I do not care for their teazing me. tell Kate I received her letter and will answer it as soon as I can conveniently.

We had a pretty good time when the sewing society met here last Thursday there was about 30 here. Stephen came down after me Saturday night so I went up to Uncle James' and went to church with them Sabbath and came home with Abbie and Tip. I cannot write any more it is getting so dark so I must say Good bye write soon and remember I am *yours only and truly* until death

                                                                    Delina

[in margins]
You sent me a stamp I will put it on this

Letter Two

                                              Champion   June 3rd/61

Dear Husband
    I received yours of the 29th Saturday and today is Sunday but I see I have dated my letter one day ahead. Well I shall not get it to the Office before that time anyhow.
Father and I went to Youngstown yesterday and gathered up all we could find that belonged to us. I guess we got most of your tools but that Pryors [?] had taken your brush and said it was away at the other end of town when we wanted to start home and did not make any move to go after it said he could not get it then or something like that I could not exactly understand so we had to come away without it I went to see Mr. Wells when we were there you don't know how I hated to. I had almost rather went to the Poorhouse to stay, but I need some money so bad, if I only could earn something in some way I would never have went near them. I had but three dollars when you went away you know and I had to pay Miss Foreman $1.75 and for the lining of your blanket, then I had but about 3 shillings left and spent most of that for paper and stamps so now I have nothing and am in need of a great many things, and what troubles me worst of all every body that you owed is dunning me Cranage [?] talks real mean about you and Dr. Sweeney is going away from Warren and wants his pay. if I can get

anything from Youngstown I will pay him but I do not know whether I can or not. Mr. W said he would lay it before the committee and see what they could do. I feel so worried about that debt at Hoyts too. I wish I had not got that shawl I feel ashamed to wear it any where they can see me but I had to have something to wear or else stay at home and not go to church or any where.

Now I expect you will think you cannot help me any now and I ought not to be troubling you with all this but if you knew how bad it makes me feel along with all my other troubles you would not blame me for wanting to unburden my heart to some one and who should I tell but you, if you do not sympathize with me I do not know anyone that will. Dan there is one thing I want to ask you do you stay 3 months from the time you got your commission or is it 3 months from the time you are mustered in. there is quite a difference you know I wish you were at home I think there are enough to do the fighting that could be spared much better than you, but since you are in for it do the best you can and come back as soon as possible. I feel so lonesome and bad sometimes, it seems as though I cannot stand it—3 months the days are *so long* I don't feel like visiting or doing any thing. I don't like to go down to Mc's for he has the blues so that he cannot eat hardly I. Baldwin has gone up. there was a mortgage on his tables and they went to pay that so Mc. will lose about 50 dollars and no knowing how much more. I feel sorry for him any thing like this troubles him so you know. Kate has had a girl to help her about two weeks now I do not know whether she can keep her all summer or not.

Mr. Bingham is here today I went to church and came home in the rain and got my feet as wet as they could be. I guess it won't hurt me though I am pretty well now.

Aunt Z [?] is no better Now dear Dan take good care of your self and don't get into danger unless it is absolutely necessary. You may talk about the glory of falling in a battle field and all that but that is nothing to me if I should lose you the fame and glory are nothing but empty chaff. Now Dan I do not wish to discourage you by any thing I have said but Dan don't stay for any longer time than you intended to at first will you tell me you won't certain it will do me lots of good. there are enough others to fill your place that are anxious to get a chance to go. If you want any thread or anything that I can send in a letter just let me know, you know I would like to do any thing for you in my power

Ever your loving wife
Delina

Letter Three

Warren   June 12th, 1861

My Dear Husband

I think if I do not begin to answer your letters pretty soon I shall get behind for I got three from you yesterday one in the morning without any stamp or post mark one at noon and one at night. The one you sent by John Smith had written with a pencil on the back "I will return on Thursday J. B. Smith" He said one of Mrs. Patch's boys gave it to him. I do not know where to find this J.B. Smith if he is going back I'd like to send this with him. I think it is so strange you do not get any letters I have written you as many as four any how since you left Cleveland and Kate says she has written 3 they were directed to Zanesville Bellair and one or two to Glover's Gap. Your letters reach us safe enough. I cannot see why ours do not reach you they were directed right I am sure. Well perhaps you will get them after while I have been up to Champion ever since you went away until this week I am down here to Mc's it has been very warm here for a day or two but it rained last night and cooled the air considerable. Kate and Mc are out in their garden setting out cabbage plants and Martha Stewart that is Kates girl is making pies in the kitchen and I am sitting in the bedroom or sitting room I don't know which they call it—writing. O I wish you were here so I could talk to you instead of writing. I can't write only this sheet full for it is all the paper I could find without going down street and I hate to do that now and precious little money I have to get any thing I could not sell any of those things in Youngstown so we brought them all home and I have varnished them up till they look most as good as new. I declare Dan I feel vexed whenever I think about it how you are away there in danger and having such a hard time of it and these lazy rich men can stay at home and take their ease and care nothing about us how we get along if they can only keep you there to do their fighting. I may get along just the best way I can I don't believe they would turn a finger over to keep me from starving. I need a little money very much indeed and went and talked to Mr. Wells about it when I was at Youngstown nearly three weeks ago. he said *perhaps* they could do something, they would write to me but I have not received a word let alone anything else. if I could only get a chance to earn something myself I would not have went near them but you know how it is I don't feel able or willing to be any body's kitchen drudge and I cannot get anything else to do It is not very agreeable to one's feelings to have to be dependent on ones friends for something to eat especially when they make you feel it either. But never mind I won't scold anymore about it if you will only come home at the end of

three months I will try to get along most any way but *don't* promise
dear Dan to stay any longer will you? I am so lonesome and homesick
for a home of our own I used to think sometimes when we lived in
Youngstown that I had a pretty hard time of it but I would a thousand
times rather live anywhere if I only had my own little family that I
then had.

I know it is necessary that somebody should go to defend our country but you have taken your turn and there's lots of others left that can
go better than you let them have a chance I am *so afraid* they will have
a great battle down there somewhere before you get home. but what
good does it do to worry about it all the time, I trust there is a God over
all who will defend the right and make all things work together for
good for those that love him and keep his commandments O! do not
forget *Him* my dear husband We are all well at present Aunt Zerviah
is very low she coughs very bad I do not think she can live very long.
We went down to the cars to see Capt. Hollis Co. off yes. morn. Some of
the boys shed a good many tears at parting. Poor fellows what a soul
sickening feeling comes over one at the thought that with some at least
it is forever I was not personally acquainted with any of them. they
went for three years. Well my paper is full and I must stop.

Yours and yours only forever

Delina

[in margins]
Write as often as you can you cannot write too often. Your letters are
the only comfort I have while you are away there I have not got any
letters from the east since I sent you that one to Cleveland I wrote
Mother a long letter about a week ago

I am making a vest for Newt I wish it was for you

Letter Four

Columbus
June 16th 1861

Dear Husband
I received a letter from you today and was glad to hear that you
had at last got one of mine. I was down to Mc's all last week came
home Friday night and your letter came Sat. so I did not get it till
today There has been Communion at the church here in Champion
today and I have been to meeting all day it has been a good meeting. I

have enjoyed it. I think Mr. Bingham preached better than I ever heard him before. I wish you had been here to have enjoyed it with me I should have felt so much better Mr. Bingham went to see Aunt Zerviah and had a long talk with her she asked him to preach her funeral sermon She said she hoped to go *home* very soon now. They do not expect her to live through tonight.

Monday Morning
I wrote so far Sunday night it was so dark I could not see a line and I have not hit them very well I see. We have not heard from Aunt this morning father is going over pretty soon I don't have the blues quite so bad as I did I am getting along better than I expected but my *dear husband* I want to see you so bad I can hardly wait. you will be home in about a month if your life is spared will you not? I have lots to tell you that I can't write.

The weather is quite changeable it was very warm some of the time last week and last night it was so cold we feared there would be a frost but there was none to hurt anything. it is quite cool today. I wish you had some of our cool breezes down there in the mountains where it is so hot we have had most too much breeze lately. The roses are in full bloom now and the little boys at school join them on their shoulders for epaulets they can't play anything but war now. Ah it is just so with us all our lives in childhood and youth every thing is fun and frolic but when it comes to stern realities how different ~~it looks~~ things appear to us. This does not seem like the same world to me that it did even two or three years ago.

Some of Capt. Asper's Co. were home on a visit and started back last Friday afternoon I saw more tears shed when they went than at any time before, perhaps it was because I just happened to see it. Dr. Woodworth has got a Co. in Warren that are on drill every night but I guess they have no intention of going. Ed. Spear Nor Laird John Crawford and several others of our acquaintances are among them. Aunt Zerviah has six brothers and they are all here now except the Dr. and he is here every few days he lives in Cleveland you know I feel so sorry for Uncle Henry he has more trouble than us. it seems as though he just commences to enjoy life when some great trouble comes to wreck all his happiness. I received a letter from Mother Hopper Friday I will send it to you she had not got mine when she wrote. She says that Charley and Ella had written to us but I have not got it. Do you known Frank L. Shafer? I [backed?] a letter to him the other day for Martha Stewart Kate's girl Martha is a pretty girl, you can teaze him as much as you please but don't tell him where you got your information. They are going to have a grand celebration at Warren the coming 4th. I will send you a paper with the program of exercises for the day. Mc talks of going in Co. with some others and having a grand ball to make some money that is the great object of his life you know to make money get rich. Well I must stop Write as often as you can I am so anxious if I don't hear from you often I am in Champion and I don't know when I can get a chance to send this to the Office.

Ever your own
Delina

[in margins] Aunt Z is a little better today not better but a little more lively

Dan you must not be so anxious to see a fight I sincerely hope you will *not* see one The less fighting the better if the rebels are only subdued.

Letter Five

Youngstown   March 26th/63

My Dear Husband

Why why don't you *write* to me. I am sick both in body and mind here it is going on to four weeks since I have got one word from you. Kate Mc. wrote to me that they had a letter from you a week ago and *I* your poor sick wife that ought to have the first claim on your attention is not worthy of a thought or word Dan is it so, the very thought is sickening I cannot believe it

but I cannot get rid of it, if you cared for me as a loving husband would you could have written me 3 or 4 times and if one letter was lost they certainly could not all be Sometimes I've thought maybe you was waiting to write until you were paid but then it is cruel to me to wait so long how do you suppose I feel when I hear that every body that has friends in the 10th Cavalry have had letters from them and people ask me when have you heard from Mr. H. I am obliged to say I have not had a letter since you were at Cincinnati. Mr. Timerman went away to Washington nearly two weeks after you left and she is not forgotten to add to her other troubles for she has money enought to live on and has had two letters from him While I have not a half dollar in the world and can think of no way to earn anything if I was able which you know I am not I have had such a pain in my side for 2 or 3 weeks I cannot go down street at all and to make the matter still worse Mrs. Timerman's boy was born night before last and she has been very sick ever since so I have been up most of two nights my throat is sore today and I am sick all over but I could not wait any longer to write to you so I've been writing this all day by spells I have not had a chance to rent the other part of our house yet and that note you left me is good for nothing to me now any how for I cannot get anything on it nor sell it and you know you only gave me about 3 dollars and I had to pay my fare from Warren and Sis's home besides most two dollars for the lumber and hauling of it to build these stairs Mrs. Timerman cannot afford to keep me and if you do not send me something pretty soon I will have to write to our folks to come and take me home if I am obliged to do that I feel as though I never *could* forgive you you did not *need* that money to lend to Lunt Brown. O my dear husband I hate to talk so to you for I love you still for our children's sake if for nothing else but you can not imagine how much you have made me suffer within the last six months if you have the least bit of love left for me in your heart write to me once more I cannot write any more now

                                                                           Delina
P.S. I wrote to you once before to Nashville. did you get it perhaps I did not direct it right I don't know how to direct this any better.

                                                                           D.E.H.
[in margins]
Caroline Fisher is doing the work for us or for Mrs. Timerman.

Letter Six

                                                                         [1863]
                                                       Youngstown   Aug. 23rd

My Dear Husband
    This is Sunday and a long lonesome day to me and would be worse still were it not for my brighteyed boy when he is asleep I am all alone. Mrs. Tim went yesterday for good she did not know as she would ever see Youngstown again and did not care much I guess. she is going to stay 2 or 3 weeks at her fathers before she goes to New York. I am going to have old Mr. Barber sleep here while I stay I don't know how long that will be, I feel kind of afraid nights after all there has been so many rows here lately. Will Fisher has just escaped with his life 2 or 3 times I got the Nashville Union out of the office the other day I suppose it came from you it is quite a good paper. Mrs. Stevens that lives in Mrs. Bakers front room has got a Parrot that talks everything she hangs it out at the door and it is a good deal of company for me it is jabbering away now its name is Judy it says "Poor Judy got the toothache oh oh oh") Just as plain as any one could Mrs. S—— thinks

she would rather have it than a baby but I don't think so at all such a baby as mine any how. Mrs. Collins was here today with hers I had heard so much about her baby being so pretty and smart but it don't notice things nor look near so bright as ours if I do say it myself and it is 2 weeks older I wish you could seem him lay here on the lounge the way his little feet and hands fly is a caution and his eyes fairly snap they are so bright I don't think his features are as pretty as Charley's hardly but he looks brighter he has changed a good deal since he was born If I did not think you could get home before long I would try to get his picture pretty soon and send it to you but I hope you can come soon What would I give if you were only here tonight. Mrs. Hurlburt's little girl was born while he was away to conference so she was not much better off than us war widows. Mrs. Alexander has got a boy 2 or 3 days old and Mrs. Kennedy (Mat) will be the next on the list I expect. Mr. Ross (the painter) got thrown out of a buggy today at Girard and badly hurt I believe his arm is broken but they think his worst injuries are internal I heard that they did not think he could live. I have not rented our house yet Folsom was here to look at it but he wanted to do off the front room and let it go on the rent but I thought I'd rather not they might cheat me like every thing and not do it to suit us either. There is another man wants to rent it by the name of Simpkins that I believe I'd rather have in it any how I don't believe they would abuse the house so much and would be just as good pay well I can not write any more tonight for Baby begins to think it is bedtime the last letter I had from you contained $5.00 and a picture of a lady I wrote you the next day after I received it. Write often

Yours Ever
Delina

Letter Seven

Warren   Nov. 6th/64

My own dear Husband
    You can imagine how glad I was to receive a letter from you yesterday dated at Cartersville for it was almost two weeks since I had heard from you and I was beginning to feel pretty blue I assure you but I felt very grateful that you was yet safe though the letter was written so long ago (allmost two weeks) that a great many things may have happened since. nevertheless I was very glad to get it and hope you are as well as when it was written. I am sorry you are having such a hard

time of it. I do hope you will get in camp some place soon and get rested but you are not so bad off as you might be as long as you are well and can get plenty to eat you can stand a good deal but I'm afraid you will get sick unless you take better care of your self. But I suppose you do the best you can under the circumstances.

Mrs. Sanderson called just as I had finished reading your letter she was very anxious about the Col. was afraid he would have difficulty in reaching the Reg. He started about two weeks ago to go back. I felt sorry for him she is so troubled about him she *knows* he is not what he should be but don't just *say* so. O if men could only feel one half the heart aches they make for those who love them best by their recklessness it seems to me they would do very different from what a great many of them do, they think I suppose that their wives at home never will know of their faithlessness and debauchery but I tell you it is not so easy as they may imagine to keep it all hid they say "love is blind" but I think some times it has "eyes before and behind and many a husband who flatters himself that his wife knows nothing about his actions only what he chooses to tell her would feel ashamed to look her in the face if he only knew how well she could read him Mrs. S. said the Col. had such a foreboding of evil that it seemed as though he was perfectly reckless it is no wonder such men are afraid to die though I suppose he is no worse or as bad as more than half the Officers in the army. May God save *my own* from the evil so that if any thing should happen to him he may be happy in Eternity for what is this brief existence compared with the *eternal future*. We are all quite well Luther grows and is just as full of mischief as it is possible for a young one to be. he just keeps me busy to watch him and after all I cannot keep him straight he will come to me after he has done some thing which he knows was naughty and say "now now now" with such a long face you could not help laughing but it won't do to laugh you know if any one asks him where his Papa is he points to the Albums or pictures on the table that is all the papa he knows it makes me feel bad sometimes I'm afraid he will never seem to you like your own child if you should be spared to come back seeing nothing comparatively of his infancy but it cannot be helped and is only one of the thousand evils that this war has brought upon us May God bless us all and make us patient and resigned to holy will while here on earth and give us all a happy family in his kingdom above in the prayers of your loving wife

Delina E. Hopper

[in margins]

There was a wedding up to Uncle James Lairds last week Sue was married to Henry Griswold of Windsor. I guess I will go to Youngstown some time this week I have been waiting this some time to hear from you but am afraid you did not get my letter telling about our affairs so I guess I'll make my own bargain with Mr. Simpkins I hope you will be paid soon but don't worry about it on my account

Letter Eight

Warren   April 9th 1865

My Best Beloved

I do not owe you a letter and if it was any one but your own dear self I would not write tonight. I have written you a dozen or fifteen letters in the last 3 months and have only received two very short ones from you. I did feel so disappointed last night for I expected to get a letter from you certain but the box was empty when I got to the P.O. Mrs. Sanderson has had several letters lately from Col. S. he says nothing about you I think if there was anything wrong with you he would have mentioned it and I cannot understand why I cannot get letters as well as any one else, but perhaps it is not your fault if I thought it was I would not write another word until I got one You used to write often and I cannot believe your love for me has grown cold and that you are indifferent about it. Some thing must be the matter with you, *do* write or get some one to for you the first chance you have

I feel more anxious than ever if possible to hear that you are safe since the glorious news of the fall of Richmond and the Surrender of Lee's Army (though we are not so sure of the last) if it is all true the war is at an end Mrs. Sanderson thinks you will all be home in two months but I cannot feel quite so sanguine as that though I hope it may be so, we will know some thing more before long I think

Luther and I are here alone tonight and we have been cracking nuts till he got tired and has gone to sleep and I sat here thinking about you and wishing it so much that you was here with us, I want to talk so many things that I cannot write and I want to see how you look and feel that the one I love best on earth is near, but as this is impossible I thought the next best thing would be to write, though I had thought I would not write today I could not help it I felt such a longing to talk to you. O if God spares you to come back safe and undefiled by the evil that surrounds you I shall be so happy I cannot be thankful enough

There was great rejoicing over the news here and all around everybody seemed to make all the noise they could Every gun in the county was brought and I saw in the Register that they had a bonfire on the Diamond in Youngstown and Speeches by the Mayor and others Rev.

Wilson was called out and he (good man that he is) proposed they should all unite in singing the doxology "Praise God from whom all blessings flow" to the tune of Old Hundred and the vast crowd sang it with a will. It done one good to hear that the people of Youngstown gave Almighty God the praise to whom it belongs first. I was up to Mr. Smith's last week to see Ems baby it is quite a fine looking boy and they are proud enough of it *but not to be compared with ours*. We are all well and want to hear from you *so bad* so please write soon and often to your own

loving wife
Delina

P.S. Julia Elliott is to be married in a week or two to Samuel Pew of this place.

D.E. H.

Letter Nine

Dec. 11, 1867
Tuesday Morning

Dear Brother Dan:

What was the matter that you did not come up Saturday we looked for you certainly. You are not sick or what can have happened. I went down street in the afternoon but not finding you went on over to Uncle Smiths to see Lillie. Aunt Eunice wanted me to stay and watch with her that night but I told her I could go better Sabbath evening so came home. Mc said Newt had been at the shop inquiring for you. When shall we look for you. I am going up to Fathers today. We expect to butcher Thursday. Newt will help Mr. Folsom and kill theirs at the same time.

I will send you a paper that has a notice of Delina's death. You can keep it or send to any of your friends I tried to get some more at the office but did not speak in time. I will get what I can of those who take them.

The days are so short that I must hurry for I want to come back before night for Mr. Warren is going to organize a regular old fashioned singing school at the church tonight and teach us the rudiments of music and I would like to review. Tomorrow night Mrs. Folsom and I are going to be initiated into the mysteries of the Templar's Would not you like to be there? Your sister

Katie Mc.

Editing a Woman's Diary

A Case Study

Elizabeth Hampsten

When Sir Philip Sidney gave the manuscript of the *Arcadia* to his sister in 1593, he called the work "a trifle, and that triflingly conceived." It was a private composition, possibly containing family jokes out of reach to those beyond the Duchess of Pembroke's circle. To Sidney, the distinction between private and public writing was clear. Private writing, not necessarily more personal, less finished, or less serious than public writing, was intended for an intimate audience. The distinction depended on the distance between writer and reader, on how much was to be explained to strangers. The differences between public and private writing come to mind now with the increasing interest in letters, diaries, reminiscences, and other writings of our near contemporaries, people who had not supposed that anyone but a few family members and friends (if they) might read them. In this vein, diaries of travelers on the trails to Oregon and California become primary sources for historians of the American West and those of ordinary women for scholars of women's culture. What is the effect of such public exposure on the writings of nonliterary and nonpublic persons? To what profit do we read them?

In 1982 the University of Arkansas Press published *Vinegar Pie and Chicken Bread: A Woman's Diary of Life in the Rural South, 1890–1891*, edited with an introduction by Margaret Jones Bolsterli. The writer is Nannie Stillwell Jackson (1854–1908), who lived on a farm near Watson, Desha County, in southeastern Arkansas. She was then thirty-six years old and married to her second husband, William T. Jackson. While keeping this particular diary (there presumably are other volumes unaccounted for) she bears the first of their two children on 15 August 1890. The household also includes her two daughters, Lizzie, age twelve, and Sue, age nine, whose father, Asher C. Stillwell, had died four years earlier. Nannie had married Stillwell in 1873, when she was nineteen, and with him also had a son, William, who evidently died before the diary begins. W. T., Nannie's second husband, was ten years younger than Nannie. He farmed and did odd jobs in the neighborhood.

The University of Arkansas Press has produced a handsome book: hard cover, 108 pages in ten-point type, with maps, photographs, scholarly apparatus that includes footnotes identifying names from *The Biographical and Historical Memoirs of Southern Arkansas* and from the United States census for 1880 and 1900 (census records for 1890 were burned), glossary, bibliography, and index, as well as Margaret Bolsterli's preface and twenty-one page introduction. Does this seemingly exhaustive scholarly treatment bridge the distance between Nannie Jackson's private writing and our public reading? Can we read *Vinegar Pie and Chicken Bread* as a book?

Nannie Jackson, the Writer

> Thursday, July, 10th. 1890. Clear & hot not enough rain yet, I finished Blanche's skirt & almost made her chimise Mr. Jackson plowed in his corn & Brother Dick hoed in the cotton, I have not been to Fannies today she came here a little while this evening, I gave her some fish Mr. Jackson bought 30 cts worth of cat fish today, no mail for any of us to day, I feel very well to night, Mr. Jackson got me ten cents worth of nutmeg & some spice too to night he did not stay out in town very late to night came home & went to bed before I got ready, Lizzie & I fixed to wash tomorrow.

While not as long as some, this entry is typical of Nannie Jackson's writing and of the diary writing of working-class women in the late nineteenth and early twentieth centuries, no matter where they lived. It lists specific facts—ten cents for nutmeg—without providing a context for the information. She almost never identifies the many names or explains relationships among people, though we can infer some of these data as we go along. Nannie Jackson also typifies other diary writers of her time in fitting entries into consistently repeated patterns. Almost every entry of hers begins by commenting on the weather. Next come reports of the day's main event (here her sewing and her husband's plowing), and then other incidents: a visit to Fannie and Mr. Jackson's shopping. Many entries end by noting whether Jackson went out in the evening or stayed home.

Nannie Jackson never writes that she is pregnant, but in the two months before her delivery she repeatedly refers to how she feels. She is often distracted from the coming birth by other ills called "chills"—

presumably malaria. "Mr. Jackson went to Dr. Chandlers this morning & got 3 doses of calomel for Lizzie & I gave it to her, she is better to night" (18 June 1880). A month later: "I had a chill & was very sick but Sue & I managed to get all the ironing done" (24 July 1880); and the next day "Mr Jackson got a bottle of quinine & ten cents worth of salts for me I had to take some I have another chill this evening."

In fact, often it is hard to tell when she is troubled by "chill" and when by her advancing pregnancy, but few days go by without some mention of her physical state. Thus through July:

> I have felt tolerable well to day . . . I am tired and sleepy . . . I did not do very much work today. . . . I feel tired and sleepy . . . I feel very well tonight . . . I feel very well to night . . . I feel very well to day. . . . I took a nap . . . did not take time to sleep any to day . . . I took my nap while Lizzie scoured.

One sign of her increasing concern about herself is the presence of Aunt Chaney, the black midwife, who stops by more and more often. On 27 July "Aunt Chaney & Emeline were here a while to night they brought me a loaf of light corn bread it is so good, Mr. Jackson & I had a good nap to day." She comes again on 1 August and on the seventh, when "Lizzie & Aunt Chaney made their bed in the kitchen & slept on the floor." On the ninth, "Aunt Chaney is here yet, I have felt better to day than I have this week"; on the tenth "Mr. Stillwell died just 4 years ago today & what a change what a change, Aunt Chaney & I went over to the McNiel grave yard & stayed a while then I came home & read some & took a nap have felt bad most all day." The next day she is not well either, and Aunt Chaney leaves "but she is not coming back unless I send for her." On the twelfth she "felt very well all day," and on the thirteenth she visited a sick friend, Mrs. May Stroud: "she is no better tonight but I cant go set up with her. . . . I feel so bad to night." Aunt Chaney is back by the fourteenth doing the wash. The flat, detailed, but unspecifying manner continues on 15 and 16 August, when Nannie Jackson manages not to say in so many words that she has borne a child:

> I had a hard chill sick all day. . . . Dr. and Mrs. Chandler was here this evening and gave me calomel Mrs. Stroud is no better Mrs. Cheatam came to see me and the baby today . . . I am still very sick and have to take more medicine Mr. Jackson has to sit up with me tonight . . . Mrs. Smith sent me some okra and greens for my dinner. I ate it and enjoyed it so much. Mrs. Chandler and Dr brought me a fine boy it's name is Davie Samuel Mrs. Cheatam and Fannie named him we will call him Davie

It takes a second reading to realize that her illness is not all due to chills in the hot and watery climate, and it can only add to one's dismay to realize that she is enduring both conditions at the same time. There are other indications of the attention Nannie pays to her pregnancy. On 4 August her husband gave her $5.25 from some butchered beef he had sold: "I have put it away to keep until I need it which wont be very long I dont reckon," and the next day he gave her $4.25 more: "& now I have nine dollars and a half in all & I am going to keep it for my own benefit when I get sick." "When I get sick" is a standard nineteenth-century euphemism for expecting childbirth.

Nannie Jackson does not reflect or offer opinions. Thus her rare elaborations emphasize crucial moments in her life. On 1 July:

> I have not felt well today am afraid I am going to be sick I went up to Fannies a little while late this evening & was talking to her, & I told her to see after Lizzie & Sue if I was to die & not to let me be buried here have me taken to Selma & put beside Mr. Stillwell & I want Lizzie & Sue to have *every thing that is mine,* for no one has as good a rite to what I have as they have I have been married to Mr. Jackson just 11 months to day & it seems like a heap longer time, maybe if we had got a long better the time would not seem so long.

Three weeks later they do seem to be getting along better:

> Mr. Jackson stayed all day with me I read some to him before we went to Mrs. Dyers & some after we came back, he went over to Dr. Chandlers with Brother Dick after supper but he did not stay long he has been so good & kind this last two weeks has not fussed about anything I have done like he used to, he got a little vexed about one of the shirts because I did not exactly understand him but I tried to fix it to suit him & believe I did manage to please him after a while.   (20 Jul. 1890)

Another event that Nannie Jackson comments on is the departure of Miss Carrie, a schoolteacher who boarded and taught the two daughters. Lizzie was leaving with her, presumably to continue at the school Miss Carrie was moving to. Again, Nannie's repeated references to a detail tell us that it has special meaning for her.

> Cool cloudy & rainy, all well this is the last day of Miss Carrie's school & they are having a candy pulling at the school house & some of the children had speeches I did not care to go   (9 Jan. 1891)

washed Miss Carries head for her today   (10 Jan.)

Miss Carrie & Lizzie left today they did not go until after dinner, oh but I did hate so bad to see them leave Brother Dick drove the wagon & took Miss Carrie's trunk & Lizzie & the valise with some clothes in it for Lizzie Sue went too they did not get back until after dark, Miss Carrie went away & forgot her pecans, oh but the room looks so empty since she left, I did hate it so bad because I could not fix a real nice dinner for them to day but we got up so late & it was long before I got the house cleaned up I did not have the chance to clean & fix chickens for a pie   (11 Jan.)

oh but Miss Carrie & I did have such a hard time night before last night for the pup whined & the baby had the colic & cried lots I was up nearly half the night & had to give him Paragoric twice, I was sorry for it was the last night she was to stay with us, in a long time & it seemed like every thing tried to make a racket & keep her a wake.   (12 Jan.)

A week before this departure, Miss Carrie was away for a few days, returning on 4 January: "Miss Carrie came home this evening she said she had a nice time." On the sixth Nannie's husband butchered: "Mr Jackson cut the bones out & fixed it to cool oh but I did get so cold holding the lamp & he got mad at me because I would not tell him what Miss Carrie & I were talking about the other night." Nor does her writing tell anyone else.

Margaret Bolsterli, the Editor

Margaret Bolsterli introduces the volume with the arresting observation that

> the value of this document lies in its tedium. . . . Mrs. Jackson exposes . . . the stifling, intellectually empty, mind-deadening quality of life in nineteenth-century rural America, which helps account for the provincial attitudes still prevalent in some areas today. (1)

And she concludes by placing in a regional context the view that the diary gives of Nannie Jackson's life: "The isolation and dullness of life there [in the Delta], the very tedium that is the stuff of this record, are the heritage of the entire rural South as well as of large areas of the rest of the country." Bolsterli compares Nannie Jackson's diary to a memoir by Henry Conklin, published in 1891 as *Through Poverty's Vale*, about a childhood of rural poverty in upstate New York; one difference is that the Conklins expected to move to new frontiers, whereas the Jacksons did not. Bolsterli ends the introduction:

After all, Henry Conklin's Uncle Joe dreamed of a farm 'that did not have a stone on it big enough to kill a chipping bird,' where the oats would grow as tall as a man. It is a sobering thought that the Jacksons owned such a farm, and the living they got from it was the realization of the American dream. (21)

The diary's historical value as a document of the time justifies, to Margaret Bolsterli, its publication—a point I want to return to.

The editorial additions are helpful indeed. Now I know that a vinegar pie is "made with vinegar instead of lemons. Lemons were a luxury in Watson in 1890" (102). Chicken bread is "coarse corn bread made without milk or eggs. It is used as feed for baby chickens, and is eaten by people as well when milk and eggs are in short supply" (101). Bolsterli might have said more about the harmful effects of mercurous chloride, the basis of the much-prescribed calomel. True, it was "used as a cathartic" as the glossary says (101), but its uses included abortion, to say nothing of the poisonous effects of its mercury. (I am left to wonder, though, about the "nice domestic skirt" that Fannie made for Lizzie with embroidery and ruffles.) Bolsterli is especially helpful for nonsouthern readers in explaining such matters as the watery topography of the Mississippi Delta; the social habit of giving gifts of food; the identification of black persons and whites by terms of address. In a footnote to the one-year anniversary of the death of a child of Nannie's friend Fannie Morgan, Bolsterli aptly comments that the child's death may account for the great amount of time Nannie reports spending with her, even though it is mentioned only this once (85). She traces nuances in the relation between Nannie and William T. Jackson (whom Nannie calls Mr. Jackson in the custom of the time)—how each depended on the other economically without feeling much affection, at least for the first year. Nannie needed his help to run the farm, and he needed her economic base and instruction in reading and writing. Bolsterli also observes differing values given to men's and women's work: men worked outdoors and made decisions, while women took care of the house and, if they worked outdoors, did only menial jobs (such as hoeing) not connected to managing property. Nannie's daughters play with dolls, clean, sew, and often hoe, but they do not think of themselves as preparing to make decisions about family business.

Insightful readings such as these make the editing indispensable to an appreciation of Nannie Jackson's writing. But Bolsterli underrates, I think, the degree of attention Nannie gives to her pregnancy, when she says only, "Although Mrs. Jackson does not mention it until the baby is 'brought by Dr. and Mrs. Chandler' on 15 August 1890, she is pregnant when the diary begins" (16). I think, as I have indicated earlier, that Nannie's consciousness of her physical condition runs through the entries, even though she makes no overt announcement (and then, "brought me a fine boy" is a rather oblique way of putting things). Indeed, our growing awareness of how conscious Nannie Jackson is of herself, how her eyes govern our view of that small space encircled by trees near Watson, gives primary value to her diary. Her women friends, the attention she pays to her two daughters, her sorrow over her first husband's death, her developing accommodation to the second (younger, ignorant, and rather insensitive as he is), her keeping the pulse of neighborhood events—all these details, laconic as may be the voice recounting them, attest to someone alive to her surroundings. I don't think that Nannie Jackson finds her life tedious or stifling. She has, of course, little choice or opportunity to know any other (she often says she reads, but does not say what, except a newspaper), but she does not complain of being bored. Her discontent and unhappiness come from missing her dead husband, from Mr. Jackson's sometimes uncouth and harsh ways, and from poverty. She writes enthusiastically about gifts of delicious foods friends bring her, occasional good moments with W. T., and other small pleasures.

Margaret Bolsterli's editing, then, seems to me in some respects at odds with itself. On the one hand, she greatly illuminates the writing, as we have seen. But on the other, I find distracting her justifications for publishing the diary, expressed, for instance, in the claim that it represents "a detailed account of routine existence in the rural South at the end of the nineteenth century" (xi). Of course it reflects its special time and place, as does most writing, but only incidentally. I would prefer that the editing concentrated on the diary as a self-contained work of literature, elucidating as necessary, instead of searching for historical applications. Footnote information, for instance, might be arranged more harmoniously with daily entries. I count 178 names in the index among 155 entries in 76 pages of text (surely with so many companions, many of them named repeatedly, the environs of Watson cannot have been unremittingly dull). A biographical glossary might have been more helpful than citation from census and biographical sources at the first mention of a person (as "Mrs. Coopwood was the wife of Benjamin J. Coopwood, a farmer near Pea Ridge"). Groups of relatives, hired workers in the Jackson household, close friends, more distant acquaintances, and the like would provide a taxonomy of Nannie Jackson's society and thus focus more sharply on her text.

Margaret Bolsterli explains why the printed diary reproduces the punctuation and spelling of the manuscript:

> In order to preserve the flavor of the document, I have made an exact copy. It seemed to me that correcting punctuation to make the material more readable would have meant changing it to some-

thing that Mrs. Jackson did not write, that the inconvenience of having to sort out occasionally erratic punctuation would be compensated by retaining the feel of the diary. This was, after all, a private record kept for her use alone and therefore one in which she did not have to pay much attention to punctuation and spelling. (xi–xii)

This question is bound to come up each time a work like Nannie Jackson's diary is considered for publication, and it deserves some discussion. I am inclined to disagree with Bolsterli's point of view on three grounds.

- Spelling and punctuation of English have been regularized only since the eighteenth century, for the convenience of printers. People do not misspell and mispunctuate on purpose; spelling in an unconventional manner is not an act of will, or I have never heard anyone who has misspelled a word claim so. For the person publicly discovered, misspelling is a humiliation, not evidence of self-expression. Wanting to "preserve the flavor of the document," in order to retain "the feel of the diary," seems mistaken (admittedly, I am a bad speller and therefore something of a biased authority on the subject). Much more important in revealing the workings of a writer's mind is the arrangement of sentence parts, the grammar, which operates for the most part independently of either spelling or punctuation. Actually, Nellie Jackson writes in a standard manner. It would be easy to "correct" her spelling and punctuation and find few mistakes in syntax. Her style is oral: she writes as one speaks, with short clauses but long stretches between full stops.
- Typesetting and proofreading "an exact copy" is more expensive than is standard typography, and editors wishing to undertake similar publishing projects may not be able to afford the expense. Furthermore, an absolutely "exact copy" may not be possible. In some people's handwriting, for instance, distinctions between capital and lowercase lettering may be ambiguous—what do you do with letters in sizes in between?
- Print exaggerates irregularities. What the eye takes in easily in handwriting may look much odder in print, and reproducing it would seem unfair to the writer, would in fact distort instead of being faithful to the original production. And finally, works like this diary should be read quickly; and irregular typography, although one soon gets accustomed to it, does slow you down.

Nannie Jackson deserves to have her writing published and read for the same reason that any other writer does: because she writes

well, because she is able to convey to us, strangers that we are, something if not everything of her consciousness. She is present.

> I did some patching for Fannie to day & took it to her she washed
> again yesterday & ironed up everything today I also took 2 boxes of
> moss & set out in a box for her, when I came back Mr. Jackson got
> mad at me for going there 3 times this evening said I went to talk
> about him, he got mad & said I was working for nothing but to get
> him & Mr. Morgan in a row, & to make trouble between them & I
> just talk to Fannie & tell her my troubles because it seems to help
> me to bear it better when she knows about it. I shall tell her
> whatever I feel like if he accused me of mean things because I was
> going to send to Redork by Mr. Morgan to get some white goods to
> make Sue & I a white dress apiece oh but I would rather he had
> treated me with silent contempt for 6 months than to talk to me as
> he did this evening & when he saw how it hurt me & made me cry
> then he wanted me to kiss him & make up, I kissed him but I can
> never get over what he said, he is going to keep on quarreling at
> me until he makes Lizzie leave home for good. Mr. Jackson took
> Mary down to the Allen place again to day he did not get back until
> 3 o clock he borrowed Sam from Mr. Morgan, & when he came
> home Sam got sick & Mr. Jackson had to drench him. . . . Tony
> sent me a bucket of blackberries & I did enjoy them so much, I sent
> Fannie a saucer full of them.   (27 June 1890)

Is it no more than Mr. Jackson deserves that the horse (Mary and Sam
are horses) he borrowed from Mr. Morgan (Fannie's husband) turns
sick on him? "Silent contempt" is a grander phrase than Nannie Jackson is used to, but then this is an unusual entry. Fannie, the friend she
often visits several times a day (and whose husband, according to a
footnote, may be a family connection), is only nineteen years old, the
same age as Nannie was on her first marriage, reminding us that this
was a time when childhoods were short. The passage is important not
only for its expression of such strong feeling but also for its glimpse of
Nannie's inner life. In a small house with little privacy and in a community where everyone else must know as much about her as she does
about them, it is all the more vital to keep some things to oneself, to
preserve the self in small secrets. The "quarreling" seems to hinge less
on Mr. Jackson's irritating paranoia than on Nannie's refusing to di-
vulge to him her more private life. He competes for her privacy with
her women friends—Fannie and Miss Carrie, for example—and surely
that must gall. But yard goods do not appear to be a serious issue, for
Nannie mentions several times buying sewing materials and even
commissioning her husband to get them for her. Nor does Nannie

sound like a selfish or particularly egotistical person. She is as generous toward her friends as they are toward her, and certainly she concerns herself with the children—here worrying that her husband will
drive Lizzie away. (Lizzie does that winter accompany Miss Carrie to
her next school, but her goal may be more to continue her education
than to escape Jackson's temper.) What is important, though, about
Nannie's sense of self-preservation is that it seems a strong motivation
for writing the diary, though she does not even there disclose the
substance of conversations and letters. But, as laconic and unemphatic
as most of her writing is, the impetus for it is much like that for her
friendships. When she says she talks with Fannie "because it seems to
help me to bear it better when she knows about it" and that whatever
Jackson says or does, "I shall tell her whatever I feel like," the same
grit seems present in her writing.

To return to the question this essay began with: can we read *Vinegar Pie and Chicken Bread* as a book? My answer, certainly, is yes; and
I think moreover that the book is a model for future editors to follow. I
do not wish to deny, however, that this kind of publication poses special
challenges. Because Nannie Jackson's diary hardly acknowledges a
world beyond the ring of trees around Watson that she speaks about so
often, public readers, strangers like ourselves, depend on the biographical and other supplementary information that Margaret Bolsterli provides. We also need some hints about reading—how to follow the "plot"
of Nannie's female friendships or her advancing pregnancy. For the
distance always will be there between such a work and us, imposing
limits we have to accept. I don't suppose we can ever know, for instance, the exact climate of Lizzie's departure with Miss Carrie, or the
fate of the older son, William, that in all these months is not mentioned. Nannie Jackson keeps much to herself. Margaret Bosterli's
own first connection to the diary was a private accident: "My mother,
as a very young schoolteacher, had boarded with Mrs. Jackson about
1907." She conveys to the rest of us that initial enthusiasm and then
shows us an engaged writer.

Institute Participants

Nancy Allen
Evergreen State College

Marlene Barr
*Virginia Polytechnic Institute and
State University*

Virginia Walcott Beauchamp
*University of Maryland,
College Park*

Elouise M. Bell
Brigham Young University

Carol Burr
California State University, Chico

Johnnella Butler
Smith College

Anne Carman
University of Missouri, Columbia

Janis Forman
*University of California,
Los Angeles*

Alice T. Gasque
University of South Dakota

Dure Jo Gillikin
*College of Staten Island,
City University of New York*

Joan Henry
*Garland County Community
College, Arkansas*

Rose Kamel
*Philadelphia College of Pharmacy
and Science*

Elizabeth Kincaid-Ehlers
Trinity College

Susan S. Kissel
Northern Kentucky University

Rayna Kline
Clark College

Margaret Murray
Mississippi State University

Linda Pickle
Westminster College

Nancy Porter
Portland State University

Janet Reed
Berea College

John Schilb
*University of North Carolina,
Wilmington*

Georgia Shurr
University of Tennessee, Knoxville

Judith Stitzel
West Virginia University

Carolyn Swift
Rhode Island College

Susan Ward
St. Lawrence University

Susan Waugh
*St. Louis Community College,
Meramec*

237

Institute Staff

Leonore Hoffmann (Director)
*Borough of Manhattan Commu-
    nity College, City University
    of New York*

Margo Culley
*University of Massachusetts,
    Amherst*

Ellen Dubois
*State University of New York,
    Buffalo*

Florence Howe
*State University of New York,
    College at Old Westbury*

Elizabeth A. Meese
*University of Alabama,
    Tuscaloosa*

Selected Bibliography and Works Cited

Letters, Diaries, and Oral Testimonies

Bishop, Nan, Sarah Hamilton, and Clare Bowman. *Nan, Sarah, and Clare: Letters between Friends.* New York: Avon, 1980.

Boone, Daniel. *The Adventures of Colonel Daniel Boon . . . to Which Are Added, a Narrative of the Captivity, and Extraordinary Escape of Mrs. Francis Scott. . . .* Norwich: John Trumbull, 1786.

Botts Family Letters. Shirley Beigel, Cincinnati.

Brett, Sally, ed. *Awakenings: Writings and Recollections of Eastern North Carolina Women.* Greenville: East North Carolina U, 1978.

    A collection of student papers, two of which include extensive correspondence: the courtship letters of Della Barlow (1867) and the letters of Rebecca Pitchford Davis to her son in the Confederate army (1861–64).

Cooperative Working Women. *Life as We Have Known It.* Ed. Margaret Llewelyn Davies. Introd. Virginia Woolf. 1931. New York: Norton, 1974.

Filson, John. *The Discovery, Settlement, and Present State of Kentucke . . . containing the Adventures of Col. Daniel Boon. . . .* Wilmington, 1784.

Fischer, Christiane, ed. *Let Them Speak for Themselves: Women in the American West, 1849–1900.* Hamden: Archon, 1977.

    Includes Abby Mansur's *MS Letters Written to Her Sister, 1852–54,* and *The Diary of Rachel Haskell, a Mining Woman.*

Fiske, John. *The Notebook of the Reverend John Fiske, 1644–1675.* Ed. Robert G. Pope. Boston: Colonial Soc. of Massachusetts, 1974.

Gilman Family Papers. Massachusetts Historical Soc., Boston.

Godfrey, Kenneth, Audrey Godfrey, and Jill Mulvay Derr, eds. *Women's Voices.* Salt Lake City: Deseret, 1982.

    A 400-page compilation of diary and journal excerpts from the writings of Mormon pioneer women.

Gwaltney, John Langston, ed. *Drylongso: A Self-Portrait of Black America.* New York: Vintage, 1981.

    Oral testimony interviews with contemporary black men and women.

Hampsten, Elizabeth, ed. *To All Inquiring Friends: Letters, Diaries, and Essays in North Dakota, 1880–1910.* 2nd ed. Grand Forks: Dept. of English, U of North Dakota, 1979.

    Contains primary documents of men and women found in the university library archives.

Heywood, Martha Spence. *Not by Bread Alone: The Journal of Martha Spence Heywood.* Salt Lake City: Tanner Trust, 1978.

Holliday, Laurel, ed. *Heart Songs: The Intimate Diaries of Young Girls*. Guerneville: Blue Stocking, 1978.

Holmes, Kenneth L., ed. *Covered Wagon Women: Diaries and Letters from the Western Trails, 1840–1880*. Glendale: Arthur H. Clark, 1983– .

> The series will be published in 10 volumes, each volume containing between ten and twenty documents, transcribed as written without internal editing, each introduced and annotated by Holmes.

Hungry Wolf, Beverly. *The Ways of My Grandmothers*. New York: Quill-Morrow, 1982.

> A member of the Blood tribe of the Blackfoot nation returned to the reserve in western Canada and questioned the older women about their lives and memories of tribal legends and customs.

Jackson, Nannie Stillwell. *Vinegar Pie and Chicken Bread: A Woman's Diary of Life in the Rural South, 1890–1891*. Ed. Margaret Jones Bolsterli. Fayetteville: U of Arkansas P, 1982.

James, Alice. *The Diary of Alice James*. Ed. Leon Edel. New York: Dodd, 1964.

Kissel, Susan, and Margery T. Rouse. *The Story of Pewter Basin and Other Occasional Writings: Collected in Southern Ohio and Northern Kentucky*. Bloomington: T. I. S., 1981.

> Contains 150 pages of letters, diaries, memoirs, and journals from the 1840s through the 1920s. The introduction contains suggestions for writing.

Lerner, Gerda. *Black Women in White America: A Documentary History*. New York: Pantheon, 1972.

Massachusetts Review 18.2 (Summer 1977).

> Contains 8 letters of Nellie Wells Kennard (1875–81) with an introductory essay by Barbara Courtney and *The White Papers: Letters (1861–1865)* of Pvt. Herman Lorenzo White, 22nd Regiment, Massachusetts Volunteers.

Moffat, Mary Jane, and Charlotte Painter, eds. *Revelations: Diaries of Women*. New York: Vintage, 1975.

Preston, Madge. Correspondence; Diaries for 1862 and 1864. MSS 978, 1861. Maryland Historical Soc., Baltimore.

———. Correspondence; Diary for 1865. McKeldin Library, U of Maryland, College Park.

———. Diary for 1868. Milton Eisenhower Library, Johns Hopkins U.

Preston, May. Correspondence. MS 978. Maryland Historical Soc., Baltimore.

Preston, William P. Correspondence. McKeldin Library, U of Maryland, College Park.

———. Papers. MS 978. Maryland Historical Soc., Baltimore.

Rosen, Ruth, and Sue Davidson, eds. *The Maimie Papers.* Old West-
bury: Feminist, 1977.
  Letters of a working-class woman to a Boston philanthropist
  written between 1910 and 1922.
Rowlandson, Mary. *A True History of the Captivity & Restoration of
Mrs. Mary Rowlandson. . . .* London, 1682.
Sanford, Mollie Dorsey. *Mollie: The Journal of Mollie Dorsey Sanford
in Nebraska and Colorado Territories, 1857–1866.* 1959. Lincoln:
Bison–U of Nebraska P, 1976.
Schlissel, Lillian, ed. *Women's Diaries of the Westward Journey.* New
York: Schocken, 1981.
Sidel, Ruth, ed. *Urban Survival: The World of Working-Class Women.*
Boston: Beacon, 1978.
  Contains oral testimonies.
Stewart, Elinor. *Letters of a Woman Homesteader.* 1914. Lincoln: U of
Nebraska P, 1961.
Summerville, Eleanor. Personal interview conducted by Colleen
Welch. April 1980.
*These Are Our Lives: As Told by the People and Written by Members of
the Federal Writers' Project of the Works Progress Administration
in North Carolina, Tennessee, Georgia.* Chapel Hill: U of North
Carolina P, 1939. New York: Norton, 1975.
Thomas, Sherry, ed. *We Didn't Have Much, but We Sure Had
Plenty: Stories of Rural Women.* Garden City: Anchor-Doubleday,
1981.

Secondary Sources

Addis, Patricia K. *Through a Woman's I: An Annotated Bibliography
of American Women's Autobiographical Writings, 1946–1976.* Me-
tuchen: Scarecrow, 1983.
Agee, James. *Let Us Now Praise Famous Men.* 1939. New York: Bal-
lantine, 1960.
Applebee, Arthur N. *Tradition and Reform in the Teaching of English:
A History.* Urbana: NCTE, 1974.
Baum, Charlotte, Paula Hyman, and Sonia Michel, eds. *The Jewish
Woman in America.* New York: Dial, 1976.
Beecher, Catherine. *A Treatise on Domestic Economy.* 1841. New York:
Schocken, 1977.
Benjamin, Walter. "The Storyteller." *Illuminations.* Ed. Hannah
Arendt. 1955. New York: Schocken, 1969. 83–109.
Bercovitch, Sacvan. *The Puritan Origins of the American Self.* New
Haven: Yale UP, 1975.
Bernard, Jessie. *The Female World.* New York: Free, 1981.
Bleecker, Ann Eliza. *The History of Maria Kittle.* 1790. Hartford, 1797.

Bradstreet, Anne. *The Works of Anne Bradstreet in Prose and Verse.* Ed. John Harvard Ellis. 1867. New York: Smith, 1932.

Carroll, Peter N. *Puritanism and the Wilderness: The Intellectual Significance of the New England Frontier, 1629–1700.* New York: Columbia UP, 1969.

Cather, Willa. *My Ántonia.* 1918. Boston: Houghton, 1954.

Coles, William E., Jr. *The Plural I: The Teaching of Writing.* New York: Holt, 1978.

Conrad, Susan P. *Perish the Thought: Intellectual Women in Romantic America, 1830–1860.* New York: Oxford UP, 1976.

Cott, Nancy F. "Eighteenth-Century Family and Social Life Revealed in Massachusetts Divorce Records." *A Heritage of Our Own.* Ed. Cott and Elizabeth H. Pleck. New York: Simon, 1979. 107–35.

Daly, Mary. *Gyn/Ecology: The Metaethics of Radical Feminism.* Boston: Beacon, 1978.

Douglas, Ann. *The Feminization of American Culture.* New York: Knopf, 1977.

Du Bois, W. E. B. *The Souls of Black Folk.* 1903. Greenwich: Fawcett, 1961.

Fiedler, Leslie A. *The Return of the Vanishing American.* London: Cape, 1968.

Franklin, Penelope. "The Diaries of Forgotten Women." *Book Forum* 4 (1979): 467–558.

Freire, Paulo. *Pedagogy of the Oppressed.* New York: Seabury, 1974.

Frontiers 2.2 (1977).
      Special issue on women's oral history.

Gilman, Charlotte Perkins. *The Living of Charlotte Perkins Gilman: An Autobiography.* New York: Arno, 1972.

———. *The Yellow Wallpaper.* 1892. Old Westbury: Feminist, 1973.

Gittelman, Sol. *From Shtetl to Suburbia.* Boston: Beacon, 1978.

Gluck, Sherna. "What's So Special about Women? Women's Oral History." *Frontiers* 2.2 (1977): 3–17.

Grele, Ron. *Envelopes of Sound: Six Practitioners Discuss the Theory, Method, and Practice of Oral History.* Chicago: Precedent, 1975.

Halsband, Robert. "Ladies of Letters in the Eighteenth Century." *The Lady of Letters in the Eighteenth Century.* Los Angeles: William Andrews Clark Memorial Library, U of California, 1969. 29–51.

Hampsten, Elizabeth. "Pen in Hand." *North Dakota English Journal* 3.3 (1978): 33–42.

———. *Read This Only to Yourself: The Private Writings of Midwestern Women, 1880–1910.* Bloomington: Indiana UP, 1982.

———. "This Is Christmas Eve and I Am in Tintah." *College English* 39 (1978): 670–78.

Hoffmann, Leonore, and Deborah Rosenfelt, eds. *Teaching Women's*

Literature from a Regional Perspective. New York: MLA, 1982.

Howe, Florence. "Identity and Expression: A Writing Course for Women." *A Case for Equity: Women in English Departments.* Ed. Susan McAllester. Urbana: NCTE, 1971. 17–26.

Howe, Helen. *The Gentle Americans: Biography of a Breed.* New York: Harper, 1965.

Howe, Irving. *World of Our Fathers.* New York: Harcourt, 1976.

Jason, Heda. "A Multidimensional Approach to Oral Literature." *Current Anthropology* 10 (1969): 413–26.

Jeffrey, Julie R. *Frontier Women: The Trans-Mississippi West.* New York: Hill, 1979.

Jelinek, Estelle, ed. *Women's Autobiography: Essays in Criticism.* Bloomington: Indiana UP, 1980.

Jordan, Teresa. *Cowgirls: The Women of the American West.* Garden City: Anchor-Doubleday, 1982.

Juhasz, Suzanne. "'Some Deep Old Desk or Capacious Hold-All': Form and Women's Autobiography." *College English* 39 (1978): 663–68.

Kolodny, Annette. "Honing a Habitable Languagescape: Women's Images for the New World Frontiers." *Women and Language in Literature and Society.* Ed. Sally McConnell-Ginet, Ruth Borker, and Nelly Furman. New York: Praeger, 1980. 188–204.

——. *The Land before Her: Fantasy and Experience of the American Frontiers, 1630–1860.* Chapel Hill: U of North Carolina P, 1984.

——. *The Lay of the Land: Metaphor as Experience and History in American Life and Letters.* Chapel Hill: U of North Carolina P, 1975.

Kuhn, Anne L. *The Mother's Role in Childhood Education, 1830–1860.* New Haven: Yale UP, 1976.

MacAlister, James. "The Study of Modern Literature in the Education of Our Time." *PMLA* 3 (1887): 8–16.

Martin, Nancy, Pat D'Arcy, Bryan Newton, and Robert Parker. *Writing and Learning across the Curriculum.* London: U of London Inst. of Education, 1976.

Mather, Cotton. *Decennium Luctuosum. . . .* Boston, 1699.

——. *Humiliations Follow'd with Deliverances. . . .* Boston, 1697.

McCloud, Emma, and James Agee. "Emma's Story: Two Versions." *Southern Exposure* 7.1 (1979): 8–26.

Montaigne, Michel de. *Essays and Selected Writings.* Trans. Donald M. Frame. New York: St. Martin's, 1963.

Myers, Robert Manson. Preface. *The Children of Pride: A True Story of Georgia and the Civil War.* New Haven: Yale UP, 1972. xi–xxv.

Myres, Sandra L. *Westering Women and the Frontier Experience.* Albuquerque: U of New Mexico P, 1982.

Neidle, Cecyle S. *America's Immigrant Women*. Boston: Twayne, 1975.

"A Notable Daughter of the American Revolution." *National Magazine* [Daughters of the American Revolution] Apr. 1923: 41–42.

Olney, James, ed. *Autobiography: Essays Theoretical and Critical*. Princeton: Princeton UP, 1980.

Olsen, Tillie. *Silences*. New York: Delacorte, 1978.

Pearson, Carol, and Katherine Pope. *The Female Hero in American and British Literature*. New York: Bowker, 1981.

Pratt, Mary Louise. *Toward a Speech Act Theory of Literary Discourse*. Bloomington: Indiana UP, 1977.

Rich, Adrienne. "Teaching Language in Open Admissions." *Lies, Secrets, and Silence: Selected Prose 1966–1979*. New York: Norton, 1979. 51–68.

Rosenblatt, Louise. *The Reader, the Text, the Poem: The Transactional Theory of the Literary Work*. Carbondale: Southern Illinois UP, 1978.

Ryan, Mary. *Womanhood in America from Colonial Times to the Present*. New York: Watts, 1979.

Schell, Herbert S. *History of South Dakota*. 3rd ed. Lincoln: U of Nebraska P, 1961.

Seelye, John. *Prophetic Waters: The River in Early American Life and Literature*. New York: Oxford UP, 1977.

Slotkin, Richard. *Regeneration through Violence: The Mythology of the American Frontier, 1600–1860*. Middletown: Wesleyan UP, 1973.

Smith, Henry Nash. *Virgin Land: The American West as Symbol and Myth*. 1950. New York: Vintage-Random, 1961.

Smith-Rosenberg, Carroll. "The Female World of Love and Ritual: Relations between Women in Nineteenth-Century America." *Signs* 1 (1975): 1–29.

Stone, Lawrence. *The Family, Sex, and Marriage in England, 1500–1800*. New York: Harper, 1977.

Stratton, Joanna L. *Pioneer Women: Voices from the Kansas Frontier*. New York: Simon, 1981.

Swift, Jonathan. "The Battle of the Books." 1704. *Gulliver's Travels and Other Writings*. Ed. Louis A. Landa. Boston: Houghton, 1960. 355–80.

Trimmer, Joseph F., and Robert R. Kettler. *American Oblique: Writing about the American Experience*. Boston: Houghton, 1976.

von Sydow, C. W. "On the Spread of Tradition." *Selected Papers on Folklore*. 1948. New York: Arno, 1977. 11–43.

Watts, Jim, and Allen F. Davis. *Generations: Your Family in American History*. New York: Knopf, 1978.

Women's Diaries: A Quarterly Newsletter. Ed. Jane DuPress Begos. Box 18, Pound Ridge, NY 10576.

Woolf, Virginia. *The Three Guineas*. London: Hogarth, 1938.